Kensington & Chelsea

Kensington & Chelsea

a social and architectural history

Annabel Walker
with Peter Jackson

John Murray

First published 1987
by John Murray (Publishers) Ltd
50 Albemarle Street, London W1X 4BD

Produced by John Stidolph
Editor – Nicola Harris
Designed by Peter Hedges
Index by Geraldine Christy
Typesetting and origination by
Fakenham Photosetting Ltd
Printed by Hazell Watson & Viney Ltd

British Library Cataloguing in Publication Data
Walker, Annabel
    Kensington & Chelsea: a social and architectural history
    1. Kensington and Chelsea (London, England)
    – History
    I. Title   II. Peter Jackson, 1922–
    942.1'34   DA685.K5
ISBN 0–7195–4344–4

End papers from a manuscript map, drawn by surveyor J P Desmaretz, of
Westminster, Chelsea and Kensington, in 1717
Frontispiece: The Albert Memorial; a chromolith of 1872

Contents

Introduction

Cheyne Walk, Old Chelsea, 1837

The names of Kensington and Chelsea run together easily, and it is now twenty-three years since they were officially joined in the creation of a new borough. An administrative boundary alone cannot unite two places, especially when they have strong individual characters, as in this case; but the parishes of Kensington and Chelsea have shared the long boundary of the Fulham Road for many centuries and have more in common with each other than with the London that grew up to the east. That seems to me a good enough reason for putting them together within the covers of a single book, and one which I hope readers will approve.

To have treated them as a single subject, however, would have been to disregard their origins as quite separate villages, so the book is divided into two parts, the first on Kensington, the second on Chelsea. In addition, the official boundaries of Kensington have not been strictly observed: they exclude part of Kensington Gardens and the museums area, but both places are so much a part of Kensington that it would have been unthinkable to consider them as belonging anywhere else.

As always, the difficulty has been to decide what must be left out, for both places have inspired the researches of local historians and the writing of histories over the last 300 years, and there is no shortage of material. But the decision to approach the subjects from a slightly unusual angle has ultimately dictated my course. The intention has been to trace the architectural and social development of Kensington and Chelsea: to describe the physical growth of the two villages and show how they attracted different kinds of inhabitants at different times, including a number of eminent writers, artists and politicians.

The illustrations from Peter Jackson's magnificent private collection, and the maps of the eighteenth and nineteenth centuries bring this development to life, and the way that the book is made up of self-contained chapters will, I hope, contribute to the clarity of the whole. I have not tried to emulate writers of the past by including the many anecdotes and histories of local families and royal residents, since they have done that so well and their books, listed in the bibliography, can still be read in the local libraries.

Of all the material available to the student of Kensington's and Chelsea's history, the *Survey of London* deserves special mention. The four volumes dealing with Chelsea were among the first to be published in the series, in 1909–1927, when only the early buildings were included; but the four Kensington volumes have all been published within the last fourteen years and are nothing less than a treasure trove of information. I have therefore had the good fortune to draw on them frequently – without them the book would be much the poorer. It is still a pale shadow of the encyclopaedic *Survey* but readers at least can be reassured that any shortcomings they may find here will be amply made good there.

The bibliography lists the books I have consulted, but I must emphasise four particular debts I owe: to the writers Mark Girouard, Donald Olsen and Nesta Macdonald, and to the Chelsea Society. Mr Girouard's work on 'Queen Anne' architecture, as found in his book *Sweetness and Light*, and the article he wrote for *Country Life* on 16 November 1972 on the Melbury Road artists' colony, 'The Victorian artist at home', are required reading for anyone interested in the borough's late Victorian buildings, as is Mr Olsen's book, *The Growth of Victorian London*. From Nesta Macdonald's booklet on the history of The Pheasantry in King's Road came much of the information contained in Chapter 35; and the Chelsea Society's annual reports have proved valuable sources of information for many other chapters.

I must also thank Mr Brian Curle and Mr John Hamp of Kensington's local history library for all their help; the staff of Chelsea Library for supplying me with a steady stream of weighty scrapbooks from the basement, even when the lift broke down; and Mrs Lorna Poole, The John Lewis Partnership archivist, for the information she provided on Peter Jones. Many thanks are also due to all the friends and acquaintances who have inquired after the progress of the book and put up with my unsociability while I was writing it; to my editor for her unfailing patience; and to my family, for being a constant support.

Kensington and Chelsea, as I have said elsewhere, mean different things to different people; but if this book can give them an insight, however brief, into how the two parishes once looked, and how they grew into the modern metropolitan districts we know today, I hope it will not have been in vain.

Brompton Road, Kensington, circa 1900

Kensington

Henry Rich, First Earl of Holland

1
Distant past and first great houses

At the time of *The Domesday Book*, the settlement of Chenesiton, derived its name probably from 'chenesi's tun', boasted few inhabitants, a priest and three acres of vineyard, together with woodland, meadows and pasture. The village that we know as Kensington developed on rising ground around its church, where St Mary Abbots stands today, bordered by a marshy flood plain and the heath of Brompton to the south and lonely hills to the north.

There were few roads in the vicinity. Kensington lay beside one ancient Roman track, the way to Brentford (now the High Street), and was linked to another, running west from the city of London to Uxbridge (now Holland Park Avenue), by a narrow lane which much later was to become known as Church Street. A number of springs rose nearby and the land was drained by Counter's Creek – now deep beneath Shepherd's Bush roundabout and the railway south of Olympia.

Kensington came into the hands of the de Vere family soon after the Conquest, an area of some 1200 acres most of which they retained for nearly 500 years, though they were usually absentee landlords. Almost immediately the first de Vere of Kensington, Aubrey, had given the church and about 250 acres to the abbots of Abingdon at the request of his dying son, Geoffry, but the rest of the estate remained intact. Altogether there were four manors: Abbots Kensington, Knotting Barns or 'Knottynghull', Earl's Court where the de Vere's, Earls of Oxford, held their manor court, and West Town, the latter including the area where the church of St Barnabas in Addison Road now stands.

The first disruption of the estate came in 1488, when the de Veres sold the manor of Knotting Barns, and by the end of the sixteenth century it had passed out of their ownership forever. All four manors, however, were reunited in the hands of Sir Walter Cope, who bought steadily throughout the 1590s and completed his acquisition of Kensington in 1609 when Earl's Court was sold to him by the Countess of Argyll, a descendant of the de Veres'.

Sir Walter Cope, 'of the Strand', advanced rapidly during the reign of James I & VI and was to become a significant figure in the history of his adopted village, for he built its first great house, long known as Cope's Castle before it was called Holland House. Perhaps if the manor house of Abbots Kensington had not been sold to Cope with the right of the lessee, Robert Horseman, to continue to live there, a new house would not have been built. As it was, Cope had no suitable home in his new domain, so he commissioned John Thorpe to design one for him on a south-facing slope not far from the village. At about the same time, he lost several acres north-east of his new house to a city merchant, Baptist Hicks, in a game of cards, and Hicks, too, decided to build a house on the hillside, the drawings for which were made by the same architect.

Hicks was also a man whose wealth and influence derived from King James. He was his financial agent in the early years and was given a peerage in 1628, taking the title of Viscount Campden, from Chipping Campden in Gloucestershire where he owned land. He called his Kensington home Campden House and died there in 1629. Cope had less time to enjoy his 'castle'. The house was not even finished when he died in 1614, though he was living there.

Thorpe's drawings show houses of similar style which must have looked fine in their rural settings, the grandest buildings for miles around. Country houses had not yet become widely popular with London's wealthy classes who still favoured the new houses being built much nearer the city, in places like Lincoln's Inn Fields and Covent Garden. Cope and Hicks had discovered the pleasures of life in Kensington which were later to draw people in their thousands and help transform a quiet village into a fashionable suburb.

Following the deaths of Cope and Hicks, the families' histories had less in common than did their houses. Baptist Hicks passed his title by special remainder to his son-in-law, Edward, Lord Noel, who supported the King during the Civil War and died at Oxford in 1643. The Noels later became Earls of Gainsborough but in 1798 the title became extinct. Campden House was let to a succession of tenants, among them Queen Anne before her accession to the throne, for whom an extra wing was built which survived until the 1940s, and the widowed Lady Burlington and her son, who was to become a famous

Holland House – the first of Kensington's 'great houses', built for Sir Walter Cope

Campden House as envisaged by John Thorpe

architect. In 1862, a fire almost destroyed the main house. It was rebuilt but in about 1900 it was demolished.

Cope's descendants followed paths which placed them much more in the public eye, though not always in a favourable light. His daughter and heir, Isabella, married the younger son of the Earl of Warwick, Henry Rich, who was later elevated to the Earldom of Holland (in Lincolnshire) and whom Clarendon described as 'a very handsome man, of a lovely and winning presence, and genteel conversation'. Unfortunately he was stronger on looks and demeanour than he was on principle, which did not prevent him from being a favourite at court with the Duke of Buckingham and, after the Duke's death, with the Queen, but which brought him to disaster during the Civil War.

Unable to commit himself for long to either side, he countenanced a meeting of Parliamentarians at Holland House in 1647, only to take up arms for the King a short time later. Thomas Faulkner, writing in 1820, described how 'his conduct was so various with respect to the King and Parliament, that neither party had the least dependence on him'. Clarendon's verdict was

perfectly poised, which perhaps Holland would have appreciated: 'He was a very well-bred man, and a fine gentleman in good times; but too much desired to enjoy ease and plenty when the King could have neither, and did think poverty the most insupportable evil that could befall any man in this world.' He died on the scaffold on 9 March 1649.

After Holland's execution the Parliamentary General, Lord Fairfax, occupied Cope's Castle, or Kensington House as it was sometimes known, and it was then that Cromwell is said to have had his famous meeting with General Ireton. Tradition has it that Cromwell chose to walk with Ireton on the slopes below the house to discuss the war because he knew that the general's deafness would necessitate a loud conversation which he did not want overheard.

After the Civil War the house passed through a quiet period in its history. Holland's widow returned, and discreetly patronised strolling players during the years of the Commonwealth when they were banned from public places. But more than a century was to pass before Holland House reached its apogee as the home of one of the most brilliant salons of Georgian London.

Detail from Kip's view of Chelsea (circa 1707) showing Kensington's houses on the skyline

2
Kensington village

In 1705 John Bowack wrote of Kensington in his *Antiquities of Middlesex*: 'This Town standing in a wholesome Air, not above Three Miles from London, has ever been resorted to by Persons of Quality and Citizens, and for many Years past Honour'd with several fine Seats belonging to the Earls of Nottingham, Warwick etc'.

The 'town' by modern standards was still a very small place, clustered round its church and surrounded by the formal avenues and gardens of its few great houses. At the farther reaches of the parish there was only a scattering of buildings: a map of 1717 (endpapers) shows a farm at 'Earles Court' and little settlements at 'Noding Hill' and Kensington Gravel Pits, the latter a wayside collection of cottages that took its name from the gravel workings on the hill. Another sizeable house, Hale House – shown as 'Hall House' by Rocque in his map of 1741–5, is sometimes known as Cromwell House because of persistent but unproven stories of its association with the Protector. Built in all probability in the seventeenth century, it stood immediately south of the present Queen's Gate/Cromwell Road junction and was demolished in 1853 when Queen's Gate was laid out. Sheffield House, which stood beside Church Lane opposite today's Sheffield Terrace, was owned by the Sheffield family and was knocked down at the same period. York and Maitland Houses, to the south, were built in the late seventeenth century, rebuilt in the eighteenth century, and survived uintil about eighty years ago, when they were replaced by York House Mansions.

The one thing which the parish of Kensington possessed in profusion was nurseries. The land in the north and west was in agricultural use but at Brompton it proved to be fertile ground for the propagation of flowers, vegetables and orchards, and map-makers of the time were meticulous in detailing the acres of plants that resulted.

The best-known nursery was that of George London and Henry Wise. Called Brompton Park, it stretched from Brompton Road up to Kensington Road and covered some one hundred acres. George London founded the nursery in 1681 and with Wise as partner had established a formidable reputation by the time Bowack wrote his history:

'And in this parish is that spot of Ground call'd Brompton-Park, so much Fam'd all over the Kingdom, for a Nursery of Plants, and fine Greens of all sorts, which supply most of the Nobility and Gentlemen in England. This Nursery was rais'd by Mr London and Mr Wise, and now 'tis brought to its greatest Perfection, and kept in extraordinary Order, in which a great number of Men are constantly Employ'd. The stock seems almost Incredible, for if we believe some who affirm that the several Plants in it were valued at but 1d a piece, they would amount to above £40,000.'

London and Wise were highly influential in weaning the aristocracy from the practice of importing plants from the Low Countries, and so successful in persuading them instead to stock their gardens from Brompton Park, that London spent most of his time travelling round the country. The gardener and writer Stephen Switzer said of him that 'It will perhaps be hardly believed in time to come, that this one Person actually saw and gave Directions once or twice a Year in most of the Noblemens and Gentlemens Gardens in England.'

The partners were supported and promoted by the eminent diarist John Evelyn, whose peregrinations seem often to have taken him to Brompton Park where he marvelled at the husbandry. Writing in 1701 in an introduction to *The Compleat Gardener*, which he translated from the French original by La Quintinie, he observed 'from the assiduity and the effects of the laudable industry of these two partners, that they have not made gain the only mark of their pains, but with extraordinary, and rare industry, endeavoured to improve themselves in the mysteries of their profession'.

Henry Wise, Brompton's celebrated gardener

Not only had they a wide variety of trees and shrubs suitable for our climate, enthused Evelyn, but they understood 'what best to plant, the humble boscage, wilderness, or taller groves with; where, and how to disperse and govern them according as ground and situation of the place requires both for shelter and ornament; for which purpose, and for walks and avenues, they have store of elms, limes, platans, Constantinople chesnuts, and black cherry trees. Nor are they, I perceive, less knowing in that most useful, though less pompous part of horticulture, the potagere, meloniere, culinarie garden.'

The partnership lasted until 1713, when London died. In the following year Wise sold the nursery: by then he had been royal gardener to Queen Anne for several years and had also bought a property, Warwick Priory, for his retirement. However, he retained the house at Brompton Park (a large building which appears to have been in existence when London bought the land in 1681) and died there in 1738. The house was later converted into three dwellings, and then used by the Science & Art Department in connection with the South Kensington Museum before being demolished in 1899 (see Chapter 12).

Kensington from the south 1750: Campden House can be seen in the distance with the old church, its flagpole to its right, and the houses of Kensington Square in the centre

The south-east view of St Mary Abbots in the mid-eighteenth century

Brompton Park nurseries withstood the pressures of an expanding city well into the nineteenth century. The local historian Thomas Faulkner could refer to the 'delightful fruit gardens of Brompton, Earl's Court, and other parts of this parish' in 1820; and even in 1851 Leigh Hunt wrote in *The Old Court Suburb* that the nursery 'is only now giving up its last green ghost before the rise of new buildings'.

In the old village of Kensington, change came slowly during the reigns of Charles II and James II. There was little cause for its expansion until 1690, when the court of William and Mary arrived at Nottingham House, later to be called Kensington Palace (see Chapter 3). Then, as Bowack explained, it enjoyed sudden prosperity:

'We can't indeed find it was ever taken Notice off in History, except for the Great Western Road through it, nor hath any thing occur'd in it, that might perpetuate its Name, till his late Majesty King William was pleas'd to Ennoble it with his Court and Royal Presence. Since which time it has Flourish'd even almost beyond Belief, and There is also abundance of Shop-keepers, and all sorts of Artificers in it, which make it appear rather like part of London, than a Country Village.'

It was definitely not a part of London, however, and its popularity was precariously founded on the presence of the court rather than on the growth of the city. After Queen Caroline's death in 1737, George II neglected the palace and Kensington lost favour and fashionable status until suburbia engulfed it much later in the mid-nineteenth century.

With the benefit of this hindsight, it seems surprising that Kensington Square should be begun, amid fields, three years before William and Mary even came to the throne. Its urban design must have looked strange indeed in such a rural setting. The square was the idea of Thomas Young, a wood-carver and joiner who acquired the land and envisaged 'a large Square of large and substantial Houses fit for ye Habitacion of persons of good Worth and Quality, with Courts and Yards before and Gardens lying backwards'. The *Survey of London* suggests that he had been inspired by such a plan while working on a house in Soho Square a few years earlier.

Young built six houses in the square but sold or leased the remaining plots to other builders. At first the rate of occupation was slow, though it improved once the court arrived in the village. Young designed a garden in the centre of the square and a bowling green to the south to attract residents, but his efforts did not reward him adequately and in 1687 he was imprisoned for debt. The bowling green became a market garden and already before 1800 one house in the square had been rebuilt.

Since then there have been many alterations and rebuildings, though Nos 11 and 12, just outside the square itself on the south side and built in about 1700, are perhaps representative of how the square looked originally. Nothing more definite can be said, since, strangely, no contemporary illustrations seem to exist.

Private houses were not the only buildings to benefit from the presence of the monarch at Kensington. The medieval church of St Mary Abbots also came

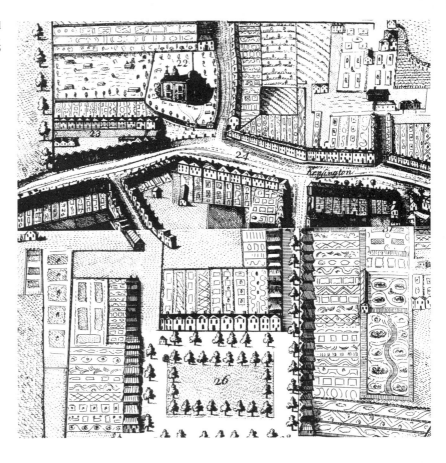

Detail from Joshua Rhodes' Topographical Survey of the Parish of Kensington, *1766*

Kensington School, designed by Nicholas Hawksmoor (circa 1709)

under scrutiny. In King William's time, Bowack explained, 'The old Church then much ruin'd and decay'd, was thought not commodious enough for the Reception of so many Noble Inhabitants, it was therefore about the Year 1694 Levell'd with the Ground, except the old Tower, and by the Incouragement and Bounty of several Illustrious Persons fairly Rebuilt, Pav'd, Pew'd, and made very Regular and Convenient.'

A few years later a new school was built for the village, on the north side of the High Street. Both a charity school and a parish school already existed, but in 1709 they were in effect amalgamated by the decision of the vestry to allow the rebuilding of the parish schoolhouse by the charity school trustees and the education of both sets of pupils under the same roof. The new building was designed by the then clerk of works at Kensington Palace, Nicholas Hawksmoor; sadly it was demolished in the 1870s. The site on which it stood is evidently one which does not tolerate lengthy occupation: the building that replaced the school was a new town hall and that, as most residents of Kensington will recall, met a sudden end only a few years ago (see Chapter 23). The only remaining pieces of evidence of Hawksmoor's building are the two stone statues of a boy and girl which now stand at the rear of the school building in Church Court, looking down on St Mary Abbots' leafy churchyard.

Within a few years of the new school being built, the village began to expand to the north, around the old manor house of St Mary Abbots, which was also known as The Parsonage. Its occupant in 1599 when Cope bought the manor, Robert Horseman, had lived on in the house and obtained nearly 200 acres from Cope's estate, but after his death his son sold the land to various buyers. By the 1720s a bricklayer named John Jones had bought the old house and land around it, and soon there were new houses behind the church as far north as Holland Street. By 1760 the manor house had disappeared. Kensington's days as a country village were numbered.

Kensington Palace in 1826, a watercolour by J Buckler

The year 1689 was a momentous one for Kensington, for it saw the arrival of royalty in the village, an event which precipitated it into the gaze of the fashionable world and set the seal on its prosperity.

William and Mary had been in England only since the previous year when they decided on the move from Whitehall to Kensington. The dampness of the riverside air at Whitehall oppressed the King, who was chronically asthmatic, and he had already authorised an extensive building programme at Hampton Court with a view to moving there. But Hampton was too far from London for convenient use, so in June 1689 it was agreed that Nottingham House at Kensington, 'being the only retreat near London he was pleased with', would become a royal residence.

Nottingham House was built in the early 1600s by Sir George Coppin on land bought from Sir Walter Cope, and here again, John Thorpe may have been the architect since a floor plan of the house by him exists in Sir John Soane's Museum. The property was later sold to Sir Heneage Finch, Speaker of the House of Commons, and passed to his successors until in 1689 it was in the hands of Daniel Finch, Second Earl of Nottingham, who was a member of William's government and who, because of his swarthy complexion and sombre expression, was nicknamed 'Dismal'.

The King paid 18,000 guineas for Nottingham House, and building work began immediately. Queen Mary seems often to have been at the house to inspect what progress was being made, and report on it in letters to her husband while he was in Ireland. In August she wrote that 'The outside of the house is fiddling work, which takes up more time than can be imagined; and while the schafolds are up, the windows must be boarded up.'

The work must have proceeded at a tremendous pace – some of it falling down and killing several workmen in the process – for the new occupants had moved in by early 1690 when John Evelyn visited Kensington and remarked on

3
Nottingham House becomes Kensington Palace

Queen Mary, by J Houbraken after a painting by Sir Godfrey Kneller

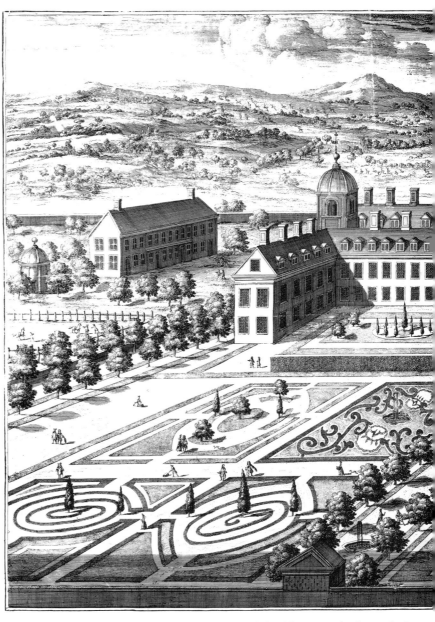

the 'straight new way' lined with lamps, which had been made through the park to the house.

Evelyn's verdict on the house was that it was 'a patched building', and even the respectful Bowack acknowledged that, in spite of its being made 'very neat and convenient, with all the proper offices', it 'wants an Air of Grandeur, and looks unlike the Palace of a King'. The Surveyor of the King's Works, Sir Christopher Wren, had been entrusted with the project, and had devised a staightforward plan, adding pavilions to each corner of the existing house, and a courtyard extending west; but the design had the air of a country house rather than a royal palace. The house given to the Duke of Marlborough in Queen Anne's reign only a few years later, Blenheim, was far grander.

Over the years, Kensington Palace (known until the eighteenth century as Kensington House) became even more of a 'patched' building than the one Evelyn had known. In November 1691 a fire destroyed the southern side of the courtyard – Defoe wrote that the Queen had suspected treason, but that the

King William III by Houbraken after Kneller

The Royal Palace of Kensington in 1724

King, 'a Stranger to Fears smil'd at the Suggestion, chear'd Her Majesty up, and being soon dress'd, they both walked out into the Garden' – and in the rebuilding, Wren's original plan was altered and the symmetry lost.

The courtyard was rearranged to make room for a larger staircase in the south-west pavilion, the Queen's Gallery was added to the north, and in 1695–6 the Clerk of the Works, Nicholas Hawksmoor, built the palace's familiar southern block, completely obscuring the façade of the old house and its two southern pavilions in the process.

Changes in the gardens were equally far-reaching. The grounds of Nottingham House had been renowned in Pepys's day – he enjoyed an evening of singing round a fountain there in 1664 – but William and Mary undertook a grand design on Dutch lines. The Brompton Park nurserymen London and Wise laid out a formal arrangement of parterres in front of the house, with a tree-lined avenue running down the centre; and when Queen Anne succeeded to the throne in 1702, she continued to extend the gardens.

William Kent's illusionary gallery on the grand staircase

The parterres were altered, because she could not bear the smell of the box hedges, and land behind the house, where there had been a gravel pit, was planted with a 'wilderness' and more gardens, the making of which, according to Bowack, required the labour of one hundred men. He thought the gardens had been 'beautified with all the Elegancies of Art', with the exception of statues and fountains, and Addison wrote in *The Spectator* (No. 477) in 1712 that 'there are as many kinds of gardening as of poetry . . . Wise and London, are our heroick poets, and if, as a critic, I may single out any passage of their works to commend, I shall take notice of that part in the upper garden, at Kensington, which was at first nothing but a gravel pit.'

Queen Anne made few alterations to the house, but in the grounds she built the beautiful orangery, thought to have been designed by Hawksmoor and modified by Vanbrugh. Her successor's mark on Kensington Palace was much more radical. George I came to the throne in 1714 and, to judge by the alterations he put in hand at Kensington House almost immediately, he felt the place old-fashioned and probably rather too homely for his tastes.

During the years 1718–21 the old house, already surrounded by later additions, was completely removed, to be replaced by a series of grand state rooms. Their decoration was entrusted to William Kent, and his brief ultimately extended to other parts of the palace, including the great staircase, for the walls and ceiling of which he painted a colourful illusionary gallery peopled with various members of the royal household, including himself and his mistress.

Various lesser alterations to the house were made in following years, including the division of rooms after the palace had been abandoned by ruling monarchs and used to house members of their families. The last king to live at Kensington was George II, and it was on the garden rather than the house that he and his wife made an impact. When Princess of Wales, Caroline had made promenades in the grounds fashionable for the court circle, and as Queen she undertook a huge project of redesign and extension. The results of her scheme can still be seen in the modern Kensington Gardens (see Chapter 16); she was also responsible for sweeping away the formal gardens in front of the palace, replacing them with the informal parkland which fashion dictated at the time, and which remain today.

The palace was neglected after her death in 1737, and George III never lived there. When Lady Mary Coke visited it in August 1768 with her friend Princess Amelia, she wrote in her journal, 'one cou'd scarcely imagine it wou'd have been worth His Majesty's while to have removed Beds that had been there so long . . . it is all so changed there is hardly any knowing it again'. In the early 1800s it was renovated and Princess Victoria spent her childhood there, but its reputation was not rescued until she opened it to the public at the end of her reign (see Chapter 21). Leigh Hunt, writing in 1855, said he could 'no more get up any enthusiasm about it as a building, than if it were a box, or a piece of cheese. But it possesses a Dutch solidity; it can be imagined full of English comfort'; it had, he decided, 'a sort of homely, fireside character'. And that, in an age when a ceremonious and stately life is no longer associated with the royal family, is probably what has made it so valuable as the home of several of its present members, including the Prince and Princess of Wales, Princess Margaret, Princess Alice, the Duke and Duchess of Gloucester and Prince and Princess Michael of Kent.

Kensington Palace in about 1690, showing the wings added on the north side in 1689–90 (from an engraving by Sutton Nicholls)

The Third Lord Holland and his wife seated in the library of Holland House; the librarian John Allen stands between them

4
Holland
House

William and Mary are reputed to have considered the possibility of buying Holland House when they were looking for a house beyond Whitehall. But even such a change in status could hardly have made it a house of more dazzling renown than it became during the first forty years of the nineteenth century, when its occupants, the Third Baron Holland and his wife, made it the centre of Whig politics.

It was natural that the Hollands should play a major part on that particular stage, being members of a staunchly Whig family. But the Whig tradition at Holland House may be said to have begun earlier, in 1716, when Joseph Addison of *The Spectator* married the widowed Countess of Warwick and Holland, and moved to the house where he had often been a visitor.

Little is known of this domestic aspect of Addison's life. He is thought to have lived at Sandford Manor, on the Chelsea/Fulham border, and to have enjoyed walking to Kensington to see the Countess and her son, Edward Henry, the future Earl. It seems unlikely that he was the boy's tutor, as some have thought, for his position in the state was by this time an important one: he was an MP from 1708, and in 1716 became a Lord Commissioner of Trade. Dr Johnson wrote in his *Lives of the Poets* that the marriage took place after 'a long and anxious courtship'; and tradition relates that it was not a happy one. But neither was it very enduring, for Addison died aged forty-seven in 1719. The story is told of the great man summoning the young Lord Holland to his bedside and saying, 'See in what peace a Christian can die'; though Horace Walpole preferred to say that he died of too much brandy.

The young earl also died young, only two years after his stepfather, and is commemorated by a monument in St Mary Abbots, though the Earl of Ilchester, writing his history of Holland House in 1937, described him as 'vicious and depraved . . . an unworthy sprig'. After his death the Holland

A view of Holland House from
The Universal Magazine

estate passed to the Edwardes branch of the family, who were created Barons Kensington in the 1770s, and it was the First Lord Kensington who sold the northern portion of the estate to the Fox family (see also Chapter 17).

The fortunes of the Foxes rested on the exploits of Sir Stephen Fox, who had made the most of his position as Paymaster-General of the forces after the Restoration, as John Evelyn noted when Fox contributed to the founding of the Royal Hospital (see Chapter 29). His son Henry, who bought the Holland estate in 1768, having leased the house since 1746, served in the government and was later made Paymaster-General like his father (though he had to relinquish the post on gaining his new title of Lord Holland). At that time it was considered legitimate for a paymaster to profit from the interest on surplus public money, but even so, Henry Fox managed to acquire an extremely dubious reputation.

Those of his two elder sons in some ways were little better, for they were busy gambling away their inheritance. Their profligacy may have had something to do with an indulged childhood, for the First Lord Holland, though relentless in pursuit of his own interests in public life, seems to have been a soft-hearted father: one of the stories told of him concerned a wall which had just been demolished, but which he ordered to be rebuilt so that his lately-arrived young son could witness its destruction.

The son in question was Charles James Fox, one of England's best-known politicians. He spent his childhood at Holland House, but never lived there in adulthood since the estate was inherited on the premature death of his elder brother by his nephew, Henry Richard, Third Baron Holland. The politics of Charles James, however, lived on in the house, cherished by his admiring nephew, and continued by the politicians, writers and historians who belonged to Lady Holland's celebrated salon.

From the turn of the century until the last ten years of Lord Holland's career, the Whigs sat almost without respite on the opposition benches. Holland House was a vital focus for the party during those years, and in the early years of government too, for a party so out of practice. This was perhaps just as well for the Hollands, since their domestic arrangements might otherwise, had theirs been a more ordinary life, have placed them beyond the pale.

The Third Lord Holland met his future wife, Elizabeth, in Italy, when she was still the wife of Sir Godfrey Webster and enjoying a somewhat unrestrained lifestyle in his absence (Sir Godfrey preferring to return to England alone). Eventually she obtained a divorce, but not before she had borne Lord Holland a son. They married in 1797, moved into Holland House later in the same year – and began to entertain almost immediately.

Over the next forty years, the Hollands' dinner parties were to be the source of many tales and witticisms, besides serving their more serious purposes. Lady Holland was a formidable hostess who thought nothing of telling a guest to leave if there were too many at table; of snubbing him if he did not come up to expectations, and of forbidding her husband to invite certain guests or eat certain foods. On being allowed a second slice of melon one evening after the intercession of one of the guests, Lord Grey, Lord Holland commented: 'Ah, Lord Grey, I wish you were always here. It is a fine thing to be Prime Minister.'

Lord Holland was not, however, the feeble character that such anecdotes might imply. He was, on the contrary, by all accounts a truly charming man. But in spite of his sound political standing and the importance of Holland House to the party, his political career was undoubtedly hampered by his wife's uncompromising character. He was made Chancellor of the Duchy of Lancaster when the Whigs gained power in 1830; but Lord John Russell, a great favourite of Lady Holland's and the main beneficiary of her will in preference to her own offspring, told her plainly that 'no man will act in a Cabinet with a person whose wife opens all his letters'.

Macaulay's first impressions of her were that 'It is to one "Go", and he goeth; and to another "Do this", and it is done. "Ring the bell, Mr Macaulay". "Lay down that screen, Lord Russell; you will spoil it". "Mr Allen, take a candle and show Mr Cradock the picture of Bonaparte." ' (The Hollands were fanatical supporters of Napoleon.) Lord Holland's widowed aunt, Mrs Charles James Fox, thought Lady Holland's high-handedness showed 'great ill-breeding and vulgarity'.

Nevertheless, Lady Holland's salon was spirited and immensely successful. Politicians such as Lord Grey and Lord Melbourne were frequent guests, the Reverend Sydney Smith, Samuel Rogers, Henry Luttrell and writers for *The Edinburgh Review* composed the core of her literary visitors, and a host of other distinguished people walked through her doors. The most enduring and faithful member of the circle was John Allen, librarian of the house from 1802 until his death in 1843, and master of Dulwich College through the influence of his patrons.

The fabric of Holland House survived its most brilliant period almost unscathed, the Hollands having neither the funds nor the inclination to set about major alterations to what must, by then, have appeared a rather outdated building. Cracks appeared in 1802, during one of their trips abroad, and radical rebuilding was suggested, but Lord Holland's sister, Caroline, who lived at Little Holland House in the grounds, realised that the diversion of water running down the hill and under the house would solve the worst of the problems.

After the Third Lord Holland's death in 1840, and that of his wife five years later, their son Henry, the Fourth and last Baron Holland, lived there intermittently, entertaining the Queen and Prince Albert at two 'Scottish fêtes' in 1849 and 1850. After his death, his widow and their adopted daughter, Marie, who became Princess Liechtenstein by marriage, quarrelled irreconcilably, and Lady Holland ran up larger and larger debts with her lavish style of living at Holland House and abroad. In 1874 she could cope no longer with her financial situation and handed the estate over to her heir, the Fifth Earl of Ilchester (the head of the elder branch of the Fox family, descended from the First Lord Holland's elder brother).

The Ilchesters made the house again a focus for society during the Edwardian period, with masked balls and garden fêtes, and guarded the rural character of its estate, despite the incursions of development on land sold off on its western flank. Woodcock were shot in its grounds as late as 1905. The Earl's widow lived on in the house after his death in 1905, until 1935; but the bombs of the Second World War put paid to the hopes expressed in 1811 by John Hookham Frere when he scratched on a window pane:

> May neither fire destroy nor waste impair,
> Nor time consume thee till the twentieth heir,
> May taste respect thee and may fashion spare.

Henry Fox, First Lord Holland

A Victorian garden party at Holland House

5
Georgian Kensington

'Kensington', wrote Thomas Faulkner in 1820, 'consists principally of one street, which extends about three quarters of a mile in length, from the Goar to Earl's Terrace. The town being in the direct road for the Western parts of England, is in a constant bustle, and resembles the most populous streets in London, especially in an evening, when the mails are setting out on their various destinations.'

Looking at Faulkner's map in his book, *The History and Antiquities of Kensington* (1820), it is hard to imagine the town being even this busy. Besides the High Street where William Cobbett had a seed farm in the 1820s, there are Church Street which was the home of Sir Isaac Newton in the 1720s – he lived where Bullingham Mansions is today, Holland Street and Kensington Square, but little else. Holland House stands in glorious solitude, and there are great stretches of fields running down to the outlying hamlets of Little Chelsea, Earl's Court and Brompton, and up the hill to Kensington Gravel Pits. Further north, the Grand Junction Canal was opened amid empty countryside in 1801.

Development in Kensington itself at the turn of the nineteenth century occurred chiefly on the Phillimore Estate, an area of sixty-four acres bought from the Campden House estate by Laud D'Oyley, and left to his daughter who had married a clothier named Phillimore. A long terrace, known as Upper and Lower Phillimore Place, was built fronting the High Street, and the east side of Hornton Street was lined with a row of houses. But not a single one of these buildings survives.

A little farther down the High Street the building of Edwardes Square began in 1811 on Lord Kensington's estate (taking his family name), and no doubt because its builder was a Frenchman, a legend was soon established that the houses were built with the idea of housing French army officers once they had helped Napoleon invade England. The fact that the threat of such an invasion was long since past by 1811 seems to have been overlooked, particularly by Leigh Hunt, who lived in the square after leaving Chelsea and, never letting facts spoil a good story, contented himself with the thought that 'It was allowable for French imaginations in those days to run a little wild, on the strength of Napoleon's victories.'

North of Kensington High Street, the hillside occupied by Holland House and Campden House was just beginning to change. Not only had the latter been altered, 'the parapets and other ornaments having been removed, and the whole covered with stucco' according to Daniel Lysons in his *Environs of London* (1795), but new houses were rising. In 1808 a builder undertook to erect seven villas in large grounds between the two mansions, north of a footpath from the town to Holland House (now Duchess of Bedford Walk, named after the duchess who lived in one of the villas until 1853). By 1817 the houses were complete and are shown on Faulkner's map, though he has marked eight instead of seven. Thomas Babington Macaulay, politician and writer lived in one, Holly Lodge. All but one have now been demolished, though four survived until the building of Queen Elizabeth College and Holland Park

The eastern end of Fulham Road in 1822; a painting by George Scharf

Section from a watercolour of Kensington High Street in 1811

Earl's Court farm (circa 1860)

The almshouses at Kensington Gravel Pits, demolished in 1821

School in the 1950s and 1960s. The surviving house, Thorpe Lodge, was decorated in the Arts and Crafts manner in 1904, and is now part of the school.

To the north of the new villas stood an older building, Notting Hill House, or Aubrey House as it is now known. It was built originally as the wells house for a medicinal spring which was discovered in about 1698 and was, for a short time, quite widely known, though by 1820 Faulkner could ascertain its position 'only after the most diligent enquiry'.

By the mid-1700s the house had been much altered, so that in 1767 it was thought a suitable residence by Lady Mary Coke, a daughter of the Duke of Argyll who had married and quickly parted from the heir to the Earl of Leicester. She had several new rooms added, and lived at Aubrey House until 1788, when she moved to Ashburnham House in Chelsea (see also Chapter 37). Her journal reveals much about the rural character of the neighbourhood, with its references to the views of Chelsea and Acton, the nightingales, her cow, 'Miss Pelham', who escaped to join a herd of cattle nearer London, the gipsies who camped in the lanes, and the roads that were so rough that her china was broken as she carried it home in her coach. Aubrey House later became a ladies' boarding school – the fate of several of Kensington's large houses – and still stands behind its wall in Aubrey Walk. Its name was changed in the mid-nineteenth century, probably in recognition of the de Vere family who had once held the manor, and one of whom was called Aubrey.

North of Aubrey House, only the small settlement of Kensington Gravel Pits interrupted the pattern of fields. Faulkner described the village as enjoying 'an excellent air, and beautiful prospects on the North'. Mendelssohn came to

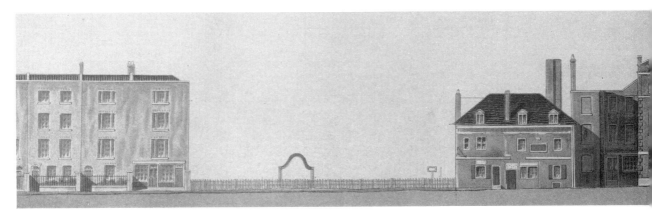

stay here, in High Row, now part of Church Street, in 1829 and the early 1830s. The lane leading to Portobello Farm (named after the place of that name in the Gulf of Mexico captured in 1739), wrote Faulkner, provided 'one of the most rural and pleasant walks in the summer'. Campden Hill Square, known at first as Notting Hill Square or Hanson's Square (after the builder) was only just beginning to take shape.

To the south, Earl's Court was equally rural, still little more than a single farm stretching westwards to the creek. The manor house and farmhouse stood near each other, on the west side of Earl's Court Lane (now Road) roughly where the station is today. On the eastern side of the lane, the first houses in what is now known as Earl's Court village were built in 1810; and in the area once known as Courtfield (the fields stretching to Gloucester Road) was Earl's Court House. Here, in the third house on the site since the seventeenth century, lived John Hunter, a surgeon celebrated in his day for his lively and enquiring intellect, who kept a variety of animals and birds in the grounds. He died in 1793, but the house survived as a lunatic asylum until 1886, when it was demolished to make way for Barkston Gardens.

Nearer Brompton Lane (now Old Brompton Road), the Gunter family ran a highly successful market gardening establishment from Earl's Court Lodge (nicknamed Currant Jelly Hall because of the family's confectionery business). But in 1805–10 they began to build there, putting up several villas eastwards along Brompton Lane.

Edwardes Square

Brompton itself comprised an area of market gardens, as shown in Rocque's map of 1741, which is now covered roughly by the streets in the triangle between Cromwell Road/Fulham Road/Selwood Terrace ('Sallad Lane' as it was known then). There were few buildings here even in 1820, but terraces were spreading down Brompton Road from Knightsbridge, earning themselves the name New Brompton and proving particularly popular with actors and musicians.

Similarly, houses were being built in Little Chelsea, a settlement straddling the boundary between Kensington and Chelsea along the Fulham Road (see also Chapter 26). Faulkner wrote that the number of houses here had greatly increased in the twenty years leading up to the publication of his book and that 'Seymour Place, Friar's Grove and Thistle Grove are amongst the modern improvements of this part of the parish of Kensington'. Seymour Place is now known as Seymour Walk, Thistle Grove as Drayton Garden but Friar's Grove has not been identified. The present Thistle Grove was originally called Thistle Grove Lane.

There was also a military academy at Little Chelsea from 1770 until about 1789, in a large house which stood beside the Fulham Road west of the present Hollywood Road, where the proprietor Lewis Lochée wrote 'several works on fortification'. The Billings, the three small streets of cottages tucked into the end of Brompton Cemetery that have become so fashionable, were not built until the 1840s and 1850s. Little Chelsea was certainly considered a desirable place, but it was a long way from being the almost constantly busy, overcrowded area it is today.

Another section of the watercolour of Kensington High Street up to the corner of Church Street

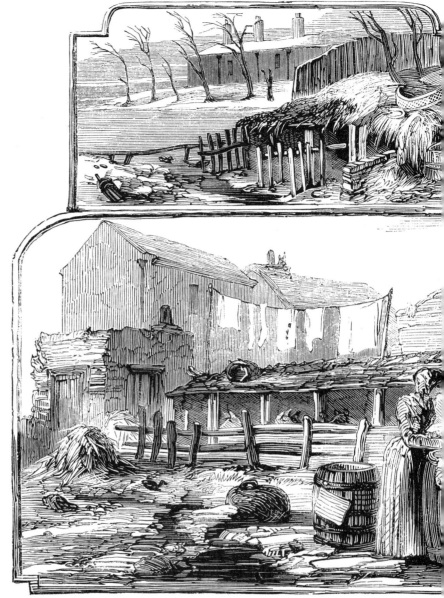

6
Potteries
and
piggeries

At the same time as houses were springing up all over Kensington for the accommodation of the comfortable middle class, one corner of the borough was developing into a slum whose notoriety was probably unsurpassed throughout London. In the same years that the dignified buildings of Onslow Square were begun, the average age at death was just over eleven and a half years for the people of the potteries and piggeries.

The area lay at the foot of the hill on which the Ladbroke estate was laid out (see next chapter), directly north of the present Pottery Lane, on badly draining clay soil between the Norland estate and Notting Barns Farm. Its first occupants were to give it its two infamous names: the brickmakers, who seem to have arrived in the late eighteenth century and later built the pottery and tile kilns one of which remains, rebuilt, in Walmer Road; and the pig-keepers, who moved there in the early nineteenth century.

Florence Gladstone, writing in 1924, asserted that the early pig-keepers

Scenes from the potteries as depicted in Historic Times, *1850*

'though uncouth and unlettered, were a self-reliant and a sober race, honest and industrious', whereas the brickmakers were 'chiefly Irish labourers of a low type'. Whatever their character, they were later joined by a motley crew who gave the place a reputation for anything but sobriety and honesty.

The making of bricks and tiles involved large excavations, which soon filled with stagnant water. The keeping of pigs entailed collecting refuse and offal from the kitchens of hotels and private houses, feeding most of it to the pigs and boiling down the fat. The combination of the two spelt disaster.

Samuel Lake of Tottenham Court Road, a scavenger and chimney sweep, was the first to keep pigs here, and he was soon joined by the pig-keepers of Tyburn who had been forced west by building development. The colony was at first sufficiently isolated to be able to go about its business unfettered; and by the time streets were being built nearby, the piggeries were so well established that developers simply steered clear.

31

Tucker's Cottage in the potteries, from Mrs Bayly's Ragged Homes and How to Mend Them *(1859)*

Shacks sprang up wherever convenient, for there was no building control in London at this time. Inevitably they were jumbled together with the pigs and ponds: indeed often the three were combined, with humans sharing their roofs with the animals and living directly over stagnant water. The ponds were filled with fetid water and the manure of innumerable pigs – the animals at one stage outnumbered people by three to one – and one lake, known as 'the ocean', covered nearly an acre. The stench was nauseous, roads were unmade and in wet weather the deep, sticky clay and open ditches made them treacherous, especially at night. The area's decline was swift, and was hastened by its reputation. It became a refuge for a variety of dubious characters, and for those who had been made homeless by slum clearances – including Jennings Place (behind Young Street) and Campden Place in Kensington (where Clanricarde Gardens was later built) – and railway development in more central areas. Later, when the railway was built across north Kensington in the 1860s (see Chapter 15) navvies moved into poor boarding houses in the neighbourhood, and gipsies often camped in the area.

The sewage authorities were unable to cope with the scale of the problem, so when cholera struck in 1849 its toll was high: the mortality rate reached 60 per 1000 living (compared with an average for London, 1846–50, of 25.4 per 1000). 43 out of every 50 deaths were of children under the age of five.

Some of the earliest attempts to help the residents of what Dickens in *Household Words* called 'this plague spot' were made by one or two Kensington ladies, and by members of local churches: notably the Silver Street Baptist and Hornton Street Congregational Chapels. Silver Street Chapel stands in Kensington Place – just off the northern end of Kensington Church Street which was once known as Silver Street – and is now called the Bethesda Baptist Chapel. Hornton Street Chapel stood at the southern end of Hornton Street until it was demolished in about 1927; a café now stands in its place. Mrs Mary Bayly, who lived in Lansdowne Crescent and wrote *Ragged Homes and How to*

Mend Them (1859), formed a 'Mothers' Society'; religious services were held in a mission room, schools were established, a temperance society was formed and in the 1860s the Reverend Arthur Robinson bought the site for St Clement's Church in Treadgold Street from his own resources.

In the 1850s the first tentative steps were taken to rid the area of pigs and provide proper drainage, though progress was continually impeded by the fact that the people were wholly dependent for their livelihood upon the animals. By 1863, however, the 'ocean' had been filled in, and in the 1870s a start was made upon the improvement of housing. By the end of that decade, the business of pig-keeping had finally ceased.

The area nevertheless remained a mean one. Instead of pig-keeping, the men turned to living off whatever their women could earn as laundresses, initially at home and later in small laundries: a local saying in north Kensington declared that 'to marry an ironer is as good as a fortune'. The owners of land north of the brickfields were busy developing it as a working-class suburb, now that the railway provided cheap and speedy travel into London, and casual labourers moved in. The respectable streets of the Ladbroke estate resolutely turned their backs on the potteries, and the railway sealed its boundaries on the north and west.

The Kensington Vestry reacted to the continuing problems with anything but alacrity until the end of the century, when it became impossible to ignore the situation any longer. In 1893 an article entitled 'A West-End Avernus' in *The Daily News* identified Wilsham Street, Kenley Street, another two streets now replaced by Henry Dickens Court, and part of Sirdar Road (modern names) as 'hopelessly degraded and abandoned'; and the social reformer Charles Booth classified Notting Dale in 1902 as 'a perhaps unexampled concourse of the disreputable classes', who however, seemed to have enough work to pay for visits to the music-hall and for summer day-trips. The mortality rate was almost as high as it had been in 1856, and eleven lodging houses accommodated more than 700 people, who, according to a special committee set up by the vestry in 1896, were 'largely made up of loafers, cab-runners, beggars, tramps, thieves and prostitutes'.

Since then the area has been largely improved and redeveloped. Avondale Park was opened in 1892, by 1906 Kenley Street had been rebuilt and Henry Dickens Court went up after the Second World War. This part of Kensington, however, is still strangely cut off, lying hidden behind the façade of the Norland estate and with the borders created by the railway reinforced in recent years by the elevated M40 and its approach road (built in the 1970s) from Shepherd's Bush.

A tile kiln in 1824

7
The Ladbroke estate

Scene at the Hippodrome: **The Last Fence**
by Henry Alken Junior

In June 1837 a racecourse was opened which a newspaper of the day predicted would form 'the greatest addition to the recreations of London which has been made during the last hundred years'. It was named the Hippodrome, and covered 140 acres of the Ladbroke estate north of the Uxbridge Road. 'The busy part of the community', said the report, 'can assemble there with perfect ease in the afternoon . . . The distance can be mastered in a moderate walk.' Such a diversion was much better than 'bustling one's way through the motley crowds compressed into a densely ambulating line in Hyde Park, or sauntering listlessly through the gloomy walks of Kensington Gardens'.

The idea of the racecourse came from John Whyte, who leased the land from James Weller Ladbroke, and arranged for two fashionable gentlemen, Lord Chesterfield and Count D'Orsay, to become its stewards. The main entrance was roughly at the modern junction of Notting Hill Gate and Pembridge Road, where Portobello Lane once met the high street of the village of Kensington Gravel Pits.

Plan of the Hippodrome racecourse in 1841

The Hippodrome might have been a great success. Racing was a popular pastime and it had a beautiful course and stabling for seventy-five horses. Racegoers could watch the sport from beginning to end from the picturesque hillock in the centre (where St John's Church now stands), and on non-racing days there were animals for hire. But local residents did not share the enthusiasm of the fashionable world.

The course, which was protected by high fencing, cut across an old footpath which linked Kensington with Kensal Green, and which was much used in preference to another, a little farther west, which led through the unsavoury and dangerous potteries. Opposition immediately made itself evident, for on the opening day a crowd broke through the fence to claim their rights to free entry.

As has always been the case, those who had just cause for complaint were joined by others. *The Sunday Times* complained that 'the assertors of the right-of-way have thrown open an avenue for the admission of every kind of

Kensington Park Gardens
as envisaged in 1853

vagabond – cigar venders (sic), ballad singers, and a very choice collection of swell mobites thronged the course'. Other papers agreed that 'every sort of ruffian finds his way to the Hippodrome': hardly the sort of reputation Whyte needed at the outset of his venture. The fashionable were certainly there too, but this was little solace since *The Sunday Times* claimed to speak on their behalf on another matter, the poor quality of the horses: 'all these persons looked upon the miserably abortive attempts at racing with the greatest disgust', it announced.

Whyte submitted to pressure and altered his course so as to leave the footpath unobstructed: the oval was compressed into a bulb-like shape farther west, stretching north almost to Little Wormwood Scrubs. It was renamed Victoria Park in honour of the new Queen, but the problems were not over. To meet the cost of the alterations, entry charges were increased, and the course simultaneously began to acquire a reputation for waterlogged ground. There were also petitions against Sunday racing. Whyte was financially out of his depth, and in 1840 handed over control to his solicitor, John Duncan, and a speculator, Jacob Connop, who, though they announced new programmes, closed the Hippodrome within a year.

Until the 1820s, the hillside on which the Ladbroke estate lay was entirely rural. It was a long way from London, and in any case its clay soil inhibited development (though in 1794 an artesian well was sunk 236 ft into the ground at Norland House, where Norland Square now stands). In the 1820s, however, James Weller Ladbroke began to grant leases to speculators who would build to a layout devised by his surveyor and architect, Thomas Allason.

This layout envisaged a road – Ladbroke Grove – leading at right angles from the Uxbridge Road (now Holland Park Avenue) and cutting through a huge circus which would be one mile in circumference, and round which houses would be built, with gardens in the centre. Allason was no doubt influenced by Nash's work in Regent's Park, which was completed in the late 1820s; but his circus was never built. Ladbroke Grove and Ladbroke Road are the only survivors of the plan, and by the time a few houses had been built fronting the Uxbridge Road and in Ladbroke Terrace, the Hippodrome had become a more attractive proposition.

When building resumed in the 1840s, however, it was to a plan much influenced by Allason's ideas; indeed it is to him and four other men that the Ladbroke estate owes its appearance, with its handsome crescents and great leafy swathes of communal gardens. Two of the early developers on the estate, Pearson Thompson and Richard Roy, both had houses in Cheltenham, and the former had employed the architect J B Papworth to lay out his Montpelier estate there.

In Kensington they enlisted the help not of Papworth, but of his pupil, James Thomson, who had also worked for Nash in Regent's Park; while Allason's role as Ladbroke's surveyor enabled him to influence the style of the development. It was Allason, for instance, who had first proposed enclosed communal gardens in his original circus layout. Initially the scheme envisaged a number of detached villas, but this was later modified to semi-detached and terraced houses which descend the hillside in a series of sweeping crescents on the south-west, and on the southern side surround London's largest private communal garden, that of Ladbroke Square.

Pearson Thompson and Richard Roy had interests only in the section of the estate west of Ladbroke Grove. To the east the developers' architects were not so imaginative, though admittedly they were dealing with less interesting contours. Thompson and Roy were also working at an earlier date, the south-western part of the estate having been the first to be developed, while later houses exhibit the florid Italianate style so popular with Victorians at the expense of the more restrained dignity of earlier designs, such as can be found in Lansdowne Crescent and at the southern end of Ladbroke Grove.

No developer hoping to create a desirable new suburb at this time could afford to neglect the provision of a suitable site for a church, which set a seal of respectability on the place. On the Ladbroke estate the crest of the hill provided a fine position for the church of St John the Evangelist, which was built in the traditional manner, to be found on similar developments all over London, on medieval lines with ragstone walls, sharply contrasting the stucco and brick of surrounding houses. It was consecrated in 1845, while ten years later the estate gained another, rather more unusual place of worship in the form of St Peter's in Kensington Park Road, a lone classical church amongst its Gothic contemporaries.

The occupants of the new houses were at first solidly middle class: merchants, army officers and professionals (their domestic servants being forbidden to enter the communal gardens unless accompanying a member of the family). But already by 1861 there were signs that the estate was not as select as its developers had hoped, for two houses in Kensington Park Gardens were divided into two dwellings, and others had been converted into girls' schools.

Houses went up faster than occupants for them could be found, especially if they were near the potteries, and this, coupled with other financial difficulties such as were common among London speculators at this time, resulted in whole streets remaining half-built and unoccupied for long periods. Ladbroke Gardens, still unfinished in the 1870s, earned itself the nickname 'Coffin Row', and this in turn dissuaded people from moving to the area.

While some speculators did well out of the Ladbroke estate, and others no doubt profited from buying and completing unfinished houses when conditions improved, others came to grief. Dr Samuel Walker was the most notorious. He had been left a fortune of some £250,000 and, hoping to raise funds for the establishment of a bishopric in Cornwall, where he held the rich living of St Columb Major, he began to speculate. He bought land in the northern, least desirable part of the estate, and his failure was so dramatic that in 1863 he removed himself from the country. His land, wrote an old inhabitant of the area, 'was covered with unfinished houses which continued in a ruinous condition for years'.

St John's Church in 1845

Gore House which stood where the Royal Albert Hall stands today

8
'Millionaires' Row' and other large houses

Kensington's status as a desirable and fashionable village was founded on its two earliest great houses, Holland and Campden, and on Nottingham House when it became a royal residence. No other houses in the area matched their standing, but a number were built later which aspired to or gained reputations of a sort, either for their design or their occupants.

Gore House was one which fell into the latter category. It was a moderately distinguished building of the 1750s, standing where the Albert Hall is today, but its place in local history was assured by its nineteenth-century tenants, William Wilberforce and, later, the Countess of Blessington and Count D'Orsay.

Wilberforce lived there from 1808 until 1821, and the chronicler of the 'old court suburb', Leigh Hunt, was not slow to point out what he felt to be the inconsistencies of a prominent evangelical living in such a place. He contrived, wrote Hunt, 'to combine the most terrific ideas of the next world (for others) with the most comfortable enjoyment of this world in his own person'.

But Wilberforce's spell at Gore House pales into insignificance beside the tenancy of his successors there. Countess Blessington's salon at the house was famous, as was the fact that her companion there was the French dandy, Count D'Orsay. Lady Blessington had been left a widow by her second husband, who had earlier taken a great liking to D'Orsay and married him to one of his daughters so that he could inherit part of his estate.

After the Earl's death, D'Orsay separated from his wife and moved into the Countess's home in Kensington. D'Orsay was several years younger than the beautiful Countess, and Leigh Hunt allowed himself to muse a little on their relationship, their 'delicate secret' as he put it, before dismissing such thoughts as narrow scandal-mongering – by others, of course.

In 1849 both the Count and Countess left England under pressure of debts and the contents of Gore House were sold over thirteen days, thousands visiting the house beforehand to view the 'costly and elegant effects . . . the property of the Rt Honble the Countess of Blessington, retiring to the continent'. The lease was bought by the chef, Alexis Soyer (see Chapter 11), and later by the Commissioners for the 1851 exhibition, who used it for educational purposes before demolishing it in 1857.

Gore House was one of a number of large detached houses along the road to Kensington. Immediately to the west was Grove House, a rather unattractive building as it appears in a photograph of 1856, which was also acquired by the Commissioners and demolished in the same year as its neighbour. And farther along, where Palace Gate now meets Kensington Road, was Noel House, named after Baptist Hicks's descendants and built in 1804 for George Aust, secretary to the Royal Hospital in Chelsea. Its pleasant gardens became a building site when it was bought in 1861 and pulled down by William Cubitt & Company.

Beyond Noel House, opposite the palace, was a pair of older buildings, Colby House and Kensington House, both dating from about 1700 though there had been an even older house there previously, occupied by the Colby family. In 1830 Kensington House became a lunatic asylum, whose primitive practices were exposed by a one-time patient, Richard Paternoster, in his book *The Madhouse System*; and a few years later Colby House next door was bought as a private residence by a later owner of the asylum, Dr Francis Philp. Having obtained the freehold for both sites, he sold them for building in 1872 and they were demolished almost immediately.

The house that arose in their place was an extraordinary example of *folie de grandeur*. It was planned as the home of 'Baron Albert Grant', cost an estimated total of £300,000, including the site, and stood for only six years after its completion, during which time it was never occupied. The flamboyant French style, with the most lavish interior decorations, must have looked oddly dated by the time it was finished, beside the new 'Queen Anne' and vernacular red-brick designs of other modern houses.

Marguerite, Countess of Blessington

Noel House, built in 1804

The eighteenth-century Kensington House

Grant was an entrepreneur of dubious character who had begun life as Albert Gottheimer and amassed a fortune by promoting and selling often worthless companies. He had also been MP for Kidderminster, 1865–8, and acquired his foreign title during a sojourn in Italy. On buying his sites in Kensington he took a robustly realistic approach to the demolition of an adjoining slum, Jenning's Buildings, the freehold of which he also owned, by paying off the inhabitants and letting them take away the woodwork. His gigantic new mansion was built, 'in all its hideous magnificence' as the local historian, W J Loftie recalled, to designs by James Knowles junior between 1873 and 1875, and its interior finished in the following year. By then, Grant's finances were precarious. Tenants for the house failed to materialise; and by 1882 the building had been demolished.

Perhaps Grant had been spurred on in his ambitious project by the large houses which arose in Queen's Road (now Kensington Palace Gardens) in the 1840s–1860s. Though this development got off to a slow start, by the time Grant started building it was inhabited by a variety of wealthy businessmen: builders, engineers, merchants and industrialists.

The land, twenty-eight acres in all, was part of Kensington Palace grounds until 1841 when it was sold for building by the Commissioners of Woods and Forests in order to provide funds for the development of other royal gardens. It included the old area known as Palace Green, the William and Mary barracks near Kensington Road, the kitchen gardens and forcing ground, and Queen Mary's 'wilderness'.

Despite some opposition, the laying out of the avenue went ahead (though trees were not planted until the 1850s and 1870s). The Commissioners were confident that their plan for a number of good-quality individual houses would be successful, but one of the first developers to take on several sites, John Blashfield, found otherwise, and was declared bankrupt in 1847, though not

40

Baron Grant's palatial new Kensington House in 1877

Baron Albert Grant as depicted by Vanity Fair *in 1874*

before he had built five houses and the lodge at the north end of the road where it meets Bayswater Road.

With an improvement in the economic climate in the early 1850s the remaining sites eventually sold, and houses were built to the designs of a number of different architects, many of them in Italianate style. Several vacant plots remained, however, since Queen Victoria objected to houses being built directly opposite the palace. Nos 4–10 Palace Green, therefore, were not built until after her death, in 1903–12.

The design of most of the houses in Kensington Palace Gardens was uncontroversial. They were occupied by large households with as many as twenty-eight servants, though Leigh Hunt wondered why anyone would live there since 'none of them have gardens, to speak of'. In the 1860s, however, two of the three old William and Mary houses that remained on Palace Green were demolished: Thackeray left Onslow Square and returned to Kensington, building himself a house of classical design on the site of No 2 in keeping with his affection for the Queen Anne period of history. He proudly called it 'the reddest house in all the town', but died only a year after moving in, in 1863. In place of No 1, a new house by Philip Webb was proposed by the twenty-three-year-old George James Howard, the future Earl of Carlisle.

The Commissioners took fright at the avant-garde plans for this brick house with steeply-pitched roofs, and it was not until Webb had modified his design with the introduction of stonework that its construction was permitted. Webb took the fact that the Commissioners could not recognise any style or period in his design as a great compliment. The house was altered in the 1950s to provide flats, and many of the other surviving Victorian houses in the avenue have suffered similarly in the course of being converted, for the most part, to embassies or for related diplomatic use.

The east side of Thurloe Square (circa 1842)

9
Expansion of Victorian Kensington

In 1888 the Kensington historian W J Loftie wrote, 'During the past few years the changes in Kensington have been so great that I doubt if any person who knew his way in it forty years ago would know his way now, if he had not visited it in the meanwhile.' The same could undoubtedly be said of parts of Kensington today (see Chapter 23), but much of the Kensington that Loftie saw develop in the forty years before he wrote his book, *Kensington Picturesque and Historical*, remains intact.

The eastern parts of the borough were particularly desirable, and a good many fashionable houses were built on the Smith's Charity estate, which originally covered eighty-five acres. Henry Smith was a sixteenth-century merchant who, according to earlier historians, had been whipped out of the parish of Mitcham as a boy for begging. On his death in 1628 he left £1000 to be used to buy land producing at least £60 per annum, which would relieve 'the poore Captives' held as slaves by Turkish pirates. Poor captives being rather thin on the ground, the trustees later successfully applied for a diversion of the funds to the other beneficiaries of his will, his needy descendants. Nowadays, the charity has various objectives, including medical research, hospitals and helping the disabled.

Two of Kensington's most charming streets, Pelham and Egerton Crescents (both named after trustees of the charity), were among the first developments here in the mid-century, attracting architects, clergymen, professionals and those of independent means as their first occupants. Their well-mannered, classical, stuccoed façades were by George Basevi, who had recently been responsible for Belgrave Square, and was appointed surveyor to the Smith's Charity in 1828.

Pelham Crescent went up in the 1830s, with Egerton Crescent, known at first as Brompton Crescent, following in 1843–7. The *Survey of London* shows that the price of a new house in Pelham Crescent was about £1000, and each one was lived in by an average of six people, including servants. By contrast, in Crescent Place nearby, the home of those who provided the various valuable local services of the neighbourhood, 105 people occupied twelve houses.

Basevi was also responsible for the design of Thurloe Square, which was built on the Alexander estate nearby in the 1840s, but in 1845 his life was cut short by a fatal fall while inspecting the west tower of Ely Cathedral.

More than 400 of the houses on the Smith's Charity estate were built by Charles (later Sir Charles) James Freake, a highly successful developer who became a friend of Henry Cole and financed the building of what is now the Royal College of Organists (see Chapter 12) from his own resources. At one time he employed 400 people, and it was he who built Onslow Square between 1845 and 1865, using a mixture of grey stock bricks and stucco. The square was built over the grounds of Cowper House, which stood where the block of flats known as Melton Court stands today; but the line of its avenue of trees which led down to the Fulham Road is preserved in the later planting of the square's gardens. At the same time, Freake built Sydney Mews between the square and the Fulham Road, part of which was used as a studio by the sculptor Marochetti. Later the whole mews was converted into studios which were rented to a number of famous artists and sculptors, including Sir Joseph Edgar Boehm, Sir Alfred Gilbert, John Singer Sargent and Philip Wilson Steer. Thackeray moved to Onslow Square from Young Street (see also Chapter 8) and Sir Edwin Lutyens was born there in 1869. Before Onslow Square was complete, more houses were also rising in Kensington's 'museum-land', on land sold off by the 1851 Commissioners: huge, tall regimented rows of ramrod houses, accompanied by almost as many mews, to cater for their affluent owners.

In the old centre of Kensington village there were fewer changes, though the Georgian vicarage which stood at the top of the first stretch of Church Street was demolished in the 1870s to make way for a new road – Vicarage Gate. A new vicarage was built at the end of the cul-de-sac section of the Gate, though this too was knocked down only recently, in 1868, and replaced by yet another version. A short walk westwards was Observatory House, knocked down after the death in 1867 of its owner, the astronomer Sir James South, and replaced by Observatory Gardens.

Only a short distance away, however, a 'new town' arose in 1837–43. This small enclave between Victoria Road and the northern end of Gloucester Road was built, on land formerly known as Town Mead, in a picturesque variety of styles, with modestly proportioned houses and the sort of 'village' atmosphere so coveted today. Leigh Hunt wrote that 'It is all very clean and neat, and astonishes visitors who a few years ago beheld scarcely a house on the spot'; he thought it a distinct improvement on 'the unambitious, barrack-like streets of a former generation'.

Leigh Hunt may have been referring to the small turret that was added to a house in Launceston Place when he voiced his reservations about the 'new town' because it featured 'one of those unmeaning, rounded towers, whose

The morning room in Linley Sambourne's house in Stafford Terrace

43

tops look like pepper-boxes, or "Trifles from Margate"'. Or he may have been talking about the end house in Kensington Gate, which also boasted a similar, but larger, turret.

Kensington Gate was built in 1850–2 by the developer of the 'new town,' John Inderwick. The site was originally known as Butt's Field and was owned by the Campden Charities, founded by Sir Baptist Hicks and his wife. The trustees built a workhouse here in 1778, but sold the property in the 1830s (a new workhouse being built in Marloes Road in 1849, later becoming St Mary Abbots Hospital). Inderwick demolished the old building and laid out Kensington Gate, which was known at first as Gloucester Square, in Italianate style. The two neighbouring houses at the bottom of Hyde Park Gate, Cleeve Lodge and Stoke Lodge, were built in the 1830s, though it is not for them but for Sir Winston Churchill's home at Nos 27 and 28 that Hyde Park Gate is now known.

North of the old village, the Pembridge area took its street names from the builder's home on the Welsh borders, and began to grow up in the 1840s, with a variety of houses, from terraces to huge villas, in the same style that was to be used at Holland Park. But it was in the southern part of the borough, at The Boltons, that the houses were built which have become its latter-day private palaces.

The distinctive layout of The Boltons was settled by 1849. It was built on the Gunter estate and its pleasant stuccoed villas with their leafy gardens were probably the work of George Godwin the younger, who was surveyor to the estate and editor of *The Builder* 1844–83, and who also designed the church in

Detail from Plan of the Parish of St Mary Kensington *by Thomas Starling, 1822 showing Little Chelsea and the junction of Earl's Court Road and Old Brompton Road, with Walnut Tree Walk (now Redcliffe Gardens) and Honey Lane (Ifield Road)*

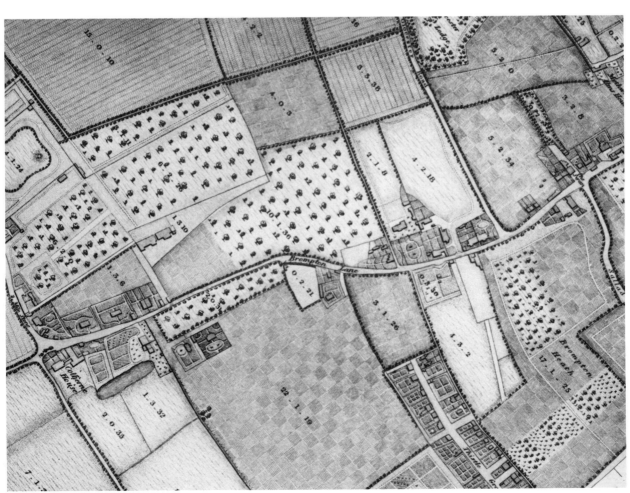

the central, oval garden. The eastern side was ready for occupation by 1852 and its first owners were members of the upper middle class, including the senior partner of Sotheby's, John Wilkinson.

However, Bolton Gardens, the first stretch of which was built westwards from the entrance to The Boltons in the 1860s, was thought superior. It was at No 2 that Beatrix Potter was born in 1866, and here that she passed her lonely childhood and adulthood until her marriage in 1913. Most of these houses, including No 2, have since been replaced by Bousfield School. Down the road were Coleherne House and Hereford House, the latter becoming an exclusive ladies' cycling club in the 1890s before both buildings were demolished and replaced by Coleherne Court (see also Chapter 21).

Hereford House is not to be confused with Hereford Lodge, which stood near where Hereford Square is now. In this latter area, near the southern stretch of Gloucester Road, five villas were built in the second half of the eighteenth century, one of which may have been the home of the builder of Hans Town, Henry Holland (see Chapter 36). In another, the Swedish soprano, Jenny Lind, stayed during visits to London in the 1840s. Like other houses which had been built to take advantage of Brompton's charming seclusion, they and their delightful grounds could not withstand the onslaught of Victorian bricks and mortar, and they were pulled down in the 1880s, when Hereford Square had already been standing next door for thirty years. The days when the area offered the opportunity for genteel retirement are difficult to reconcile now with the crowded, cosmopolitan atmosphere of modern Gloucester Road.

The same area, 58 years later, from a map issued by the Cannon Brewery (1880). The area to the east of Earl's Court Road – shown as 'land laid out for building mansions' – and the site of Evelyn Gardens were the last to be developed

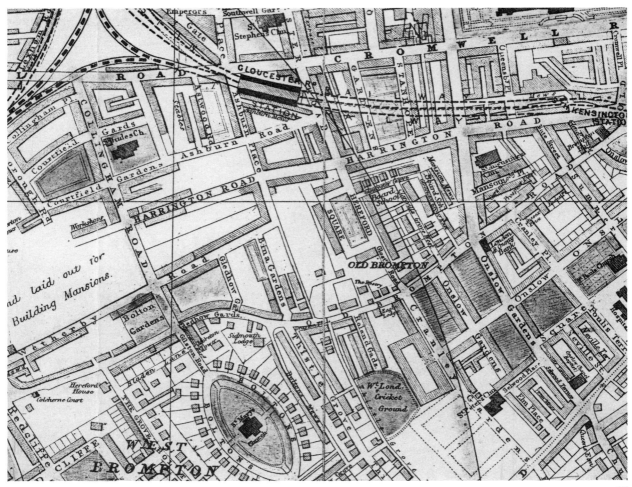

View of Kensal Green Cemetery in 1838

10
Burial grounds

It seems only natural that the burial of London's dead took place, until the mid-nineteenth century, largely in the city's graveyards; until one considers the consequences. Dickens gave a graphic hint of the horrors that lay behind their walls in *Bleak House*, when one of his protagonists finds the body of her former lover among 'piles of bones' and her guide explains, 'they was obliged to stamp upon it to git it in'. Dickens was not exaggerating.

By the 1830s, London's graveyards were literally overflowing. Graves became shallower, their occupants were ejected before they were decomposed to make room for others, and ships' ballast was used to raise the height of the soil so that an extra tier of graves could be dug. In some churches, candles would not burn in the vaults. Elsewhere, steps had already been taken to solve the problem of overcrowded city graveyards, most notably in Paris where the Père-Lachaise cemetery was opened in 1804. England's first cemetery is said to have been the Rosary in Norwich, established in 1819; Liverpool's Necropolis opened six years later.

In London the campaign for public cemeteries was started by a barrister, George Frederick Carden, in 1824 in *The Penny Magazine*, and by 1830 he had enough support for the creation of the General Cemetery Company. In the intervening years a number of architects had also shown interest in the idea, including one, who had drawn plans for an extraordinary pyramid containing many thousands of tombs, to be built on Primrose Hill. Carden's proposals received added impetus when the first wave of cholera began to wash over the country in 1831–2, for its origins in contaminated water were at first unsuspected, and it was thought to spread in filthy conditions and foul air.

A bill 'for establishing a General Cemetery for the Interment of the Dead in the Neighbourhood of the Metropolis' was passed in 1832 and with it came the incorporation of the General Cemetery Company, the first of eight such commercial companies that were authorised between 1832 and 1847. Vicars were compensated for the loss of burial fees by a fee paid to the incumbent of the parish in which the body originated.

Land had already been acquired for the company by a member of its provisional committee, the banker Sir John Dean Paul, who bought fifty-four acres in the then totally rural area of Kensal Green, adjoining the Harrow Road, for £174 per acre. Discussions went ahead immediately as to the layout of the cemetery and the design of its buildings. A battle over architectural styles ensued during which Carden and the Gothic faction proved unable to withstand Paul's preference for the Grecian style; in 1833 Carden left the company.

The cemetery of All Souls was laid out to plans by one Liddell, who had worked under Nash at the office of the Commissioners of Woods and Forests; and the buildings – a gateway and two chapels – designed on austere Greek lines by John Griffith (despite the fact that a competition for the project had been won by a Gothic design). Most of the building work, including the perimeter wall and great entrance arch, was complete by 1834, and in *The Penny Magazine*'s illustration of August in the same year, the cemetery appears as a grand country park – by that time only 193 interments had taken place and made little impact on the scenery.

At Brompton the impact on the landscape of the West London and Westminster Cemetery was considerable. Its grand design and stately buildings were introduced into a largely rural landscape of market gardens in the early 1840s on forty acres of land bought from Lord Kensington: an ambitious architectural feat beside which modern cemeteries pale into miserable insignificance. From the entrance lodge on Lillie Road, a long drive led the length of the site to an octagonal domed chapel. Down the western boundary was a wall of catacombs. Trees beside the central drive gave way to arcades (below which were more catacombs) which opened into a circle, at the east and west edges of which other chapels were planned, though never built.

The building of Brompton Cemetery was a project fraught with difficulties. The company's finances never matched its ambitions, and in 1844 its architect, Benjamin Baud, was sacked after a dispute over money.

The company was founded in 1837, and the architectural competition it held for the design of the site was won by Baud, who had worked with Sir Jeffry Wyatville at Windsor Castle and whose one and only major work seems to have been the cemetery. The ground was consecrated in 1840, before building work was completed, and its disorderly atmosphere, resembling a building site, was blamed by some directors for the cemetery's slow start in attracting burials – there were only eighty-nine in 1841.

While Brompton gradually established itself, the public debate on the question of interment became increasingly urgent. In 1849, after another cholera epidemic, Edwin Chadwick accused the cemetery companies of failing to improve conditions, and the Metropolitan Interments Act that followed in 1850 gave the Board of Health the power to buy private cemeteries, and to close the old city graveyards. Brompton was to be the only cemetery purchased under the Act before it was repealed in 1852 to make way for new legislation empowering London vestries to provide burial grounds of their own. The last plot at Brompton was sold in 1956; Kensal Green is still in use.

London's early cemeteries were fully expected to be regarded as parks for the enjoyment of the public, and were designed and planted with this in mind, as early guide books to Kensal Green make clear, detailing the flora and extolling the virtues of the landscape and views. At Brompton the directors consulted the landscape gardener, J C Loudon, who made a special study of cemeteries culminating in a book on the subject, and who was buried only a few years later at Kensal Green.

The number of tombs and mausolea have obscured the landscape designs, but have become a spectacle in themselves. The Kensington historian Loftie reported in 1888 with great distaste that 'the vulgarity of a majority of the monuments is very painful', but today they are more likely to be found fascinating for their representation of the changing fashions and aspirations of several generations. There are temples and obelisks, shrines and simple headstones; fine sculpture, ridiculous pomposity and banal tributes to the dead.

In Brompton, a prize-fighter is commemorated by a recumbent lion and a sculler's tomb is topped by a boat; angels hover above the Corinthian tomb of

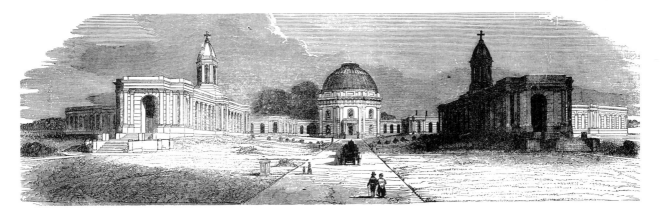

Mary Gibson at Kensal. There are many familiar names: at Kensal, the Duke of Sussex, son of George III; Thomas Barnes, editor of *The Times*; Gaetano Bartolozzi, engraver (see Chapter 33); the tightrope walker Blondin; Brunel, father and son; Decimus Burton; George Cruikshank; Leigh Hunt; Kiralfy (see Chapter 20); the publisher John Murray; the painter Smirke; Thackeray; Trollope; and the circus owner, Ducrow, who had inscribed on his extravagant mausoleum, 'this tomb erected by genius for the reception of its own remains'. At Brompton: George Borrow; Sir Henry Cole; George Godwin the younger, editor of *The Builder*; Emmeline Pankhurst and Val Prinsep (see Chapter 17), are among the famous names commemorated there.

The other two cemeteries in the Royal Borough are far smaller and hidden behind high walls in Chelsea. The Jewish burial ground at Queen's Elm was bought by a society of Jews in 1813 and contains simple rows of headstones with inscriptions in Hebrew and English. At the Moravian private burial ground off Milman Street, however, the layout is more ordered, with the area quartered for the separate burial of married and unmarried males and females.

The Moravians came to Chelsea in 1750, when Count Zinzendorf bought Lindsey House in order to establish a settlement for them which was to be named 'Sharon'. The sect was founded in the fourteenth century in Moravia and Bohemia, deported in the sixteenth century, when they settled in Poland, and recognised by the Church of England when in 1742 the Archbishop of Canterbury granted them a licence.

The Moravian chapel at Chelsea in 1828

Zinzendorf built a chapel and minister's house behind Lindsey House, in what had been the stable yard of old Beaufort House, and established the burial ground where, it was rumoured (falsely), the Moravians were buried upright so as to be ready to spring up at the resurrection. Several Moravians did move to the house, but the venture was not a success and after the Count's death the property was sold in 1770 (see Chapter 25). The old chapel is still used by a congregation of about forty, mostly of Caribbean descent since the Moravian missionaries were active among their eighteenth century ancestors, but the enclosure is now closed to new burials. The out-buildings there have been converted to artists' studios.

A bird's-eye view of Brompton Cemetery, drawn in 1849

11
The Crystal Palace

The transept of the Crystal Palace in 1851

The hopes and optimism, and lofty aspirations of those who planned the Great Exhibition of 1851 were expressed by Prince Albert when he addressed a banquet held for its promotion. He saw man as 'approaching a more complete fulfilment of that great and sacred mission which he has to perform in this world', which was, he believed, 'to conquer nature to his use, himself a divine instrument'. The exhibition of 1851 was to 'give us a true test and a living picture of the point of development at which the whole of mankind has arrived in this great task, and a new starting-point from which all nations will be able to direct their further exertions'.

This gigantic 'living picture' was displayed in 1851, largely due to the presence in the Society of Arts of the Prince and another man of immense energy and enterprise, Henry Cole, who had worked in the Record Office, the Post Office and the Treasury and had a growing reputation as a publicist. As a result of the enthusiasm of these two, the society held an exhibition demonstrating good industrial design in 1847 – the year in which it received its royal charter – and decided to follow it annually with others culminating in a large national version in 1851. But by 1849 the success of the project led the Prince to the decision that the 1851 event must be international.

The combination of the Prince's inspiration and Cole's determination was vital. There was tremendous opposition to the idea from *The Times*, which thought that the project failed to justify the upheaval and expenditure it would cause, and from the reactionary MP for Lincoln, Colonel Charles de Laet Waldo Sibthorp, who based his campaign on the proposed felling of trees on the site of the exhibition building in Hyde Park. Support for the exhibition in Parliament was jeopardised by the death of one of its most influential

supporters there, Sir Robert Peel, two days before a debate on the sanctioning of Hyde Park as the site.

Matters were not eased by the building committee's design for the exhibition hall, which they had produced themselves, after rejecting all competition entries (in the tradition of all good architectural competition organisers). The vast brick building was crowned by a large dome and convinced many people that the Exhibition Commissioners had no intention of pulling it down later, as they had promised, but would leave it as a permanent and monstrous intruder into the open space of the park.

The problem was overcome by the unsolicited interference of Joseph Paxton, who had started his career as an Under-Gardener at the Horticultural Society's Chiswick grounds (see Chapter 43) and become the Duke of Devonshire's Gardener and adviser. He suggested a vast variation on the theme of the greenhouses he had built at Chatsworth, to be built of iron, glass and wood, an idea which he first sketched on blotting paper while at a meeting of a disciplinary railway board. The design was published in *The Illustrated London News* in July 1850, and the building committee was forced to concede the appropriateness and cost-efficiency of the proposal.

Thus, after battles in the press and Parliament, the building of the celebrated 'Crystal Palace' went ahead (the nickname is said to have been invented by *Punch*). It stood just beyond the Kensington parish boundary, stretching from a point near today's Alexandra Gate, where the road to the Serpentine bridge enters the park, to the barracks, and the novelty of its prefabricated construction soon made it one of the sights of London, well before it was complete. Its vast iron frame dominated the park. The glass was

'Visitors from the country', as depicted in The Illustrated London News

View of the Crystal Palace from the north bank of the Serpentine

Paxton's glazing wagon

made by Chance Brothers, who had been using the sheet method only since 1832, and who had to employ thirty extra glass-blowers from France to meet Paxton's order for 293,655 panes; and Paxton had invented an ingenious trolley which ran along the gutters, enabling workmen to fit glass panels into the roof.

The roof had originally been designed as a flat surface, but Paxton altered it later to accommodate the three trees that were saved from the axe, thus creating the great arch of the transept. One of the trees was dubbed 'Sibthorp's elm' in recognition of the MP's campaign for its retention – though Sibthorp remained implacable. By December 1850 there were over 2000 workmen employed on the site.

Whatever the public had thought of early proposals for the Great Exhibition of the Works of Industry of all Nations, nothing but fervent enthusiasm and an almost religious intensity of admiration for mankind's achievements was evident on the opening day, 1 May 1851, as a crowd of over 25,000 filled the Crystal Palace for the occasion. Albert and Victoria conducted the opening ceremony, attended by two of their children, Princess Victoria and the Prince of Wales, and the Queen wrote of the occasion in her journal:

'This day is one of the greatest and most glorious days of our lives . . . The tremendous cheering, the joy expressed in every face, the vastness of the building, with all its decorations and exhibits, the sound of the organ (with 200 instruments and 600 voices, which seemed nothing) and my beloved husband, the creator of this peace festival ''uniting the industry and art of all nations of the earth'', all this was indeed moving, and a day to live for ever. God bless my dearest Albert, and my dear Country, which has shown itself so great to-day. One felt so grateful to the great God, whose blessing seemed to pervade the whole undertaking.'

The building was colossal. Its length measured 1848 ft, compared with St Paul's Cathedral's 515 ft, and it was 408 ft wide, with a nave that was 63 ft high, and a vaulted transept reaching 108 ft. There were over 100,000 exhibits, the value of which was probably about £2 million (excluding the Queen's Koh-i-Noor diamond), covering 'works of industry and art', from agricultural implements to ostrich-feather head-dresses, from Sheffield plate to a stuffed elephant (which was provided for the India section by the museum at far-flung Saffron Walden), and from the much-admired crystal fountain, by F and C Osler, to a 'sportsmans knife' with a bewildering array of eighty blades and instruments.

There were raw materials, decorative arts, machinery, jewellery, stationery and clothing. The British & Foreign Bible Society complained that their stall had been sandwiched between a distilling apparatus, a railway model and a malt machine. The western half of the palace was reserved for exhibits from Britain and the Empire, and the eastern half for those of visiting nations. Stalls cost nothing, but the public paid for tickets ranging in price from a shilling to five shillings for the exclusive Saturday afternoons.

Messrs Schweppe provided refreshment, selling nearly a million Bath buns and thirty-three tons of ham, among other things (though no alcohol was available) and across the road in Gore House, Alexis Soyer, the famous chef of the Reform Club, dispensed a more lavish cuisine in his Gastronomic Symposium of All Nations, amid a lurid colour scheme and down a 300-foot table under a loggia in the garden. Filtered water was provided for the exhibition by the Chelsea Water Works Company.

Beyond the glass walls of the exhibition, the influx of thousands of people from the provinces and overseas to the capital caused relatively little disruption. There was an increase in general sightseeing, and nearby roads sometimes jammed with traffic, but the extra police drafted in to cope with an expected rise in crime had little to do. Street accidents increased, but the only major 'incident' at the Crystal Palace itself was caused by one of the people who had been most fearful of trouble. The elderly Duke of Wellington insisted on visiting the exhibition on what turned out to be its busiest day, 7 October, when no fewer than 93,000 people were there. The excitement caused by his arrival gave those farthest away the impression that the building was collapsing (a fear that had been voiced in the early days of the project), whereupon they stampeded the exits.

The Great Exhibition closed to the public at the end of 11 October, though during the following two days it was open free of charge to exhibitors and their families. By 11 November, it had been cleared and emptied. The Commissioners made a handsome profit of £186,437, of which £5000 was presented to Paxton, who was later knighted.

Despite Henry Cole's attempts in the press, under the not very subtle pseudonym of Denarius (carbon) to argue the case for retention of the building, it was sold for £75,000, dismantled in the summer of 1852 and removed to Sydenham in south London, where it later burnt to the ground in 1936. It was certainly a popular landmark and place of entertainment in south London, but its later role could never rival its original one as the gargantuan showplace of early Victorian Britain in all its confidence, prosperity, curiosity and vulgarity.

'Going to the exhibition', as seen by George Cruikshank

12
The making of museum-land

The success of the Great Exhibition in 1851 left the Commissioners with a surplus £186,000 in their hands, and a clear recommendation from Prince Albert as to how this should be spent. His wish was for London to possess a cultural and educational quarter where the arts and sciences could be promoted and taught, in a way which would be of practical use to industry and make Britain the leading country of the industrialised world: once again Prince Albert was the inspiration, while the execution of his ideas was mainly the achievement of Henry Cole, head of the Department of Science & Art.

'South Kensington' was the invention of the 1850s, and a name which rolled sourly round the mouths of those who resented the power accumulated by Cole and his department, and the money spent on building on the Commissioners' estate. As the buildings rose, compromises were made, both in what was built, and with the original ideas. Modern opinion may question the wisdom of establishing such an overpowering grouping of scholarly institutions, but would at least acknowledge, in an age when building even on a minuscule site is fraught with problems, the boldness of such a plan in a city where grand designs are few and far between.

In 1851 the land stretching from Kensington Gore southwards to Thurloe Square in Brompton was largely undeveloped, with only a few houses lining the northern road, and Brompton Park House standing on the southern edge. Cromwell Road did not exist, and there was as yet no station. The Commissioners bought a total of eighty-seven acres here, and by 1856 had laid out the main roads: Cromwell Road, Exhibition Road and Prince Albert's Road (later renamed Queensgate); and in the same year the area was designated 'South Kensington'.

The high-minded project got off to a somewhat bathetic start when the first 'temporary' buildings were erected for the South Kensington Museum (later the Victoria and Albert Museum) on ground immediately to the east of old Brompton Park House (see Chapter 2). Shortage of funds at a time of war in the Crimea and uncertainty as to which institutions might actually remove themselves to the new quarter, meant that the plans made for a dignified edifice were abandoned, and replaced by large corrugated iron sheds. These served the purpose of affording shelter to the Department of Science & Art's miscellaneous collections, but quickly earned the nickname, the 'Brompton Boilers' which tended to detract from their serious purpose. The department itself was also installed here, as were its Science Schools and Normal Training School of Art (later the Royal College of Art); and over the years, more buildings were added, by Francis Fowke and Henry Scott of the department, some more successful architecturally than others.

Brompton Park House was linked to the 'Boilers', and wooden sheds were put up behind. The entrance to the museum was a distinctly unimpressive wooden lean-to, and the press, though often happy to praise the contents, were impatient with the hotch-potch exterior of what was meant to be one of

Britain's great showplaces. In 1889 *The Art Journal* claimed the situation was 'assuming the proportions of a national scandal'.

West of Exhibition Road, a building had arisen in 1862 which attracted even stronger contempt. In 1858 the Society of Arts, encouraged by the popularity of its 1851 exhibition and with one eye on the possibility of moving to South Kensington from the Adelphi, proposed another international exhibition to rival its predecessor, with the emphasis to be on the industrial arts. Francis Fowke of the Royal Engineers, who worked in Cole's department, was given the task of designing a gigantic building which would house the exhibition immediately to the south of the Horticultural Gardens which were then just about to be laid out for the Horticultural Society and were also designed in part by Fowke, together with the architect Sydney Smirke.

The exhibition was planned for 1861 but was postponed when war broke out in Europe in 1858. Prince Albert died in December 1861, so the exhibition was held in the following year without his beneficial presence, and also without the anticipated visit by the Queen, factors which affected its popularity. It attracted more than six million visitors, but there was no profit, and 'opinion' was howling for the demolition of the prefabricated building: *The Art Journal* called it 'the most worthless and the vilest parody of architecture that it has been our misfortune to look upon. There is not a railway-engine house in existence that would not scorn to be compared with it.' It was demolished by 1864.

The Horticultural Garden also had a limited life. Designed in an excruciatingly formal Italianate pattern, with arcades running up either side to a large conservatory at its northern end (which stood where the 1851 exhibition memorial now stands, behind the Albert Hall), it was opened in 1861, principally as a refined resort for members of the RHS (the society obtained its royal charter in 1860), which at some future date might be surrounded by a

The South Kensington Museum, otherwise known as the Brompton Boilers

The National Training School for Music when first built, now the Royal College of Organists

Alfred Waterhouse's Natural History Museum, which replaced the 1862 exhibition building

quadrangle of public buildings. But the Prince and Cole were both concerned to give it more general appeal, and it was later opened to the public on the anniversaries of the Prince's birthday, despite the society's misgivings.

However, by the 1870s, buildings designed for annual exhibitions had encroached on part of the garden, the RHS's finances were in disarray, and the Commissioners had abandoned the idea of a quadrangle and wanted to build a science museum across the site. In 1888 the society left, and the laying out of Imperial Institute Road (now no longer a through road) and Prince Consort Road began. The curving line of the two roads built later to lead from Prince Consort Road up to the Albert Hall, trace the original boundary of the garden in the days when it represented the northern edge of the Commissioners' development of their estate.

On the site of the vast 1862 exhibition hall, a new building was planned. This was to be another large edifice, a museum of natural history (the British Museum collection which had outgrown its accommodation in Bloomsbury), patents, and other exhibits not yet decided upon. A competition for its design was won, ironically enough, by Fowke, originator of the 'vilest parody' which had just been pulled down. But in the following year, 1865, Fowke died suddenly at the age of only forty-two, and responsibility for the building was given to Alfred Waterhouse, then a young and rising architect. Waterhouse was later given leave to drop Fowke's plans and submit his own, and so it was that the great blue and buff Natural History Museum was built fronting the Cromwell Road.

The Romanesque style, the terracotta walls, the innumerable delightful creatures that decorate both the exterior and interior, and the huge, soaring space of the great hall, may constitute for some present-day visitors one of the most splendid public buildings in London, especially since it was cleaned in 1974–5, but it was not universally welcomed. Loftie declared that the new Natural History Museum and the City Institute (since demolished) were 'built in defiance of all the rules of proportion laid down by the architects of the last

The Imperial Institute, of which only one tower now remains

generation, and equally in defiance of all the rules of taste on which in our own time Mr Ruskin and other writers have so strongly insisted'. Indeed, he had nothing good to say about South Kensington at all: 'That such buildings as those of the late Captain Fowke, of the late General Scott, of Mr Waterhouse, RA, or of Mr Colcutt, his pupil, should be chosen as the home and headquarters of English art training, is in itself nothing less than a national misfortune', he decided.

His comments came in 1888, eleven years before work at last began on the South Kensington Museum to give it a respectable façade, and twenty-one years before the building that provided it, designed by Aston (later Sir Aston) Webb, was opened by King Edward VII. It had been given its present name by Queen Victoria when she laid the foundation stone in 1899. One wonders whether the new, solid and monumental V & A, would have given Loftie any reason to change his mind.

The 'museum-land' of South Kensington grew steadily throughout the second half of the nineteenth century and has continued to change in the present one. The Science Schools – now the Henry Cole Wing of the V & A – were built in 1871; the Imperial Institute by 1893, though all that now remains of it is its tower; the florid National Training School for Music, now the Royal College of Organists, in 1894; the Royal School of Needlework and the Royal College of Science, both in about 1900 and both now demolished; and the Science Museum in 1928. Imperial College now has several modern buildings, and the Royal College of Art is housed in a block built in 1960–2 on Kensington Gore.

It is an area that has managed perhaps surprisingly well to preserve its origins, considering the obstacles that always fall in the path of such grandiose and long-term plans. Prince Albert's wish that it should be devoted to the practical application of science and art for the furtherance of industry and prosperity is not evident everywhere, but it is at least one which is probably as well understood today as it ever has been since the Prince's day.

The old church of St Mary Abbots just before demolition in 1869

In the great expansion of Victorian London, certain parts of old Kensington were overwhelmed by the demands of an increasing and changing population. Such was the fate of the parish church of St Mary Abbots. Having been built for a small, rural village, albeit in a style that was considered at the time suitable for the accommodation of royalty, the church was unprepared for the growth of its congregation in the 1850s and 1860s, and by 1866, not only were the modest proportions deemed unsatisfactory, but its very walls were found to be on the verge of collapse.

No illustrations exist of the medieval church, but its tower survived until 1770; the historian John Bowack described it in 1705 as 'low and built of Flint and rough Stone, with little Art or Order', and it must indeed have been low since, in drawings of the William and Mary church viewed from the east, it is scarcely visible.

The rebuilding of the church in the 1690s was intended to make it a place of worship fit for the King and Queen who had recently established themselves at Nottingham House (see Chapter 3). Of the total cost of about £1800, the King donated £300, Princess Anne gave £100, and the Bishop of London, its patron, £50. The shortfall was made up by the sale of sittings in the pews. At first these cost little, the church being large enough to accommodate the local population easily; but later, demand for pews grew so strong that their owners not only sub-let, but made quite a profit when moving away from the parish. The situation became so grave that the churchwardens eventually consulted counsel in order to alter the original agreements and restrain the enterprising parishioners.

A sketch of the interior of old St Mary Abbots, made just before its demolition in 1869, shows its homely scale, with galleries above the box pews on either side, a flagstone floor, walls covered in memorials, a pulpit and reading desk (donated by King William) facing each other across the chancel steps, and a coved and decorated ceiling. Despite its charming appearance, however, the building was in a precarious state by the time the drawing was made, and indeed had had a life dogged by instability.

An early attempt at aggrandisement was made in 1770 when the last remaining remnant of the medieval building, the tower, was demolished: in view of the running repairs and excavations that had gone on around it, both before and since the 1690s, it did well to survive so long. A new tower was built in 1772, with a small square clock turret rising from its parapet, crowned by a white cupola on pillars and a weather vane at the very top. Such a decorative addition did much for the otherwise plain exterior of the church and no doubt helped to qualify it as a suitable subject for the various drawings and paintings that were made of it at this time.

13
St Mary Abbots

The proposed design of the new church as shown in The Illustrated London News *in 1869*

In her book on the church, *St Mary Abbots Kensington*, Judith Guillum Scott suggests that the recurrence of structural faults may be explained by the shifting of the gravel on which the building stood and by the springs and wells in the area; Holland House was certainly affected in this way (see Chapter 4).

By the 1860s, however, the church itself was no longer admired. *The Church of England Magazine* of 7 March 1860, not surprisingly a supporter of the Gothic style, referred to it as 'a most ungainly modern building' (it was by then about 170 years old) and Leigh Hunt concluded that it was notable 'for nothing but the smallness and homeliness of its appearance'.

A report on the structure by an architect, Gordon Hills, painted the grim picture. Invited to survey the church with a view to making yet more repairs, he wrote on 1 October 1866:

'I have arrived at the opinion that no further expense ought to be incurred upon the old building but such as is necessary to render it safe for temporary use and that there is no wise alternative but to provide for a new Church . . . I found the walls (except in the Tower) constructed outside of the poorest and worst description of bricks I have ever seen in a public building . . . The heart of the walls consists of masses of stone, chalk and flint, evidently the material of the older church taken down when this one was built about 1690 and this old material has very little adherence in itself or to the bad facing. The walls are everywhere penetrated with wet to the inside.'

Hills rounded off his summary by alluding to 'the notorious ugliness of the building because I may add in conclusion that the reason is totally wanting

The new St Mary Abbots before the building of its tower

here which would in a work of beauty or antiquity call for a sacrifice of money or even of convenience for the sake of preserving an ancient memorial'.

The decision was taken to build a new church. A building committee unanimously agreed that Mr (later Sir) George Gilbert Scott should be appointed architect and Scott told the vicar, Archdeacon Sinclair, that he thought the site was 'hardly to be surpassed for convenience or grandeur of position'. Down came the ricketty old building, and up rose the present St Mary Abbots. There was a consecration service in 1872, but neither the vicar nor the architect lived to see its completion, which came seven years later when the 278-foot tower and spire were finished – built in imitation of the beautiful spire of St Mary Redcliffe in Bristol. (The total height was said, at the time, to be 278 ft, but the *Survey of London* reports that a recent measurement found it to be about 250 ft excluding the vane.) The ceremony on that occasion involved the vicar of the time, the Reverend Edward Carr-Glyn, climbing the scaffolding and laying the top stone with the help of a silver trowel which had been presented to him en route, a spectacle which occurred in a stiff breeze.

Soon after the building of the new church, R Weir Brown, author of *Kenna's Kingdom* (1881), was saddened by the way the churchyard had been railed off. Having gained admission he was shown by the gardener the shed in which lay the monuments from the walls of the old church. 'They seemed, indeed, in hopeless confusion; bits of marble were everywhere; some very small for it had been necessary to take the monuments to pieces on their removal.' The memorials were reinstated, however, inside Scott's sober Gothic church, together with King William's pulpit, and include a tablet commemorating the life of Archdeacon Sinclair. Later, in 1889–93, the cloisters were added which afford such a delightful winding approach to the church from the corner of Church Street.

Holy Trinity Church at Brompton, built in 1826–9

It was while Sinclair was vicar of St Mary Abbots that Kensington was divided into smaller parishes, as was the policy of the Bishop of London of the time, Charles James Blomfield. In the Georgian period one or two proprietary chapels had been built, including one at Brompton (in Montpelier Street) but church building got under way in earnest during Victoria's reign. Some were funded jointly by the state and the Church Commissioners – Holy Trinity, Brompton, was one of these – but others were built entirely at the expense of local developers, such as St Paul's, Onslow Square and St Peter's, Cranley Gardens.

Developers were keen that their areas should have impressive churches to lend tone and thus make their houses more desirable. The *Survey of London* observes that, while the Commissioners' churches were often built of cheap bricks, the estate churches were lavishly faced in ragstone. 'High' churches also favoured brick, not only because it was felt to be appropriate for an urban setting but also so that they had the maximum funds available for internal decoration.

Many of Kensington's churches struggle on, with depleted congregations and mounting repair bills. Some have found alternative uses; some, like Holy Trinity, Brompton, have become fashionable venues for weddings and baptisms. Perhaps they have fared comparatively well for city churches in the twentieth century, being in an area of London that has enjoyed a stable, settled and traditional population; but Kensington is now on the international map, with fewer and fewer residents who are 'locals' of long standing, and more and more to whom the parish church means little if anything; though anyone who has walked up Church Walk or Holland Street on a winter's evening and heard the bells pealing out across the old village, would surely be interested in St Mary Abbots' survival.

The opening of the Royal Albert Hall by Queen Victoria in 1871

'On Monday morning her Majesty so far broke through the seclusion which she has observed for some years past as to be present at a great public ceremonial not absolutely connected with her high state functions. The occasion, however, was one which not only warranted, but almost demanded, such a departure from her late mode of life, for it was to add all the solemnity of state to the commencement of a building destined to perpetuate, in a most enduring form, the services which the late Prince Consort rendered to the advancement of science and art.' (*The Illustrated Times*, 25 May 1867).

14
The Royal Albert Hall

The year was 1867; the occasion was the laying of a foundation stone at the site of the Royal Albert Hall of Arts & Sciences. The high solemnity and ceremony of the day was in keeping with the elevated aspirations of those involved with the project, for their aim was to build a hall adjacent to the new cultural centre of South Kensington which would inspire the 'moral improvement of the people'. The death of Prince Albert, the originator of the idea, added a note of reverence to the scheme.

The Prince had first suggested the building of a hall in 1853, and two years later he commissioned a refugee German architect, Gottfried Semper, to draw up plans for an unusual quadrangular development of shops, flats and galleries at the centre of which would be a hall for the performance of music. The plan came to nothing, but the concept of such a hall lodged firmly in the mind of Henry Cole, who, with characteristic tenacity, pursued its realisation for another fifteen years until the building finally took shape at the northern end of the Exhibition Commissioners' estate.

Cole evidently favoured a hall for the masses, so that they would be lured from their 'debasing pursuits'. When the idea for another international exhibition in 1861 was adopted, he envisaged the hall as an integral part, a vast building seating 30,000 where choral singing could take place. Again the idea was abandoned; and when it resurfaced after the Prince's death in 1861, it was in a much modified form, a meeting-place for minds rather than a music-hall, in line with the hopes expressed by Albert at the opening of the Horticultural Society's garden in 1861 that South Kensington would soon be a place where 'science and art may find space for development'.

Such a wish also found favour with people of influence who took a dim view of the hordes that might descend on South Kensington if a huge popular amphitheatre were built. The view was freely expressed later when it was proposed that the Albert Hall Commissioners take over the running of the Horticultural Gardens, whose visiting crowds might boost hall attendances: *The Times* stated its concern about the 'human garbage from the purlieus of the Strand and Haymarket' that might be attracted to the 'comparatively pure atmosphere of South Kensington'.

When the Queen gave her approval to a memorial to the late Prince Consort which would include not only an obelisk or statue in Hyde Park but also a hall on the lines of that which he had envisaged, Cole managed to obtain an audience with Her Majesty, to be absolutely sure of her support, and to confer with her private secretary, General Charles Grey, who had served the Prince in the same capacity and was enthusiastic about the plan.

But all available funds were exhausted on Sir George Gilbert Scott's Albert Memorial; and it was then that Cole resuscitated a scheme for funding the hall which he had first concocted while in Europe in 1858, and which was later to create problems for the administrators who had to balance the books. The proposal was to sell seats at £100 each, in the hope that members of the royal family would lead the way in subscribing, and that some sort of official support would also be forthcoming. Eventually it was: the Commissioners gave the site above the Horticultural Gardens, where Gore House had stood, for the building of the hall on a 999-year lease at the nominal fee of one shilling per annum, and also provided £50,000 in the form of the purchase of seats. And at a meeting in Marlborough House in July 1865, the Prince of Wales presided over a meeting that, at last, made the building of the hall a certainty.

Queen Victoria laid the foundation stone in May 1867, dressed in mourning and welcomed by a large crowd which had gathered along the route and in a specially-erected marquee on the site. Admitting to the assembly that 'it has been with a struggle that I have nerved myself to a compliance with the wish that I should take part in this day's ceremony', she announced that she wished the hall to bear 'his name to whom it will have owed its existence'; and proceeded to spread the mortar with a trowel of solid gold.

The building of the Albert Hall by the firm of Lucas Brothers – who accepted £38,000 worth of the cost in the form of seats – took four years. There had been many designs since the original proposal of 1853, in which the hall varied from a rectangular to a circular form and with which several architects were involved, including Gilbert Scott. Ultimately all thought of reconciling the design of the hall with the memorial opposite was abandoned and the architectural profession was dropped in favour of two engineers, Francis Fowke, who died in 1865, and Henry Scott (see also Chapter 12) who determined the hall's final form, based on Fowke's designs.

The elliptical hall was built in red brick and terracotta, and its height of 155 ft must have made it appear monumental viewed from the north, without the large mansion blocks that now flank it on a similar scale. Three huge porticos marked its north, east and west entrances, and a terracotta frieze ran round the building below the cornice, its sixteen sections designed by different artists and depicting the arts and sciences. The canopy was added later, in the 1890s. Inside, the building was designed as an amphitheatre, with three tiers of boxes around an arena, above which the balcony sloped away to a gallery. Above, a calico 'velarium' was suspended from the roof in imitation of those used in Roman amphitheatres. This was later replaced by an aluminium ceiling in an effort to reduce the echo, and more recently still by suspended diffusers.

Loftie, writing in 1888, described it as a building 'which the want of any kind of proportion reduces to an insignificance from which lavish ornament cannot rescue it'. But generally its ponderous, squat dignity seems to have been welcomed, and certainly made a favourable impression on the American writer Moncure Conway, who felt that 'no building so stupendous and noble'

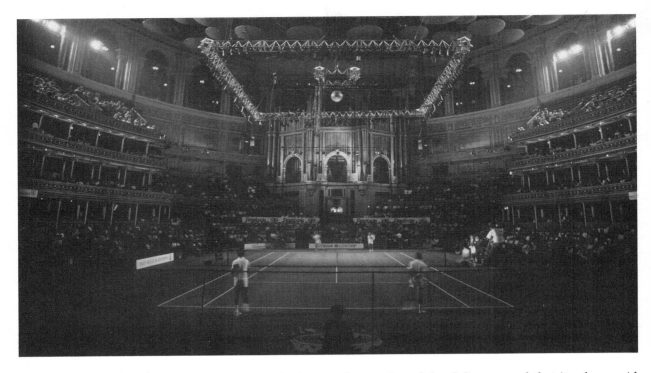

had been built since the erection of the Coliseum, and that its place amid European civilisation was comparable to that of the Parthenon (*Travels in South Kensington*, 1882).

At the opening in 1871, the Queen commented that the hall 'looks like the British Constitution', and certainly the details of its construction were weighty enough: six million bricks were used in its walls, and its double-domed roof was supported by an iron framework weighing 400 tons. Fifteen tanks of water holding 1400 gallons were placed above the gallery in case of fire, and the 11,000 gas burners that lit the interior could be ignited by electric sparks in ten seconds. The great organ contained 10,000 pipes.

Beside such statistics, Cole's original figure for an audience of 30,000 perhaps would not have seemed out of place, but the final figure was much lower at 7000. Of these, more than 1000 were seatholders, and it was to them that the management was forced to turn when it was found impossible to cover running charges: in all the planning of the hall, no allowance had been made for financing it beyond completion of the building work.

In addition, performances were not always fully attended, for the distance of the hall from South Kensington station proved off-putting. Plans were made for an underground railway or tramroad along the route, but this was reduced to a tunnel walkway that never went farther than the old entrance to the Horticultural Gardens just north of Cromwell Road, where it is still used today.

The Commissioners tried to ease the financial difficulties by buying Lucas Brothers' seats, and making these together with their own available for letting; but more drastic measures were necessary. In 1876 the management asked seatholders for an annual levy of £2 per seat, and resistance to the proposal no doubt gave a certain bitter satisfaction to enemies of the hall who disapproved of it as an extravagance, and who resented the ambitions of Henry Cole and his department.

The Building News was among those who spoke their minds: 'The building cost over £215,000, though few would think so, to look at it', the paper railed in March 1876. 'It has been kept up to afford maintenance to a useless staff of officials, who have long traded on the successful manipulation of the associations, which, in the public mind, cling round the memory of the good man whose name the building bears.' The paper described the levy as an 'attempt to fleece the shareholders' and concluded: 'If the House of Commons once sets itself seriously to investigate the accounts of the sums of money which have been squandered in the Court suburb during the last fifteen years to the disgrace of art and the retardation of science, there will be an unpleasant time of it for a few people whose names we could mention.'

The measure was adopted, however, and was the first of several levies on seats; the latest came in 1986 when a sum was fixed of £210 per annum per seat. The management also battled through many arguments before it was settled that seatholders could be excluded from the hall on a certain number of days per year so that it could be let for privately organised functions.

At first, the events held within its walls conformed strictly to the definition of arts and sciences stated in its charter: concerts by the Royal Albert Hall Choral Society (later the Royal Choral Society) and various exhibitions and demonstrations of scientific innovations. Henry Cole gave a convoluted explanation as to why a wine club should be allowed to keep wine in the hall's cellars: 'Wines involve chemistry, Natural History and the Art of using the Grape', he said; therefore the cellars may 'be said to have been used for Science and Art'.

But in 1886 a supplemental charter increased the uses to which the hall could be put, and soon boxing, political meetings, fancy dress balls, temperance rallies and bible-bashing evangelical gatherings all found shelter beneath its dome. Trade fairs, the Chelsea Arts Ball (from 1910 until 1985), basketball championships and clairvoyance demonstrations followed. But it is appropriate to Cole's ambitions for the hall that it is best known today for 'the Proms' which were first held there in 1941 following the bombing of their original home, the Queen's Hall, Langham Place. *The Building News* showed perhaps the clearest understanding of the true role of the hall when it invited it to 'stand forth honestly as a high-class place of entertainment'.

The last night of the Proms

Kensington Canal, with Brompton Cemetery in the background

15

Kensington Canal and the railways

In the great transport revolution that introduced railways to London, the absorption of both Kensington and Chelsea into the capital was inevitably hastened; but at the same time, neither parish suffered greatly from the ravages that afflicted more central areas. While great swathes were cut through the streets of St Pancras and the East End to clear a path for the lines from north and east, the western approaches still consisted mainly of fields and nurseries. The demolition of only a few houses was necessary to bring the District line under Campden Hill to Kensington High Street, and Earl's Court was still a small farm settlement when its first station was proposed in 1864.

The next few years saw an extraordinary outburst of activity; from companies wanting to build lines, from outraged residents, and from developers and landowners, some of whom, such as Lord Kensington, had foreseen the benefits, while others simply made the most of them once the railways had arrived.

The idea for Kensington's first railway sprang from efforts to make the Kensington Canal more profitable. This canal had been built in the 1820s by a group of men headed by William Edwardes, second Lord Kensington, to make Counter's Creek navigable from Counter's Bridge (below today's Olympia station) to the Thames. No doubt the example of the Regent's Canal, which had just been built between Paddington and Limehouse, spurred the company on; but the canal attracted little traffic, cost far more than anticipated to build and was adversely affected by tides.

In 1836 the canal was bought by a newly formed company, the Birmingham, Bristol & Thames Junction Railway (later named the West London Railway Company). They laid a track from the canal basin at Counter's Bridge north to the Great Western and the London & Birmingham railways at Willesden, in the hope that they would use the line and canal for access to the docks down river. But this short railway was no more successful than the canal. It often failed to keep to its timetables, was pilloried by *Punch* so that it became known as 'Punch's railway' and was closed within six months of opening in May 1844.

Eventually, however, events caught up with it and gave it a purpose. The population was growing, and so was railway enthusiasm – there had been 1428

A pen and wash picture by Walter Greaves of the canal where it was crossed by Stanley Bridge and the King's Road

lines promoted in 1845 – and in the late 1850s it was decided to fill in the moribund canal and extend the railway past Earl's Court and Sandford Manor to the Thames, where it would link up with the railways south of the river. This new line, known as the West London Extension Railway, opened in 1863, with a station in Kensington called Addison Road (now Olympia) – which was an important stage in the transportation of milk from the country into London – and at Chelsea just below Stamford Bridge. It is now used as a by-pass route for trains travelling between northern England and the south coast.

In the same year that the extension railway opened, the world's first underground city railway, the Metropolitan, was inaugurated from Paddington to Farringdon, and inspired a tidal wave of proposals for others: 259 were presented to Parliament in 1864. The plethora of schemes and companies jostling for a place in the development of London's railways appears, by today's standards, a huge and disorderly muddle, with rival trains running over the same routes, stopping at adjacent stations and terminating abruptly where their writ ran out.

Thus, a plan for an inner circle by the Metropolitan Railway's engineer John (later Sir John) Fowler was approved, but only for extensions to its line, from Paddington to South Kensington, and from Moorgate to Tower Hill. The gap between South Kensington and Tower Hill was to be filled by the Metropolitan District Railway, a different company which also proposed two spurs: from South Kensington through Gloucester Road and Earl's Court to a junction with the extension railway at West Brompton, and from Kensington High Street down through Earl's Court and back up to Addison Road.

The two companies did not amalgamate until the London Passenger Transport Board assumed responsibility for the underground system in 1933; and the two stations at West Brompton, one for the extension railway and the other for the district, though they stood next to each other for over seventy years until the former closed in 1940, were never united. The two stations at Notting Hill Gate were connected only in 1957–9.

Kensington's original stations were South Kensington, High Street Kensington, Gloucester Road and West Brompton, built between 1865 and

*The 'cut and cover'
method in operation
near Kelso Place*

*Detail from a map produced by the
Birmingham, Bristol and Thames Junction
Railway Company in the 1830s,
showing the route of the Kensington Canal*

Interior of the Kensington Station (now Olympia) in 1868; one of the stations on the newly-opened West London Extension Railway

1869, but South Kensington and the High Street were both altered and given arcades in the early 1900s. Earl's Court was built in 1871 and reconstructed twice, with a new entrance opposite the exhibition stadium added in 1937.

An already established and desirable residential area such as South Kensington was an attractive source of custom for the railway companies, though their very arrival changed that custom, since the proximity of a station obviated the need for horses and carriages, and made the place attractive to a slightly different, commuting kind of middle class. But in North Kensington the effect of the railways was more dramatic.

Beyond the spaciously laid out Ladbroke estate there was, until the 1860s, little but the fields of Portobello and Notting Barns Farms, with the slum of the potteries to the west. But in 1864 a feeder line from the original Metropolitan line at Paddington opened across the fields of Notting Dale to Hammersmith. The Portobello estate quickly became covered with suburban terraces – though some larger houses were built near Ladbroke Grove station – and between the new, raised railway and the brickfields and potteries to the south, a new slum developed.

At the turn of the century the borough saw the inauguration of the 'tube' train. Previously, the undergrounds had been built by the 'cut and cover' method, whereby a deep trench was cut in the ground, an iron arch laid, and the ground filled in above. Now, thanks to the development of a tunnelling shield by the engineer, James Henry Greathead, the electric 'tubes' could be built deep below the rapidly growing and densely built city. Electricity was supplied by the Lots Road power station in Chelsea, opened in 1904, and many of the stations were designed with the distinctive oxblood-red glazed faience tiles that can still be seen today.

The first tube line, the Central London Railway, was opened between Bank and Shepherd's Bush in 1900 by the Prince of Wales, with one of its stations at Holland Park; the Piccadilly line followed in 1907. At first passengers reached the platforms by lift, but in 1911 Earl's Court was the scene of a great innovation. 'London has come into line with New York', declared *The Illustrated London News* on 14 October, 'in the matter of the Escalator, and two moving staircases now connect the Piccadilly "Tube" and the District Railway at Earl's Court Station'. A man with a wooden leg known as 'Bumper' Harris was retained to spend all day riding on the escalators to demonstrate their safety, and *The Illustrated London News* offered its own helpful tips: 'Should a passenger wish to move faster than the stairs, he can walk or run up or down them as they are "going" in the usual way.'

The 'moving staircase' at Earl's Court Station, 1911; the first of its kind

16
Kensington Gardens

The plan for what we know as Kensington Gardens, a place so familiar to generations of children, was first drawn up in the 1720s. In the early years of royal residence at Kensington, the development of the gardens had been limited to the area immediately surrounding the house and stretching north to the Oxford (Bayswater) Road, although Queen Anne had enclosed a deer park to the east. But it was during the reign of George II that the modern gardens took shape, largely due to the energies of his wife, Queen Caroline.

Designs for extensive parkland east of the palace were first made while George I was still alive, by Wise and Bridgman (the latter succeeding Wise as Royal Gardener in 1728). They entailed the creation of a large basin (the Round Pond) from which radiated three avenues; a long lake created from a series of ponds linked by the Westbourne River (the Serpentine); a broad avenue running north to south (the Broad Walk); a mound topped by a revolving summerhouse, and wide expanses of grass planted with trees. Faulkner noted with approval in 1820 the break with the tradition of 'tiresome uniformity' in gardens which this landscaping represented, though in another ninety years another writer on Kensington, Ernest Law, was to complain of the 'tedious monotony' of landscape gardening and welcome the return to 'old-fashioned formal gardens' when the new sunken garden near the Orangery was opened in 1909. Such is the vacillation of taste.

Queen Caroline expended not only a good deal of energy on the landscape project but also considerable sums of money, much of which was spent on the creation of the Serpentine between 1730–1. The work involved was prodigious: the accounts of Charles Wither, Surveyor-General of Woods, included the digging out of '74,644 Cube Yards of Earth'; the grubbing-up and moving away from the waterline of 105 oaks, elms and willows; the removal and replanting

A view of the Serpentine in Kensington Gardens in 1832

A scene in Kensington Gardens with a military band

of twenty large elms which involved eighteen horses and sixty men; the digging of a large well with elm pipes to it from the pond, 'for drawing down the water of the pond at pleasure'; the supply of ropes, wax, pitch, tallow, oakum, straw, and 'Hayseed to sow the Slopes'; and the making of a 'large Shelter Shed for the Workmen to retire to in bad weather'.

Beyond the Serpentine a trench and low wall were built to separate the gardens from Hyde Park, a recently imported idea from France named a 'ha-ha', according to Faulkner, because of the surprise of 'common people . . . at finding a sudden, and unperceived check to their walk'. The bridge over the Serpentine between the two parks was built in 1826 – probably on the site of a dam marked in Rocque's map of 1736 – and a few years later the Westbourne, by then an open sewer, was diverted to prevent the lake filling with noxious mud.

Water was supplied instead by the Chelsea Water Works Company, which was already pumping water into the Round Pond from the Serpentine outfall at Knightsbridge. Not until 1869, however, was the thick, putrid mud removed, causing a predictable assault on all noses in the neighbourhood.

During Queen Caroline's time the gardens were opened to the public on Saturdays and by the time Faulkner was writing the walks were open every day. In spite of their loss of exclusivity, however, they were evidently still a place in which to be seen: Faulkner described the walk leading to the palace as 'crowded on Sunday mornings in the spring and summer, with a display of all the beauty and fashion of the great metropolis'.

By the Victorian era, Kensington Gardens had become the natural place to which nannies and nursemaids took their charges for an airing; but it is with fairy-tale children rather than the mere mortal version that the gardens have been associated ever since J M Barrie created Peter Pan in 1904. Barrie was living in Gloucester Road and fond of strolling in the gardens where he first met the Llewellyn-Davies boys, who lived in Kensington Park Gardens and were to be the inspiration for his celebrated story. After the deaths of their parents, he became their guardian.

A photograph, taken in 1906 by Barrie, of Michael Llewellyn-Davies at the age of six, dressed as Peter Pan, formed the basis of Sir George Frampton's

The Summerhouse

statue of 'the boy who never grew up', which was erected secretly overnight on 30 April 1912 in the gardens so that it would appear as if by magic the following morning.

Peter Pan is not the only statue in Kensington Gardens. There is Queen Victoria, by her daughter Princess Louise, beyond the east front of the palace; King William III to the south – presented to Edward VII by the Kaiser in 1907; G F Watt's sculpture, *Physical Energy* (1904); and the Elfin Oak, a carved tree-stump by Ivor Innes in the playground.

And there is the Albert Memorial. Such an ornate, formal structure seems to have little in common with the gardens, and it stands in what was once part of Hyde Park. The walls of the gardens ran from Kensington Road opposite Palace Gate, slightly away from the road along the carriage drive and up to the bridge over the Serpentine, thus excluding what was to become the site of the memorial, but after it was built, the boundary was moved to the Alexandra Gate.

Prince Albert had expressed the hope that no statue of him would be made in his own lifetime; but after his early death at the age of forty-two, a memorial of some sort was inevitable, and a design by Sir George Gilbert Scott was

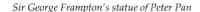

Sir George Frampton's statue of Peter Pan

chosen. Scott described his design as 'a vast and magnificent shrine or tabernacle' protecting the statue of the Prince, inspired by the Eleanor crosses. It was flanked by sculpture 'illustrating those arts and sciences which he fostered, and the great undertakings which he originated'. Building was begun in 1864 and completed in 1872, though the statue itself was not put in place until 1875, and gilded in the following year (the gilding was removed in 1914–15). Above the statue of the prince, by J H Foley, the memorial is richly decorated with bronze, enamels and glass mosaics. Beneath, a sculpted frieze runs round the podium, depicting poets, musicians, painters, architects and sculptors, while the eight groups of statuary represent the industrial arts and the four quarters of the globe. At the time of writing, the memorial needed several million pounds spending on its restoration.

Plans were originally entertained to alter the line of Kensington Road to take it nearer the memorial, but they were never carried out. Neither were calls heeded for a screen of trees between it and the Albert Hall, to disguise the architectural incompatibility of these two monuments to Prince Albert's memory; so that today they remain, contemplating one another across the busy road, a disparate but impressive couple.

The Albert Memorial and the Albert Hall

Yachting on the Round Pond in 1874

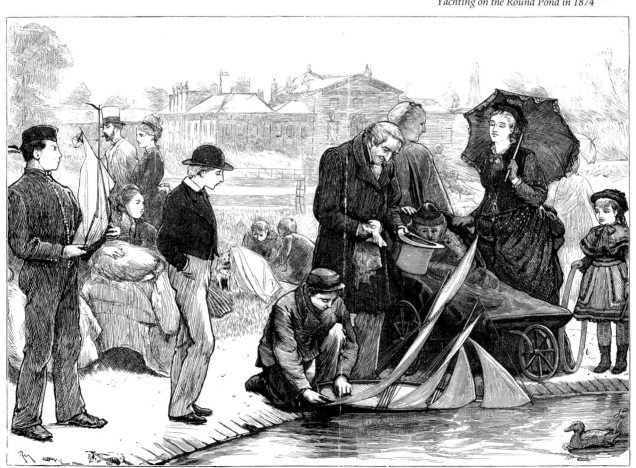

G F Watts' new house in Melbury Road, designed by F Cockerell and George Aitchison

17
The Melbury Road artists' colony

The life of a successful Victorian artist could be an affluent one, and nowhere was this more apparent than in the Melbury Road area, adjoining Holland Park. At one time it boasted no fewer than six Royal Academicians as residents. The presence there of Frederic Lord Leighton is sometimes credited with this popularity, but the origins of Kensington's superior 'artists' colony' lie in a meeting between the Fourth Lord Holland and the artist G F Watts in 1843.

The estate attached to Cope's Castle, as Holland House was originally known, had once stretched from the house almost to the Fulham Road, but in 1768 the owner and descendant of Cope, William Edwardes (later First Baron Kensington), sold the northern half to Henry Fox, First Baron Holland (see Chapter 4) and in 1823 the Fox family began to develop the land. In that year Addison Road was laid out, and three years later work began on the church of St Barnabas, designed for the Church Commissioners by Lewis Vulliamy. The curve in the road was made to avoid the ponds which stood here, next to the old manor of West Town which was consequently also known as The Moats. Development proceeded slowly at first, but by the late 1870s most of the estate between Kensington High Street and Holland Park Avenue, from Addison Road to the railway, was built up: the Gothic terrace in Addison Road was built in 1850, and the two roads of ornate villas known simply as Holland Park were begun in 1860, with their now characteristic canopies added later.

In the 1840s the Holland estate was still rural in character; the park surrounding the house was far larger than today, and where Holland Park Road now runs, there was a farm with a flourishing dairy (which survived incorporated in other buildings on the High Street until the 1960s). This was the background of Lord Holland when he met G F Watts in 1843 in Italy; and this was the scene to which Watts later introduced his friend Thoby Prinsep when he was looking for a house after thirty years in the East India Company.

The Prinsep family took possession of Little Holland House, which stood on the site of the present No 14 Melbury Road, in 1850. Watts came to live with them, and the artistic connection, together with the sociability of Mrs Prinsep, gave the house a reputation as an artistic salon. One enthusiastic visitor, an American called Mrs Twisleton, described the house as a place 'where everything is free and green, and beautiful . . . the rooms are low and large, and wainscotted', and her hostess as full of 'exuberant cheerfulness and beaming kindheartedness'. George du Maurier, however, found the effusiveness unsettling and wondered 'if they are sincere', and Mrs Prinsep's rather different attitude towards Watts's young bride, Ellen Terry, is thought to have contributed to the almost immediate failure of the marriage.

The Prinseps' son Valentine – on whom du Maurier based the character Taffy in his novel *Trilby* – became a professional artist and a friend of another, and rather more talented, rising star, Frederic Leighton. It was the decision of these two young painters to build themselves houses that created the Melbury Road colony, though the styles of their homes were quickly superseded by the Queen Anne revival designs of Norman Shaw.

By the 1860s Lady Holland's extravagant lifestyle had created debts that were too great a burden for even the extensive development of the estate to bear, and she was forced to sell more land. Two plots in Holland Park Road, which had been laid out originally as a mews for houses fronting the High Street, were sold to Prinsep and Leighton in 1864, though Lady Holland claimed to find the process of selling land for building 'a very bitter and sad pill'. Later, in the 1870s, she was forced by her financial situation to sell the entire estate to a relative, the Fifth Earl of Ilchester (see Chapter 23).

The two houses were built simultaneously, but in very different styles. Prinsep had his designed by Philip Webb in subdued Gothic, with steep gables and two large pointed arch windows in the north-facing studio; while Leighton, following the classical, Mediterranean style of his paintings, chose a

G F Watts in the garden of Little Holland House with the almost completed statue of Physical Energy

Residence of the late Lord Leighton. No. 2 Holland Park Rd. Kensington.

Leighton House, showing the Arab Hall on the left

Inside Lord Leighton's Arab Hall

relatively austere classical form devised by his friend George Aitchison, who later recalled that 'Every stone, every brick – even the mortar and the cement – no less than all the wood and metalwork passed directly under his personal observation.'

Leighton was a charismatic figure. Aitchison later said that he had appeared in Rome in 1853 'a light-haired, handsome, dashing young fellow of twenty-two, with fine manners, who let the most brilliant as well as the wisest sayings fall from his lips in his sprightly and animated conversation'. His first picture was exhibited at the Royal Academy when he was only twenty-five, and was bought by the Queen; and he went on to become President of the Royal Academy in 1878.

His house was designed to revolve around his work, with modest public rooms on the ground floor, one bedroom and a large studio. The interior was decorated with brilliant blue tiles by William de Morgan in the entrance hall, ebonised woodwork throughout, and a plaster cast of part of the Parthenon frieze in the studio, but it was not until Aitchison added the celebrated Arab Hall for Leighton in 1877–9 that the house gained a reputation for lavish decoration. Built into this hall, an imitation of the Muslim palace of La Zisa in Palermo, are Leighton's collections of ceramic tiles, together with a mosaic frieze by Walter Crane and a 'zenana' oriel window brought from Cairo. At the centre of the domed room, amid its shimmering colours of blue, jade, gold and silver, is a small fountain, trickling ceaselessly into a pool of black marble.

Leighton entertained lavishly and highly successfully. In addition to the normal round of parties he also held annual musical evenings, one of which Mary Gladstone recorded in March 1882: 'Pictures and pretty people all in

Tower House, now 29 Melbury Road

picturesque confusion, tapestry and lovely screens with hangings and a gallery with beautiful children gazing down.' Such occasions helped establish him in the world of fashion, and his house was part of his bid for position. As Mark Girouard showed in his article, *The Victorian Artist at Home* in *Country Life*, 16 November 1972, and in his book *Sweetness and Light* (1977), the idea that an artist's house should reflect the nature of his work was a recent one, developing only as the Victorian age accorded artists a status and income they had not previously known. Melbury Road was the scene for the emergence of the purpose-built studio house where a new kind of artist painted a new style of picture for a new breed of capitalist collectors.

After Leighton and Val Prinsep built their houses, others followed. The fantastic Tower House, the French Gothic folly of the architect, William Burges, was begun in 1876, though its interior was unfinished at Burges's death and not completed until the actor, Richard Harris, bought the house, in 1969. The decoration rivalled Leighton's Arab Hall in its extravagance: stone corbels, painted walls, friezes, carving and stained glass, with furniture designed to match.

To this bizarre collection of disparate architectural styles was added the gentle domestic elegance of Norman Shaw's Queen Anne designs when the artists Marcus Stone and Luke Fildes (later Sir Luke) commissioned him in 1875 to create Nos 8 and 31 Melbury Road respectively (modern numbers). Fildes wrote of his house, 'I consider it knocks Stone's to fits', and it is his house in particular, looking down the road from behind its garden wall, which seems still to evoke the secluded, leafy character of the area as it was in the 1870s.

In 1875 the lease on Little Holland House expired and it was demolished. Other houses were built, for Watts, the sculptor Hamo Thorneycroft and the artist Colin Hunter, and Holman Hunt lived in the road for the last few years of his life. The architect Halsey Ricardo was responsible for one house there before its owner, Sir Ernest Debenham, commissioned him to design the distinctive No 8 Addision Road in 1905, in green, blue and cream. Many of the studio houses of Melbury Road are now flats. Only Leighton House, bought in 1926 by Kensington Borough Council, remains as it was built, though its half-empty rooms and lifeless studio are pale reminders of the urbane artist and his elegant parties.

Little Holland House, home of the Prinseps

John Everett Millais

18 The battle of the styles

The Victorians did not hold London's Georgian streets in high esteem. They thought them dingy and monotonous: Leigh Hunt called them 'unambitious' and 'barrack-like'. But the Italianate style with which they lined their own new streets, though superficially more decorative and considered at the height of their popularity to rival the palazzi of Italy, began to appear equally uninspired to sections of the architectural press, and by the time the last residential plots on the 1851 Exhibition Commissioners' estate were being taken in the 1870s, writers were lobbying for change.

Change was inexorably on its way in the form of the 'domestic revival' in architecture (see also Chapter 40). Reacting against the sterility of builders' debased Italianate speculations, architects were developing a style based on seventeenth and eighteenth century English and Flemish vernacular traditions. The use of brick was central, since it allowed more freedom for expression than stone and was more 'honest' than the outmoded stucco; and it was also recommended on the grounds that it could withstand the grime of London's atmosphere more successfully than other materials.

The northern end of the 1851 Commissioners' estate, by the end of the nineteenth century, found itself the setting for a number of houses inspired by the Queen Anne revival of the 1870s: not because of speculative building but because the site offered opportunities to several wealthy young men who were keen to have such houses built for themselves by fashionable architects such as Richard Norman Shaw. The Commissioners' enlightened attitude towards these houses, which differed so radically from neighbouring streets, sprang from their desire to see building of quality on their estate.

Some of the brick houses of this period have since disappeared, demolished to make way for the expansion of Imperial College, or destroyed by bombs in the Second World War. Those that remain have mostly been converted to flats.

Lowther House, designed by Norman Shaw:
it now houses the
Royal Geographical Society

Indeed, many large Queen Anne houses built as speculations, by developers newly enamoured of the style, represented the swan-song of the spacious family town house in London. Even as they were rising, Norman Shaw and others were designing the high-class 'mansion' blocks of flats which became the fashionable new homes of a less affluent, more practical era.

The Queen Anne houses in the Queen's Gate area, however, were individual commissions by prosperous patrons of architecture, and the work done for them makes the classically inspired house built at the same time for the artist John Everett Millais, in nearby Palace Gate (No 2), look very conservative, if not plain old-fashioned by comparison. The first to go up was Lowther Lodge, on the corner of Kensington Road and Exhibition Road, designed by Shaw and built in 1873 for William Lowther MP. It was the only one of its type in the area, resembling a country residence rather than a town house in its rambling plan and irregular style. It was sold in 1912 to the Royal Geographical Society which extended it in 1928–30 and continues to occupy the building. Shaw also designed four houses in Queen's Gate, two of which, Nos 196 and 170, have survived; and another Queen Anne architect, J J Stevenson, was responsible for the two houses known as Lowther Gardens which were built in 1877 on the corner of Prince Consort and Exhibition Roads (and now house the National Sound Archive).

The domestic revival was not adopted in sizeable speculative developments in Kensington until the 1880s, but thereafter it was widely accepted as the successor to the Italianate style and became common wherever there was room left to build. Such an opportunity arose when Kensington House was demolished in 1882 and its site opposite the palace was sold. The buyer was Jonathan Carr, who had already speculated in the creation of a fashionable suburb at Bedford Park in Chiswick, with architectural contributions from Norman Shaw and others; and he aimed at a similar project here. The site was

Lowther Gardens in Queen's Gate, designed by J J Stevenson and A J Adams

named Kensington Court and Carr employed J J Stevenson to design the first houses on the eastern side, which were built by 1886 and had their own private electricity supply from a specially built generating station nearby. Stevenson designed a few more houses on the estate but thereafter he and Carr appear to have had nothing more to do with the development, which was filled up with more houses and some flats.

In south-west Kensington, the effect of the new architectural trends took a more dramatic form when the firm of Ernest George & Peto designed twenty-nine large houses in Harrington Gardens and Collingham Gardens. Amid the acres of nondescript middle-class streets that were spreading across this part of the borough, these buildings sprang up as flamboyant monuments not only to a new way of architectural thinking, but to a way of life which was already doomed to decline. The houses were built between 1880 and 1888 by Peto Brothers, both the builders and one of the architects being sons of the mid-Victorian contractor, Sir Samuel Morton Peto. They embraced a lively range of vernacular styles, disdained conventional internal layouts and orderly lines of façades, and flaunted Flemish gables, tall chimneys and leaded lights.

Contemporary 'informed' opinion was mixed on the manifestations of the domestic revival. Some thought it refreshing, others were irritated by what they saw as its studied 'quaintness'. Loftie took to Kensington Court, describing it as 'a kind of museum of beautiful buildings', but could not cope with excesses he found elsewhere. In the newly inhabited area south and west of Cromwell Road, he wrote, 'Street after street, and square after square, are built in red brick and terra-cotta after designs by various eminent architects of the school founded by Mr Norman Shaw, but far outstripping his views, and plunging into the wildest extravagances of what may be called eclectic art.'

The influence of the new red-brick architecture was lasting, and lent itself well to designs for the mansion blocks which were beginning to rise in London.

Flat-living was an alien concept to the Victorians, with unfortunate French connotations: it was well known that the French led ill-ordered and unhygienic lives in their cramped apartments, and the possibility of sharing a roof with people not of one's own class caused the English middle class great consternation. But lack of space in London and increasing numbers of people living in subdivided houses made blocks of flats an obvious development, and Kensington received its share.

Probably the best known was, and is, Albert Hall Mansions, partly because of its situation but mainly because of its architect, Norman Shaw. It was built in the 1880s after Shaw had been to Paris to study the design of apartments there, and had spacious flats with accommodation for servants, and a northerly façade overlooking Kensington Gardens with characteristically Shavian shaped gables and shallow oriels at fifth-floor level.

Others followed: Campden Hill Court in 1898–1900, Coleherne Court (where the present Princess of Wales lived before her marriage) in 1901–4, and York House in 1904–5, the latter built on the site of two older buildings, York House and Maitland House. In 1907 Oakwood Court near Holland Park, newly built, was advertised in a *Souvenir* of the Royal Borough as having flats which were 'constructed on the latest scientific principles, with separate Sculleries, Pantries, and Servants' accommodation'. The latter feature was vital. Flat-dwellers might have to put up with living in far greater proximity to their servants than they had done in the past, but every flat provided in some way, however modest, for their accommodation, so that respectability might be preserved.

Nos 39 and 41 Harrington Gardens, designed by George and Peto

Herbert Gribble's winning design for Brompton Oratory

The Church of the Immaculate Heart of Mary, as the Brompton Oratory should be correctly called, owes its existence to the great changes that affected English Catholics in the nineteenth century. In 1828 came the Catholic Emancipation Act, and in the 1840s John Henry Newman's Oxford Movement led to his own and others' conversion to the faith of Rome. Then in 1850, the Catholic hierarchy was re-established after a break of three centuries. Not all the changes were to the Catholic layman's liking, but they encouraged an assertion of the faith of which the oratory was a bold and magnificent expression.

Until the middle of the nineteenth century, the site on which the Brompton Oratory stands lay beyond the spreading streets of Brompton. There had been a building there for some time: an eighteenth-century house and wax-bleaching shop was enlarged in the 1820s by Robert Pollard to create a boys' school called Bemell House. But development was concentrated to the south of Brompton Lane (as Brompton Road was known) and, as Edmund Daw's map of the parish of St Mary Abbots in 1852 shows, the gardens of Brompton Park were still more or less intact to the west. Opposite stood the Bell and Horns Inn (see Chapter 13) and to the rear was Holy Trinity Church, built in the 1820s.

In such surroundings the great oratory church would have looked extraordinary. But the Congregation of Oratorians began their life at Brompton modestly, thirty years before their new building arose and before they could know that they were helping to bring fashionable prestige to the area.

The original 'oratory' was simply the place where people gathered to hear the words of St Philip Neri in sixteenth-century Rome. Later, he became the leader of an informal community of priests and, after his death in 1595 and canonisation in 1622, oratories spread throughout Europe. It was not until the 1840s, however, that the movement reached England via John Henry Newman.

Newman's famous conversion to Catholicism in 1845 had been followed by a visit to Rome, where he had been ordained priest. Returning to England on Christmas Eve, 1847, he established the oratory in the Midlands and was joined there by another convert, Frederick William Faber, who had been living with a band of followers on the Catholic Earl of Shrewsbury's estate.

In 1849, Faber came to London and established the capital's first oratory in a converted building in King William Street off the Strand, in order to pursue the Oratorians' aim of urban evangelism. The house soon proved too small, and so with the help of a few Catholic grandees, the community began to look for a site where it could build a new church in the Italian style, 'with eventually a stone façade and Corinthian columns'. When they settled upon Brompton, Faber enthused that it was 'the Madeira of London', but Newman was unimpressed. He had been instructed by Pope Pius IX to work among the upper classes and thought the location 'a neighbourhood of second-rate gentry and second-rate shops'.

The site was bought for £16,000 in 1852 and work was soon under way on a new house, designed by J J Scoles in a plain Italianate style, with its own private chapel and library. This is the building which still stands today; and a temporary church followed. Funds for a more elaborate church, it was felt, could be collected later. In the thirty years during which this 'temporary' building was in use it was altered many times and the interior made increasingly elaborate; but nothing could disguise the fact that it looked more like a large shed than a church and the Catholic community of Kensington was no less concerned about the appropriate appearance of their place of worship than were the Anglicans of St Mary Abbots (see Chapter 13).

At the time that the Oratorians were appealing for funds – 1874 – the Gothic elevations of St Mary Abbots had been standing for only two years, and the spire was not yet built. The Gothic style of architecture was almost unquestioned, at this time, as the proper dress for a place of worship, in both Anglican and Catholic circles: the leading architect of the Gothic Revival, after all, was a Catholic convert, A W Pugin. But the Oratorians were the leaders of an ultramontane revival in England and all their inspiration came from Rome, which left them in no doubt as to the appearance of their proposed new building: 'Italian Renaissance' was the style stipulated in their instructions to the architects competing for the job of designing it.

The differences between Pugin and the Oratorians became known as the 'Rood Screen controversy' because of Pugin's fanaticism for a reversion to the mysteries of the medieval mass behind its rood screen. By contrast, Faber held 'popular services' at the oratory in a mission spirit which brought in thousands to what the Oratorian Father Sebastian Bowden described in *The London Oratory Centenary 1884–1984* as 'Processions with banners and images, confraternities in their habits, festoons and lights innumerable, orchestral and popular music – all that makes a Catholic feast . . . as completely and simply as in a Catholic country.' Pugin, who considered Gothic to be the only truly Christian architecture, was horrified by the Oratorians' Italianate interpretation of Catholicism.

Having decided on the building of a new church and received £20,000 from the Fifteenth Duke of Norfolk for the purpose, the congregation held a competition for its design in 1877. In fact, a design by the obscure architect who was to win the competition, Herbert Gribble of Plymouth, had already appeared in *The Building News* of March 1876. The paper at first claimed that this was the plan favoured by the congregation but had to apologise the following week, saying that it was 'merely a suggestion'.

It seems unclear as to the truth behind this *faux pas*, but Gribble certainly had links with the Oratorians. Not only was he a recent convert to Catholicism, but he had worked in the office of the Catholic architect, J A Hansom, at Arundel and had been involved with the building of the church of St Philip Neri there in the late 1860s–early 1870s; in the Duke of Norfolk's home town it would not have been surprising if their paths had crossed.

Gribble's entry for the competition – which was not the same as that published earlier – was one of thirty, which included work by George Gilbert Scott junior, Henry Clutton and E W Godwin. The competitors were given no

The altar of St Philip Neri

guidelines as to cost, and the entries' estimates varied from £35,000 to £200,000, a fact which made life difficult for the architect Alfred Waterhouse, who had been called in to report on the designs. He narrowed the choice down to four, and the Fathers decided upon Gribble's. Needless to say, their choice was not universally approved.

There was some misunderstanding of Waterhouse's brief, which seems to have been to advise rather than adjudicate; and the early publication of Gribble's first design prompted some peeved letters to the press. An anonymous 'competitor' wrote on the subject to *The Builder* on 3 August 1878:

'It is, of course, no business of the public or the profession how the Fathers spend their money. They are perfectly at liberty either to take advantage of so rare an opportunity and such princely funds to erect a building which shall be emphatically *usui civium decori urbis* – something on the lines of the Early Renaissance, and recalling the hopes of its vigorous dawn, like our own Gothic revival, to be so soon and so sadly dashed; or they may, if they prefer, erect a building with all the coarseness of St Peter's or St Paul's carefully copied, and all their redeeming merits carefully eliminated. True artists may weep, – as they weep over the Albert Memorial, the new Foreign Office or the new Law Courts, – at magnificent opportunities frittered away on gilding and tinsel, on vulgarity and deformity, or mere masquerading . . . But, sir, the public, and the profession especially, have a right to complain . . . when the Fathers advertise for designs, put some thirty members of the profession to an expense of many hundred pounds, and then give the first premium to a design which they have had before them for years. . . .'

The appearance of such an imposing building on the site was also a blow to the standing of Holy Trinity, though initially the latter seems to have had few admirers to regret its disappearance behind the bulk of the oratory: *The Builder* in 1843 thought the exterior of Holy Trinity 'most unsightly'. Nevertheless, its eclipse by the new Catholic church can hardly have been welcome. Loftie, writing in 1888, describes the oratory as being 'thrust most awkwardly, and indeed, architecturally speaking, impudently, almost against the corner' of Holy Trinity.

The oratory was unfinished when its dedication service took place in April 1884, lacking its outer dome and its façade. It is easy to forget, when reading of the ceremony that attended the occasion, how relatively humble the building looked without its now familiar Portland stone façade, pediment, pilasters and statuary, topped by the dome and lantern. Nevertheless, the service was impressive. Cardinal Manning gave an address to a congregation that included not only the most eminent Catholic laymen in the country, but sixteen bishops, 250 clergy, a choir of 150 and an orchestra of forty.

Newman did not attend the service; it seems he was concerned at the ostentation of the building. Father Faber had been dead for twenty years; Gribble too, died before the church was complete, half-way through the construction of the façade in 1894, at the age of only forty-seven. The dome was added, to a design by George Sherrin, in 1895–6.

The interior was designed by an Italian architect living in Kensington, Commendatore C T G Formilli; he gave it its bright colour scheme, the relief figures and panels, the gilding and the pulpit. Gribble had proposed a splendid *baldacchino* for the high altar but this was never built. The Italian character of the place was emphasised by the addition of several church furnishings from Italy: an altar and reredos of 1693 which was placed in the Lady Chapel, and marble figures of the twelve apostles, carved in the late-seventeenth century for Siena Cathedral.

The oratory enjoyed the attentions of a number of wealthy patrons apart from the Dukes of Norfolk, six of whom are commemorated in the clerestory windows of the nave: Mrs Elizabeth Bowden, for example, gave St Wilfrid's Chapel in memory of Father Faber, and Mrs Daglish-Bellasis gave the outer dome. By the time it was completed, the oratory had already become the fashionable focus for Catholics from miles around.

It was the growing significance of Kensington to the Catholic church that prompted the building of Our Lady of Victories at the western end of Kensington High Street in 1867–9, and this church became the pro-cathedral, seat of the Archbishop of Westminster, until Westminster Cathedral was consecrated in 1902. (Our Lady of Victories was destroyed by a fire bomb in 1940 and rebuilt to designs by Adrian Gilbert Scott in 1955–8.) Then in 1874 the English Catholic hierarchy decided to establish in the same area a college 'for more advanced studies for the higher classes of the laity'. Thomas John Capel, a prelate who moved in fashionable Catholic circles, opened the college in the same year at Abingdon House, a Georgian building which stood where Cheniston Gardens is today; but a few years later he resigned and the school folded. Debt was given as the official reason, but it seems that the true explanation lay with his homosexual connections. He was soon declared bankrupt, left the country and died in California. His skill at converting upper class Protestants earned him an unflattering portrait as Monsignor Catesby in Disraeli's novel *Lothair*.

View of the Oratory (circa 1890)

Entertainment at the Royal Kent Theatre in 1830s

20
Earl's Court and public entertainment

In the days when Kensington was a small village, Pepys and his contemporaries used to enjoy a ride out from London to a tavern there, or to a pleasant garden. The Victorians were much more demanding. They were more numerous, better educated and more mobile; they were also hungry for knowledge and had an apparently insatiable appetite for the curiosities and wonders of life. The Great Exhibition of 1851 (see Chapter 11) was both a reflection of this and a stimulation to such an appetite, and as the century progressed, mass entertainment came to be provided on an increasing scale, culminating in Kensington with the Big Wheel at Earl's Court.

The pleasure-gardens of the eighteenth century were forerunners. There was one at Cromwell or Hale House where 'feats of horsemanship' were performed; and at the Florida Gardens off Hogmire Lane, a German gardener converted his grounds into a place of public amusement. He later went bankrupt and the Duchess of Gloucester, George III's sister-in-law, had a house built on the site, the house later taking her name and in turn providing the reason for the renaming of Hogmire Lane, Gloucester Road.

Kensington also briefly had its own theatre. The Royal Kent Theatre stood in what is now Old Court Place and opened in 1831. But it was a short-lived enterprise: in 1838 the company playing there made off with the takings, and by 1850 there were five new houses on the site.

In early 1851, William Batty, the owner of Astley's Amphitheatre in Westminster Bridge Road, bought a long-established nursery on Kensington Road (where the artist Samuel Palmer is thought to have had a cottage) and opened what became known as Batty's Hippodrome, where de Vere Gardens stands today. Batty aimed to attract visitors to the Great Exhibition with his fantastic programme, which included ostrich races, a monkeys' steeplechase, brass bands, comic scenes and chariot contests in an arena of which not a trace remains.

Contemporary periodicals show it as a large and splendid coliseum decorated with coats of arms and flags, and it was claimed that it held 14,000,

'Ascent of Mr Hampton's "Erin-go-Brach" balloon, at Batty's Royal Hippodrome, Kensington', in 1851

though the true number was probably far smaller. Performances began at five o'clock each day and reserved seats cost three shillings, but third-class seats could be had for sixpence. *The Lady's Newspaper* thought the displays of horsemanship and chariot-racing 'about the most exciting subjects for contemplation in or near the metropolis'. Its fortunes were closely tied to the Great Exhibition, and it was open for only two seasons. Building began on the site in the 1870s.

Kensington's largest and most successful place of public entertainment was at Earl's Court. The name may now conjure visions of nothing but trade shows, but for years before the present building went up, the same ground was the scene of a series of notable exhibitions that introduced exotic cultures and unheard of curiosities to a public as yet unspoiled by the mass media.

The land on which the exhibitions were held became available as a result of the layout of the District and Western Extension Railways (see Chapter 15) as well as others over the border in Fulham. There was a triangle of waste ground and several other, barely connected patches, which the first exhibition organiser, John Robinson Whitley, described as nothing but 'a cabbage-field and a sea-kale swamp' when he found it in 1884.

The land had been bought a few years earlier by Monsignor Capel (see also Chapter 19) for the building of a Catholic public school, but the plan had come to naught. The site suited Whitley's purposes, for he was planning an American trade exhibition and needed somewhere with good communications – it was near no fewer than four stations, Earl's Court itself, West Brompton, West Kensington and Addision Road (now Kensington Olympia).

When the exhibition took place in 1887, its character had changed. Several exhibitors having dropped out, Whitley had signed up Colonel William Cody, better known as 'Buffalo Bill' and his 'Rough Riders and Redskin Show', consoling himself with the thought that cowboys and Indians were 'every bit as much a genuine product of American soil as Edison's telephones or Pullman's railway cars'. Thus the trade fair became as much an entertainment

Chariot racing at Batty's Hippodrome

A hand-bill for the Earl's Court American Exhibition

as an exhibition, setting the standard for years to come at Earl's Court and proving immensely popular with the public.

An arena was built on the main triangle, and an iron and glass exhibition hall arose on another strip of land. Beyond that were gardens with a switchback railway, a toboggan slide and the largest bandstand in London. Whitley employed 2000 men working day and night shifts to prepare the site and build the seven bridges required to link the different areas, and the grounds were planted with trees, shrubs and flowers native to North America.

Rocky Mountain scenery was erected in the huge arena to set the scene for Buffalo Bill's troupe, which included 110 Indians complete with families, about 150 cowboys and their 'broncos' and ponies, sixty-four tents, a dozen wagons, eight steers, sixteen buffaloes, 300 saddles, various weapons and the famous Deadwood stage-coach, not to mention the gun-toting Annie Oakley.

In order to receive the American businessmen who came over for the exhibition, Whitley organised a Council of Welcome composed of various eminent gentlemen, and this formed the basis of the 'Welcome Club', which had its own villa in the grounds, facing the bandstand, and a summer season of garden parties which were a feature of pre-1914 London life. The author of *London and the Western Reaches*, Godfrey James (1950), recalled sitting in the garden, before the days of wireless, seeing the results of the America's Cup series signalled by flares: red for a lead by the defender, green for the challenger, Sir Thomas Lipton.

Nearly 15,000 people visited the American Exhibition each day for five months, including the Queen and Gladstone. Whitley followed it up with more: an Italian exhibition in 1888, French in 1890 and German in 1891 – all with elaborate painted scenery to create the appropriate setting – before retiring at the end of 1891.

His successor at Earl's Court was the Hungarian showman Imre Kiralfy, who had staged various spectacles in America and at Olympia before buying the Earl's Court lease in 1894. He rebuilt the site and opened with a spectacular 'Empire of India' exhibition, complete with an Indian village imported from Poona, 200 native craftsmen, a herd of elephants from Burma and a 'jungle' of stuffed animals.

In 1897 he held a 'Great Naval Spectacle' in the Empress Theatre on an adjoining site, in which dummy ships manoeuvred in a concrete tank holding a million gallons of water, and explosions were created by the dropping of sodium from the roof. One day the sodium store overheated and exploded, destroying the offices and killing two people and several cab-horses. His 'Greater Britain' exhibition of 1899 involved the accommodation of 200 Zulus and their families in a specially built village, and in 1904 the canals of Venice were reproduced in the theatre.

Spectacular as these shows were, the most dramatic feature of Earl's Court during these years was the Great Wheel, built in 1894–5 on the lines of the Ferris Wheel at the Chicago Exhibition of 1893. It rose 300 ft into the air and carried forty cars, each capable of holding forty passengers. *The Builder* thought the cost of such a thing should have been 'devoted to some more useful end than carrying coach-loads of fools round a vertical circle', but the public loved it, and were not at all deterred by its one major hitch, when it stuck one summer night with a full load of people who had to spend the night aloft. On their return to solid ground they were each given a £5 note, which not only averted criticism and stimulated free publicity, but inspired the music-hall song, 'I've got a five-pound note'. The wheel was dismantled in 1907 and sent to the scrap-heap. By then Kiralfy had left for the White City, but exhibitions continued until 1914, when the grounds were used to accommodate Belgian refugees. After the First World War the site was partly derelict, but in 1935 the lease was granted to Earl's Court Ltd, which opened an ice-rink and built the present exhibition hall.

The place of such nineteenth-century amusement grounds could be said to have been taken in our own century by the cinema, and Kensington possesses one of the earliest purpose-built theatres for the showing of films, the Electric Cinema Club in Portobello Road, built in 1910. It later became a music-hall but was altered very little, and is now a cinema again. The Coronet on Notting Hill Gate, on the other hand, started life as a music-hall and became a cinema in the 1920s. Marie Rambert (later Dame Marie) established her Russian School of Dancing in an old Congregationalist school in Ladbroke Road in 1929 and named it the Mercury Theatre; the Rambert ballet school remains there still.

Earl's Court as it was at the time of the American Exhibition in 1888, seen from Lillie Road; today's exhibition building occupies the site on the far right

The big wheel

Shopping after dark in Brompton Road, 1895

21
The Royal Borough

Towards the end of her long reign, Queen Victoria turned her attention to the old royal palace in which she had been born and where she had lived until her succession to the throne in 1837. Kensington Palace had been deserted by monarchs at the end of George II's reign, and during Victoria's time was occupied by various members of the royal family – the future Queen Mary was born there in 1867 – but it was falling into decay. As early as 1838 its partial demolition had been suggested, but the Queen was attached to the place – 'the poor old palace', as she referred to it – and vigorously opposed a suggestion that it should become the home of the National Gallery.

In the year of her diamond jubilee, Victoria decided that her subjects' curiosity should be gratified by the opening of the palace. In the following year a notice appeared in the press, announcing that 'the State Rooms at Kensington Palace, in the central part of the building, which have been closed and unoccupied since 1760, together with Sir Christopher Wren's Banqueting Room, attached to the Palace, shall after careful restoration be opened to the public'. Walls had to be rebuilt, roofs reslated and floors renewed, before the decorative work inside could be restored, having reached an advanced state of neglect. Ernest Law, writing in 1899, described dirt-encrusted woodwork, broken balusters, smoke-blackened paintings and 'damp oozing from the walls'. The job was done at last, and the palace was opened to the public on the Queen's eightieth birthday, 24 May 1899.

It was in the same year that the London Government Act was passed, which made various changes in Kensington one of which was that it became a borough. Two years later it took a leap in status when the new King, Edward VII, conferred on it a new title. The Secretary of State for the Home Department wrote to the mayor announcing that he 'commanded by His Majesty to inform you that in accordance with the expressed wish of Her Late Majesty that her birth at Kensington Palace should be so commemorated, His Majesty has been graciously pleased to command that the Borough should in future be designated "The Royal Borough of Kensington"'. In a 1910 booklet on the borough, Ernest Woolf wrote smugly that 'there were considerable heartburnings and envies amongst the other London Boroughs, which, even after a lapse of nine years, have not been altogether alleviated'.

Another change made by the Act was the alteration of Kensington's boundaries, so that the palace was taken from what had been the parish of St Margaret's, Westminster, and included in the new Royal Borough; though part of South Kensington's museum-land and the eastern part of Kensington Gardens remained outside, as they do to this day.

The boundary also affected the northern part of Kensington. Hitherto, its border had reached just beyond the Great Western Railway but had excluded most of Kensal Town, which was part of the detached portion of Chelsea and had become a notorious slum. But in the 1899 reorganisation, this curious outpost of Chelsea was abolished and proposed for division between the new boroughs of Kensington and Paddington.

The outgoing Kensington Vestry was not pleased. At a meeting in June 1899, it resolved that 'it is most undesirable that the Borough of Kensington should have any portion of Chelsea (detached) added to it, as under the special circumstances of the case, that area can better be dealt with, and, it is believed more acceptably to the inhabitants of both Parishes, by being retained as part of the Borough of Chelsea'. Despite its protests, however, the new boundary was drawn round the northern edge of Kensal Town, presenting the new borough council with a problem on a similar scale to the potteries, which was yet to be

An invitation card from the publisher Andrew Tuer and his wife for a party at Church Walk Gardens in 1882: the site is now occupied by a block of flats, Ingelow House

The Plough Inn at Kensal Green, a favourite haunt of the artist George Morland

solved (see Chapter 6).

Kensal Town began life as an isolated hamlet situated on high land, where a tavern known as The Plough became a popular resort after a walk across fields from Kensington – George Morland is said to have painted there. When the Grand Junction Canal was dug to the south of the settlement in 1801, its isolation was emphasised, and in 1838 the Great Western Railway created another barrier on the north. For a long time there were only two exits, one north and one south, and between the two the settlement, now known as Kensal New Town, expanded and degenerated quickly into a slum. Charles Booth described it in 1902 as 'just as full of children and poverty as was the old woman's dwelling in the nursery rhyme'.

Though not as vicious as some of London's slums, it was endowed with outward conditions almost as bad. Booth catalogued them: 'windows broken and dirty; boys and girls, of from twelve to sixteen, looking ill-fed; ragged, hatless, and unwashed; trousers in tatters, skirts frayed and draggled; and toes showing through miserable boots'. Some of the houses were 'colonized by riff-raff driven from the slums of Tyburnia, on the construction of the Great Western Railway', and other inhabitants lived off their wives' earnings as laundresses, work which gave the area the nickname 'Soapsuds Island'. Among an influx of Irish from Lisson Grove (which the Great Central Railway had recently ravaged) begging was 'chronic'.

Booth's map of Kensington in his *Life and Labour of the People in London* (1902), showed it to be predominantly a wealthy area, but there were gaps in the great swathes of yellow that denoted wealth. North Kensington suffered from overcrowding and too many mean lodging houses; and in what is now known, somewhat optimistically, as Earl's Court village, Booth found the women's morning work 'enlivened by gossip and nips of gin'. The more respectable streets of the neighbourhood were also perceptibly on the decline: Booth noted that 'the tide of fashion and favour which for some time flowed towards Brompton exhausted itself in the Wild West of Earl's Court'.

Otherwise, Kensington was a prosperous place. It was the home of 'higher government officials, lawyers, heads of City houses, etc, etc', and Booth's yellow ink, his highest category, delineated Addison Road, the heart of the Ladbroke estate, Pembridge Square and much of Brompton and the museums area. Today it might highlight other areas, but it would certainly be equally prolific.

Until the second half of the nineteenth century, London's high streets were lined with a motley collection of small shops and their signboards and awnings. Those who patronised the shops were local folk, or the servants of grander inhabitants, the latter confining themselves to visits by carriage to their tailors.

But the Victorian age brought great changes. The huge increase in white-collar workers and a comfortable middle class created a demand for more than the mere necessities of life, and a need for a different kind of shop to satisfy it. And as London's suburbs grew, Kensington's shop-keepers found themselves in the midst of this new clientele. Their response to the challenge made their stores some of the most popular in the metropolis.

Kensington High Street bears little resemblance today to its appearance in the 1860s, when it was a narrow thoroughfare crowded with traffic and bordered by a jumble of buildings. In 1868 the Metropolitan Board of Works embarked on a street-widening and slum-clearing programme which resulted in the rebuilding of shops between Young Street and the new station. And the first half of the present century saw even more radical changes as the Barker's empire constructed its two great palaces of commerce. Since then, Barker's operations have contracted to the eastern end of its main building, but at one time the company's tentacles spread beneath the road to its north side, and into the old houses of Kensington Square, an overpowering force which, though a huge commercial success, was not always welcomed by nearby residents.

John Barker was born in Maidstone in 1840, and apprenticed to a draper at the age of twelve. In the 1860s he worked at Whiteley's, the store which became a famous institution in Westbourne Grove, but left in 1870 to set up on his own in two of the new shops in Kensington High Street. He had moved into an area where several local businesses were already doing well: Seaman Little

22
The great stores

Harrods in 1892; two years before it was decided to put up a completely new building

& Company had been there since 1861; the Toms family had had a 'toy and fancy repository' for more than thirty years when one of their number went into partnership with a local draper, Charles Derry, in 1869; and the Ponting brothers had come to London from Gloucestershire in the 1860s, working in Westbourne Grove before opening their own shop shortly after Barker, in 1873.

All these establishments prospered rapidly, drawing customers not only from the expanding immediate neighbourhood, but from farther afield since the railway deposited passengers practically on their doorsteps. They extended into adjoining premises, rearranged their lengthening shop-fronts, and diversified their wares, adding everything from ironmongery to the novel and highly popular ready-made lady's dress. They drove out smaller tradesmen and caused congestion in the side streets with their delivery vans.

But beside the onslaught of Barker's expansion, others paled into insignificance, and sooner or later succumbed. Seaman Little & Company were the first to go as Barkers swept into their buildings in 1894, Pontings followed in 1907, and in 1920 Derry & Toms were merged with their competitor, leaving Barkers in possession of the entire southern frontage to the High Street between Young Street and Wright's Lane. Both Pontings and Derry & Toms, however, retained their own names and something of their own identities until they were finally closed in 1970 and 1973, respectively.

A little nearer London, Harrods was expanding with similar rapidity. Henry Charles Harrod had started his first shop as a wholesale grocer and tea dealer in Stepney in 1835, moving to Eastcheap in 1849, and buying premises in Brompton from a friend four years later. His son, Charles Digby Harrod, took over in 1861, at a time when this part of London was being transformed from an undistinguished and haphazard ribbon of buildings into a fashionable suburb. The shop spread into neighbouring premises and one-storey extensions built out over front gardens (a common development still evident along the north side of Notting Hill).

Barkers in 1893

Pontings and Derry & Toms in 1926

Kensington High Street before the road was widened again in the twentieth century: the town hall can be seen on the left, and the station on the right

In 1894 a complete rebuilding was decided upon by the board (Harrods having become a limited company in 1889). They chose as architect C W Stephens, who had worked for their rival, Harvey Nichols (founded in the 1850s, though Benjamin Harvey had opened his draper's shop in 1813). It was a good year for Stephens, for at the same time as he was given the Harrods commission he also secured the job of designing Claridges.

Harrods in its new guise, a vast and elaborately decorative edifice of terracotta and plate glass occupying an entire island site (though part of it was at first used as flats) was complete by 1912. It had made history several years earlier, however, when the first escalator in Britain was installed within its walls. This was simply a gently inclined conveyor belt running between two hand-rails; but Harrods felt the need to anticipate its possible effect on customers by posting an attendant at the top armed with sal volatile and brandy.

Rebuilding on a more modest scale had also been going on in the Barker's empire in Kensington High Street, but in 1929 reconstruction on a grand scale began at Derry & Toms. The work was directed by Barker's own architect, Bernard George, with the help of an American, C A Wheeler of Chicago: for the American, Gordon Selfridge, had set the pace in department store design with his stunning, steel-framed, neo-classical building in Oxford Street in 1909. The new Derry & Toms boasted lifts in onyx and marble surrounds and an elegant fashion theatre, and its exterior was decorated with a stylish frieze of alternating relief panels and figured metal grilles.

Its most famous feature, however, was the roof garden, which was opened in 1938. Carefully laid out with drains, layers of rubble and soil, and a water

supply from an artesian well, the garden had a sun pavilion at its centre and was divided into three areas: a 'Tudor Court', an English woodland with a lake and waterfall, and a Spanish garden. Though closed intermittently in recent years, it was kept open throughout the Second World War and has now re-opened as a night-club with an open-air restaurant in the summer.

The reconstruction of Barkers which resulted in the handsome building that now dominates the top of the High Street took place gradually, between 1927 and 1958. By the 1920s Barkers had grown to the point where it owned houses on all sides of Kensington Square immediately behind the store, and was proposing the demolition of three of them in order to build a new loading bay. Residents' fears were therefore alleviated by the rebuilding plans of 1927 which left the square untouched.

In fact, Barkers had given up neither their plans nor their holdings in the square – by 1939 they owned two-thirds of its houses. But the loading dock was

The first escalator to be installed in Britain, at Harrods in 1898

98

eventually built elsewhere, many of the houses in the square were listed, and its residential status has outlived the expansionary heyday of the department store. Behind Barker's great bronze-framed windows now, the shop itself (part of the House of Fraser since 1957) has shrunk into one end, relinquishing much of its space for offices.

The expansion of Kensington High Street's other famous store, Biba, was brief indeed. Having begun as a small boutique in Church Street in 1964, it became a highly successful part of the 'Swinging Sixties'; but by the time Barbara Hulanicki and her husband Stephen Fitzsimon had created what *The Times* described as 'five floors of incredibilia' in the old Derry & Toms building in 1973, the best years were behind them. Biba on a grand scale caught the full force of the recession; its parent company, Dorothy Perkins, was bought by British Land and the shop was closed in 1975.

Biba – the face of Kensington in the 1960s

The Harrods sale

The Ismaeli Centre on Cromwell Road

23
Modern Kensington

Kensington's history is brief, but crowded. It is unlike those provincial towns that were already holding important markets and building cathedrals in the early Middle Ages, and a parvenu compared with the Roman city of London itself. But in a rapidly expanding metropolis, where villages can be, and have been, consumed without trace, it has fared tolerably well. Its old centre still retains something of its character, though the church and most of the houses have been rebuilt since their earliest days; and many of its later streets are intact, for they have adapted highly successfully to the twentieth century.

There have been many losses too. Apart from the obvious ones, the open spaces, there are few of Kensington's large old houses still standing, and hardly anywhere that still breathes the atmosphere of leafier times, when the barriers between town and country were fewer, and farms still coexisted with brash brick terraces. In Melbury Road and Holland Park there are perhaps brief glimpses of it, and Church Walk, where Ezra Pound lodged as a young man, still conveys a village ambience. But in Earl's Court Road, where there was a farm as late as the 1860s, and in the starkly metropolitan streets in the seedier quarters of the Portobello estate, all reminders of the recent rural past are gone.

One of Kensington's last green patches disappeared quite recently, when the new town hall was built. Until the Second World War this site was occupied by four detached houses: the eccentric Victorian Abbey House at the southwest corner, Niddry Lodge and the Red House at the top, and Hornton Cottage on the east side. But during the war the Abbey was damaged by bombs, and in 1946 it was sold to the borough.

The new library, described appropriately by its architect E Vincent Harris as 'a building of good manners', was opened immediately to the south in 1960, and in 1968 permission was granted for the building of Sir Basil Spence's town hall, after a public inquiry. Baroness Spencer Churchill had already planted a giant redwood in memory of her husband, Sir Winston Churchill, on a site carefully marked so that it would be enclosed by the new development, and other trees on the edge of the site were shored up during the massive building operation.

In 1973 the sump and car park foundations were laid in 'the big pour', a continuous pouring of concrete which began at 7 o'clock in the morning with the arrival of sixteen lorries, and continued until half past five that evening with a steady stream of twelve lorries per hour. The resulting building, which was officially opened in 1977 and serves the borough of Kensington and Chelsea as created in 1964, is a dramatic and spacious arrangement of brick, concrete and glass, but its 'good manners' do not extend to an empathy with the surrounding brick and stucco terraces and their gardens.

On the hill behind the new town hall, two landmarks have been lost: the Grand Junction Water Works Company's tower, which was demolished in 1970 and Tower Cressy, a Victorian folly, in the 1940s. Beyond, Notting Hill Gate was relentlessly redeveloped after the last war with a staggeringly unimaginative line of box-like buildings which now look as shoddy as anything they replaced. Kensal Green and parts of north Kensington have also been steadily redeveloped since the turn of the century to eradicate the slums that grew up there.

Kensington escaped relatively lightly from the bombing raids of the Second World War, but its most famous landmark, Holland House, suffered a direct hit. Having seen most of its farmland built over in the nineteenth century, its parkland had also contracted in the twentieth when Ilchester Place and Abbotsbury Road were created in the 1920s. After standing derelict for several years after the war, the house and fifty-two acres were bought from the Earl of Ilchester by the London County Council in 1951 and most of the damaged building demolished, leaving only the arcades, part of the ground floor and the east wing, where there is now a youth hostel. In 1959 a new addition to this was opened, designed by Hugh (now Sir Hugh) Casson and Neville Conder.

A later, and much more attractive building by Casson, Conder & Partners was built in 1980–3 on an empty island site between South Kensington station and Cromwell Road for the Ismaeli community: a striking combination of grey and blue granite with angular teak-framed windows. It contrasts favourably with the blue, tent-like Commonwealth Institute (opened in 1962 as a successor to the old Imperial Institute of South Kensington) which sits so self-consciously on the edge of Holland Park.

More changes are taking place on the site of the barracks which stood until very recently between Church Street and the palace. They were built in 1856–8

Church Walk

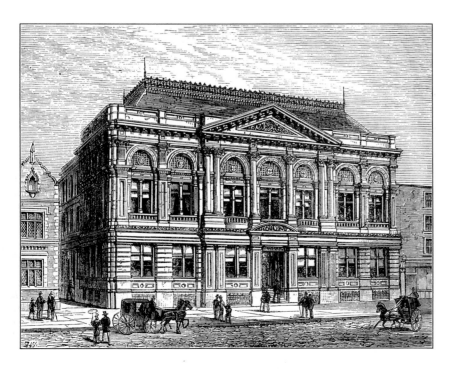

The Kensington town hall of 1880

Armoured maiden at the Notting Hill Carnival

Kensington's new town hall, designed by Sir Basil Spence

on the site of the palace's old kitchen gardens, over the site of a proposed road which had not materialised, and in place of which the footpath was created which is still much used today. The barracks ceased to be used as such in 1972, and are being replaced by flats and a shopping centre, which will no doubt change the character of Church Street and perhaps return to it something of its old status as centre of the village.

Kensington's most contentious building in recent years was the old town hall, an undistinguished though not unpleasing Victorian building which was built in the High Street next to the Vestry Hall (now a foreign bank) in 1880 as a result of an unsatisfactory design competition. When the council's plans to redevelop the site were publicised there were calls for the building to be listed, but before this could be done, a demolition gang was sent in one weekend in 1982, and by the Monday morning there was a gaping hole where the façade had been. While uproar ensued over the council's underhand behaviour, the building remained in this unseemly state until it was finally pulled down in 1984 and the very modest present block was built to designs by Sir Frederick Gibberd & Partners.

Such battles are inevitable in every high street, and Kensington has its share of mediocre buildings which should be allowed to make way for replacements, in the event of worthy new designs being forthcoming. It is right that the borough, one of the most prestigious and affluent in London, should encourage outstanding new buildings as well as conserving the old. The latter it has proved it can do in its conservation areas; of the former there is less evidence.

The affluence of modern Kensington is at once both a continuation and a change from its past. Its Victorian streets and squares were built for professional and independent classes and still house their modern counterparts, though families are less in evidence than in the nineteenth century. Its mews and artisan terraces have long since been 'gentrified'; but the number of residents of long standing dwindles as property changes hands every few years for increasingly large sums which only high earners can afford.

Those who provide the essential services to such a community can rarely now afford to live nearby, as they did once. But there is still variety in the borough. There are unmodernised streets, rented accommodation and a multi-racial population in northern Kensington, council housing in Kensal Green. Students still live in parts of South Kensington, and Earl's Court is well established as the Australian quarter. In All-Saints Road, Notting Hill, the reputation is of a different kind: it was classed by police in 1987 as one of the three most difficult inner-city areas in the capital. The Notting Hill Carnival has

The Notting Hill Carnival in Ladbroke Grove

developed into a major annual event, for many races as well as the West Indians who started it in 1966, and seems to have shaken off the violent reputation it acquired in the 1970s. Portobello Road, which has had a market almost from the time when it was first built up in the 1860s, may now be lined with pricey antique shops at its southern end, but further along it still has the clothes and food stalls for which it was traditionally known.

Kensington, in short, means different things to different people; and yet it has a distinct identity of its own. Perhaps that identity derives from its stuccoed villas, or its garden squares; perhaps from its associations with Prince Albert or with the great Victorian middle classes. More probably, it is fostered by the unique combination of these and other facets. Faulkner would not recognise all the areas that were developed after he wrote his history of Kensington in 1820, but he would certainly be familiar with the 'constant bustle' of the High Street, and, one hopes, with those aspects of the place that have survived to remind us of our history.

Chelsea

24
Early history and Sir Thomas More

No one quite knows how Chelsea acquired its name. Nineteenth-century historians of the village devote many pages to etymology, but they all arrive at similar conclusions. The Anglo-Saxon version of Cealchythe, or Celchyth, may mean a chalk-hythe, or wharf; or it may derive from chesel-ea, a chesil, or gravel bank. Chelsea lies on gravel, not chalk, thus supporting the latter theory; but it may have been used as a landing place for chalk from elsewhere.

Whatever the explanation, the name 'Chelsey' was in common use by the sixteenth century, and by the 1700s was being used with the spelling we know today. It was a pleasant place, only a few feet above the Thames but high enough to provide the first stretch of good land west of Whitehall: *The Domesday Book* records a vineyard there as well as pasture and ploughland. On either side lay the marshes of the Five Fields (now lower Belgravia) and Fulham, and the boundaries of the manor were marked both east and west by streams, the Westbourne and Counters Creek respectively. To the north lay the heathland of Brompton and the hills at Kensington.

The Thames was the village's lifeline and archaeological finds in the river indicate its early use. In the 1730s the historian Maitland, in the course of searching for the point where Caesar crossed in 54 BC, discovered a ford, 'about ninety feet west of the south-west angle of Chelsea College Garden (the Royal Hospital); whose channel, in a right line from the north-east to the south-west, was no more than four feet seven inches deep', and which he felt sure had once

Previous page: 'Chelsey Colledge', circa 1700, now the Royal Hospital

106

been lower, before embankments and bridges had been built along the shore. In 1856, when the foundations of Chelsea Bridge were being laid, workmen discovered skulls and weapons which dated from the Iron Age, and the Celtic Battersea Shield which was found in the river is now in the British Museum.

Until 1900 the parish of St Luke's, Chelsea, also included a detached area covering about 140 acres immediately to the north of Kensington, later known as Kensal New Town. Somehow this became attached to the Chelsea manor, perhaps when it belonged to the Abbey of Westminster in the early Middle Ages, and remained a part of the parish until it was divided between the new boroughs of Kensington and Paddington in 1899. To the inhabitants of medieval Chelsea, it was a remote rural outpost (see Chapter 21).

Chelsea in the early sixteenth century was a tranquil, rural spot, a very small village with a medieval church and only one large house, that of the Earls of Shrewsbury (see Chapter 25). It was here, set back from the Thames and where Beaufort Street now runs, that the newly knighted Sir Thomas More built himself a house that has been famous ever since, even though the building itself stood for little more than 200 years before completely disappearing.

More was born in London in 1477/8 and educated at Lambeth Palace, Oxford and the Inns of Court. As a young man he spent four years at the Charterhouse before marrying Jane Colt in 1505, and entered King Henry VIII's service in 1518, becoming Under-Treasurer in 1521 and Lord Chancellor

Sir Thomas More

Kip's view of Chelsea from Britannia Illustrata *(circa 1707) showing Beaufort House and its gardens, with Gorges House to its immediate left, Lindsey House in front, and Little Chelsea in the top left corner*

Beaufort House, an illustration of 1834
copied from Kip's view

in 1529. He lived with his family in Bucklersbury in the city of London, marrying the widow Alice Middleton after Jane's death in 1509, but at some point in the early 1520s they all moved to the new house at Chelsea. In 1523/4, More also owned Crosby Hall which was moved to Chelsea in 1908, though there is nothing to show that he ever lived there (see also Chapter 44).

There are no illustrations of More's house other than Kip's view, which was drawn more than 150 years after it was built, during which time it had been altered by successive owners. But the style of the Tudor house can still be seen in the drawing, and if we detach it from its formal setting and place it amid groves of trees, with a simpler garden and a view of the wooded river banks, we may gain an impression of how it looked in the 1520s and 1530s. Ellis Heywood, writing in the 1550s, described it as being 'surrounded with green fields and wooded hills . . . covered with lovely flowers and the sprays of fruit trees'.

Desiderius Erasmus wrote much on the subject of his close friend, More, and the combination of his vivid descriptions and a vision of Tudor Chelsea tends to make one link the two together. But Erasmus never saw the Chelsea house; his last visit to England was in 1517, though he met More at Calais and Bruges in 1520/1. Nevertheless, his words best illuminate the family life of one of England's most famous men.

Erasmus wrote in a letter to Ulrich von Hutten that More lived with his second wife, Alice, who was several years older than her husband and whom More had married almost immediately after Jane Colt's death for the sake of his children, 'as pleasantly and sweetly as if she had all the charms of youth. You will scarcely find a husband who by authority or severity has gained such ready compliance as More by playful flattery . . . With the same address he guides his whole household in which there are no disturbances or strife. If such arise he immediately appeases it and sets all right again, never conceiving enmity himself nor making an enemy. Indeed there seems to be a kind of fateful happiness in this house so that no one has lived in it without rising to higher fortune; no member of it has ever incurred any stain on his reputation.'

Erasmus's words today have an ominous ring, but More lived with his family at Chelsea for over a decade before Henry VIII's patience with his principles ran out and he was condemned to death. The household was a large one: as well as More, his wife, three daughters and one son, there were Margaret Gigs, a foster-daughter; Anne Cresacre, his ward who married his son John; his stepdaughter Alice; William Roper, later his biographer, and husband of his favourite daughter Margaret; and his two other sons-in-law, William Dauncey and Giles Heron.

Many visitors came to Chelsea, among them the most powerful people in the land, but in spite of his high office, More led a simple life. He entertained his humble neighbours, and looked after the poor of the village. He liked to sit upon the flat roof of his gatehouse and contemplate the view; and he sang in the choir of St Luke's. A popular anecdote in Roper's *Life of Sir Thomas More* tells how the Duke of Norfolk came to Chelsea and was astonished to see him at church in the role of a humble parish clerk.

When Holbein came to England from Basel in 1527 with a recommendation from Erasmus, he was entertained at Chelsea. He had already illustrated More's *Utopia*, and now he painted at least two portraits of his host, as well as a family group, the sketch for which survives and shows More surrounded by the women of his household, together with his son John and the 'fool', Henry Patenson. When the King saw Holbein's pictures in More's house he is said to have exclaimed, 'Is there such an artist alive, and can he be had for money?', an inquiry that led to Holbein's appointment as Court Painter.

The importance of study in More's family is evident from the group sketch, in which several figures hold books. In a letter to his children's tutor, Gunell, he wrote that he preferred 'learning joined with virtue to all the treasures of kings', and that 'if a woman . . . to eminent virtue should add an outwork of even moderate skill in literature, I think she will have more real profit than if she had obtained the riches of Croesus and the beauty of Helen. I do not say this because of the glory which will be hers . . . but because the reward of wisdom is too solid to be lost like riches or to decay like beauty.'

Holbein's drawing of More (fifth from the left) and his family

More's tomb in the church

James Hamilton's map of Chelsea, 1664

More was never deceived by high office into making his happiness dependent on the King, as many others did. Roper tells how Henry liked to confer with him on 'matters of Astronomy, Geometry, Devinity, and such other Facultyes, and sometimes of his worldly affaires', but that More learned how to 'dissemble his nature' to make himself less sociable so that he could 'goe home to his wife and children (whose company he moste desired)'.

One incident recorded by Roper presaged the great man's fate. It took place at Chelsea where Henry liked to visit his Chancellor and where, on this occasion, in the garden 'walked with him by the space of an houre, holdinge his arme aboute his necke'. When the King had left and Roper expressed his delight in his affection for More, the latter replied: 'I find his grace my very good lord indeed, and I beleeave he dothe as singulerly favour me as any subjecte within this realme. Howbeit, sonne Roper, I may tell thee I have no cawse to be proud thereof, for if my head could winne him a castle in France . . . it should not faile to goe.'

More was beheaded on 6 July 1535 after a year's confinement in the Tower. The act of attainder against him expelled his family from their house, and Lady Alice moved to the old parsonage nearby. More's head was stuck upon a pole until his daughter recovered it and had it placed in the Roper family vault in St Dunstan's, Canterbury; his body was buried in the chapel of St Peter's ad Vincula in the Tower.

Whether it remained there or was returned to Chelsea – and if so, by whom – is something of a mystery. John Aubrey stated in his *Lives* that it was 'interred in Chelsey church, neer the middle of the south wall', and in a letter to *The Times* on 11 May 1935 Reginald Blunt wrote that nine coffins were removed from a vault at this point in 1872, when his father was rector and was having heating installed in the old church. The coffins were taken to the new St Luke's in Sydney Street, and, said Blunt, 'Rumour, I know – but probably ex post facto rumour – had it that one of the coffins was much shorter than the rest.'

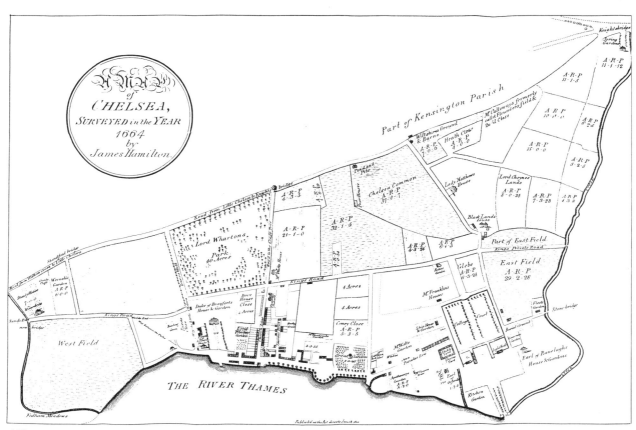

A view of Henry VIII's manor house based on an illustration in Faulkner's history of Chelsea

25
Riverside palaces

'The village of palaces' is an old name for Chelsea, and an apt one. Though the neighbouring village of Kensington became known as 'the old court suburb', Chelsea has an older claim to royal connections, for there were members of royalty living here long before their successors discovered Nottingham House; indeed, before even the first great houses of Kensington had been built.

Chelsea's attractions were simple: a pleasant rural atmosphere, and a highly convenient setting beside the great highway of the Thames, only a short distance from the city of London. Henry VIII developed a liking for the place during his visits to Sir Thomas More, but it was not until he had sent his stubborn Chancellor to the block that he took steps to follow his example and build himself a house. Ironically, neither his new manor nor any of the other aristocratic buildings of the period ever supplanted More's house as the most famous and best-loved in Chelsea's history.

The story of this and other Chelsea houses is peppered with the names of illustrious families, of whom lengthy tales have been told, and who were often related by marriage. To add to the complexity, the houses' names tended to change according to who owned them, and those by which they are now known, in some cases, were adopted many years after they were first built.

Thus, More's home is generally called Beaufort House, though it was not until 1682 that it was sold to Henry, Marquess of Worcester and later Duke of Beaufort. Perhaps the fact that a beautiful view of the house by Kip was published during his period of ownership helped to perpetuate the name. The view shows later additions to the house, such as gables, but not the wing which ran north from the eastern end which was probably added by Lady Dacre in the late 1500s. Information on how the house looked in Lady Dacre's time comes from plans made by John Thorpe at about the turn of the century, though it is not known whether he was actually employed to alter the building.

Various minor changes were made over the years by different owners, which may account for the curtly expressed view of John Evelyn, the diarist, when he was involved in the sale of the house in 1679. He thought it 'ill-contrived' and even after further alterations by the Duke of Beaufort, felt that 'he might have built a better house with the materials and the cost he had been at'. Nevertheless, Bowack claimed in 1705 that Queen Mary's search for a house beyond the damp air of Whitehall led her to consider Beaufort House, but added, most mysteriously, that she was prevented 'by some secret obstacles'.

The house stood empty for several years between the Beaufort family quitting it and Sir Hans Sloane buying it in 1736. He is said to have paid £2,500 for it, but this was to be no guarantee of its future, for he had it pulled down three years later. Only the gateway designed by Inigo Jones survived and was taken to Chiswick; its move being thus commemorated by Pope:

> Oh gate, how com'st thou here?
> I was brought from Chelsea last year,
> Battered with wind and weather;
> Inigo Jones put me together,
> Sir Hans Sloane
> Let me alone,
> Burlington brought me hither.

Signs of Sir Thomas More's old estate have not quite disappeared from Chelsea however. Here and there an old brick wall survives in a garden to remind the owners that they live on the site of one of the loveliest homes in Tudor England.

In Kip's view, another gabled building can be seen looking east across the forecourt of Beaufort House. This was Gorges House, built in about 1600 by the Second Earl of Lincoln when he lived at Beaufort House and given to his son-in-law, Sir Arthur Gorges. It lasted an even shorter time than its grander neighbour, being demolished in 1726, but the third house in the picture has survived up to the present day.

Lindsey House, as it is now known, began life as the principal farmhouse on More's estate, and was later occupied by King Charles I's physician, Sir Theodore Mayerne. Around the time of his death in 1655 it was altered extensively, when it gained its distinctive mansard roof and round-headed dormer windows, and the Third Earl of Lindsey made further changes when he moved there in about 1671. Bowack described the house in 1705 as 'after the modern manner'.

Its most renowned occupant was undoubtedly Count Zinzendorf, who arrived in 1750 from Upper Lusatia in Saxony to establish his colony of

Detail from Kip's view, showing (top) Gorges House and Lindsey House

The entrance to Lindsey House

Moravians, a religious sect which had originated in Bohemia and was given shelter by the Count during an era of persecution in Poland and Moravia (see also Chapter 10). He was also the last owner to enjoy the house in its entirety, for shortly after his death in 1760, it was divided into seven houses, one of which was later the home of Marc Isambard Brunel and his son Isambard Kingdom. Lindsey House is now a part of Cheyne Walk and still stands overlooking the Thames, though with the juggernauts thundering past its front wall, and houses hemming it in on its three other sides, it is difficult to imagine how it looked in quieter times.

To the east of this corner of Chelsea where three large houses were to stand together, Sir Thomas More built a chapel and library and this was probably the building that was given to Margaret and William Roper and which became their home. It stood near where Crosby Hall stands today, and became known as the Moorhouse, so that many people believed it to have been More's own home (as they believed, at various times, of several other Chelsea houses).

The property was sold by the Lincoln family in 1622/3 to Sir John Danvers, and here he created a small estate: plans for a new house were made by Thorpe (though it is not known whether they were executed) and the garden was designed in the newly imported Italian style. Some time after Danvers's death, Pepys visited it and thought it 'the prettiest contrived house I ever saw in my life' and in 1691 Aubrey left a vivid description of the 'very elegant and ingeniose' house and its grounds.

From the hall, he wrote, 'you are entertain'd with two delightfull Visto's: one southward over the Thames and to Surrey: the other northward into that curious garden', where there was 'a kind of Boscage (wildernesse) of Lilac's, syringa's, sweet Briar etc: Holly-Juniper and about 4 or 5 Apple trees and peare trees', as well as a bowling green, sculpture, a grotto and 'stately great gravelled Walkes'. Bordering these walks were 'Hysop, mixt with severall sorts of Thyme' on which Danvers 'was wont in faire mornings in the Summer to brush his Bever-hatt . . . which did perfume it with its naturall spirit; and would last a morning or longer'.

After the death of Lady Danvers – who by a previous marriage had borne two famous sons, Lord Herbert of Cherbury and the poet and divine, George Herbert, and whose funeral sermon was preached in Chelsea Old Church by her friend, the poet John Donne – Danvers espoused the Parliamentary cause. The Chelsea historian Faulkner had harsh words for him, writing that he 'always embraced the religion and interest of the prevailing party'; he was one of the signatories of the King's death warrant, and died before the Restoration could bring retribution. His house was condemned in 1696, and a street begun which can be seen in Kip's view. Kip also showed the gardens, but not the house, though it is thought to have stood until about 1720. The new street,

Danvers House as redrawn from the Thorpe manuscripts

Danvers Street, and Paultons Square now cover the beautiful gardens.

The old manor house at Chelsea stood just beyond and north of the church, at what is now the top of Lawrence Street, and for many years was the home of the Lawrence family. A nineteenth-century watercolour in Chelsea library was long thought to represent the old house as it was when occupied by the Duchess of Monmouth in about 1714 and known by her name, but it has since been established that, by then, the old manor had been demolished and its place taken by a block divided into four, one of which was the duchess's home. The building was later used for a time for the manufacture of Chelsea porcelain (see Chapter 30) before it too was pulled down in the 1830s.

Nearby stood Shrewsbury House, Chelsea's oldest great house, built early in the sixteenth century for the Earls of Shrewsbury, which has now been replaced by a block of flats that still bears their name. This house was also one of the last to disappear from the riverside. It became a 'stained paper manufactory' amid the cramped and crowded conditions of the wharves until 1813 when, says Faulkner, 'the materials were sold piece-meal by a speculating builder'; but a few fragments remained until the shop, of which they formed a part, was demolished in 1931. A house designed by Lutyens replaced it; but this lasted only four years before suffering the same fate.

The Shrewsburys were an eminent family, one member of whom, the Fourth Earl, had accompanied Henry VIII to the Field of the Cloth of Gold. In 1568 the Sixth Earl, who was married to the difficult and demanding 'Bess of Hardwick', was given custody of Mary, Queen of Scots, whom he treated, according to the historians, with all deference and generosity, but who did not return the compliment; so that when Queen Elizabeth sent him on a mission to Lancashire he thanked her for ridding him of 'two she-devils'.

The great houses of Chelsea were thus in the hands of several notable families when Henry VIII made his entrance into this prosperous rural scene. Having no property there, he came to an agreement with the Lord of the Manor, Lord Sandys, whereby the latter gave up his manor to the King in exchange for Mottisfont in Hampshire. Henry chose a site for his house near the river, now occupied by 19–26 Cheyne Walk, and created a 'great garden' to the north and east. The only illustration of his palace is to be found in Faulkner's *An Historical and Topographical Description of Chelsea 1829* where it is shown from the north, a view said at the time to have been taken from an old roll.

Here Henry's daughter, later Queen Elizabeth I, spent her early days. After her father's death she was joined by his widow, Catherine Parr, and later by Lady Jane Grey, and the story of their lives together at Chelsea is told with great gusto by A. G. L'Estrange in his *Village of Palaces* (1880). Catherine was courted here by the ambitious and unscrupulous Sir Thomas Seymour and was troubled after their marriage by the lecherous games he played with the fourteen-year-old princess. Elizabeth was removed from Chelsea, Seymour later went to the block and the next owner of the palace, the Duke of Northumberland, met the same fate when he tried to place his daughter-in-law, Lady Jane Grey, on the throne. The palace's last royal occupant was Anne of Cleves, who died there in 1557/8.

When Henry's manor came into the hands of the Duke of Hamilton in 1639, he built a western extension which was the last of Chelsea's riverside palaces. It became the home of the Bishops of Winchester shortly after the Restoration, and remained so until its demolition in 1828. *The Gentleman's Magazine* wrote at the time that 'it must excite the regret of the Architect as well as the Antiquary, to witness the gradual demolition of every antient fabrick in the vicinity of London'.

The manor, including the royal manor house itself, was bought in 1660 by Charles Cheyne, later Viscount Newhaven and Lord Cheyne. But the family did not remain long in Chelsea. In 1712 the Second Lord Cheyne was made Lord Lieutenant of his native county, Buckinghamshire, and sold the manor to Sir Hans Sloane, who lived in the house only during the last few years of his life (see Chapters 26 and 28). It was pulled down shortly afterwards, in about 1755.

On what was once a green and wooded river bank, only Lindsey House now remains as a reminder of the magnificent series of houses that graced Chelsea's shore.

A view of Chelsea and the Thames in 1750

In 1705, John Bowack described Chelsea as 'a large Beautiful and Populous Town' in which lived 'many Honourable Worthy Inhabitants, being not more remarkable for their Titles, Estates, Employments, or Abilities, than for their Extraordinary Civility, and Condescention, and their kind and facetious tempers, living in a perfect Amity among themselves'.

The village clustered round the old church of St Luke's (now rebuilt and known as the Old Church), by the banks of the Thames on which it was so dependent. The river provided a livelihood for local working people, and furnished others with the easiest means of communication with London, though by Bowack's time roads to the city were also evidently in frequent use, since he writes that a man may 'in less than an Hours time either by Water, Coach, or otherwise, be at the Court, Exchange, or in the midst of his Business. The Walk to Town is very even and very Pleasant'.

Chelsea's main streets led north towards the King's private road (designated as such by Charles II to provide a direct route to Hampton Court), west towards Beaufort House, and east to the Royal Hospital, but none was known by its modern name. Westwards from the church ran Lombard Street and Duke Street, with buildings on both sides of the road and an arch between them, blocking off the river at this point. Church Lane, now Old Church Street, was the home of Bowack himself, and was built up as far as the King's Road, on the corner of which a new parsonage was built in the early eighteenth century (the older one had stood west of Beaufort House).

To the east of the church were several great houses, separated from the river by a roadway and ending where the road forked into two: Robinson's Lane (later called Queen Street and now Flood Street), and Paradise Row (now the lower part of Royal Hospital Road), where a fine row of houses was built in the late seventeenth century (and demolished in 1906). At the stableyard of the hospital the lane turned left to traverse the edge of College Court – now Burton's Court – for there was no road directly in front of the hospital until the mid-nineteenth century.

26
The early village

Little Chelsea in 1780

To the north there were a few buildings at Blacklands, the house Charles Cheyne occupied before moving to the manor house. Blacklands Lane later became known as Marlborough Road, after Lady Matthew's house there was turned into the Marlborough Tavern – and Marlborough Road was later renamed Draycott Avenue. Across the lane lay Chelsea Common, where a cowkeeper tended the commoners' cattle. This was a lonely place where many a traveller lost his purse to footpads. In 1729, for example, it was reported that 'On Sunday Morning last about 8 o'clock Mr Rogers of Chelsea crossing the Common in order to go to Kensington was knock'd down by two Footpads who robb'd him of his Money and beat him in a barbarous manner and then made off across the Fields towards Little Chelsea.'

On the western side of the common was the Queen's Elm, a place that retains its name to this day. The story goes that it is the site of an elm tree beneath which Queen Elizabeth I took refuge during a downpour, while on a visit to Lord Burleigh, who may have lived at Brompton Hall (which stood near the present South Kensington station) and who certainly owned Beaufort House in Chelsea for a while. The local historian Reginald Blunt found the elm referred to as 'the Queen's Tree' in parish records as early as 1586.

Nearby, on the boundary between Kensington and Chelsea, lay the hamlet of Little Chelsea, with several worthy inhabitants. There was Robert Boyle (1627–91), a physicist, chemist and founder member of the Royal Society; and the Stanley family at Stanley House. This building was originally erected by Sir Arthur Gorges (see previous chapter) in the early 1600s and called Brickhills, but was rebuilt in the late seventeenth century by a member of the Stanley family into which Gorges' daughter had married. In the nineteenth century the house became the College of St Mark, and new buildings by Edwin Blore were added in 1843. The College of St John from Battersea was united with it in 1923, and in the 1970s, when 'Marjon' moved to Plymouth, the site was bought for Chelsea College.

Nearby stood Shaftesbury House, which had been built in about 1635 but which was altered when the Third Earl of Shaftesbury bought it in about 1700. His stay in Little Chelsea was brief: in 1706 his constitution was assailed by the 'great smoak' of the neighbourhood – perhaps the river mists – and he took refuge in Hampstead. The house later became a workhouse belonging to the parish of St George's, Hanover Square, and was pulled down in 1856 to make way for St Stephen's Hospital.

As in Kensington, there were a number of nurseries in the area, and

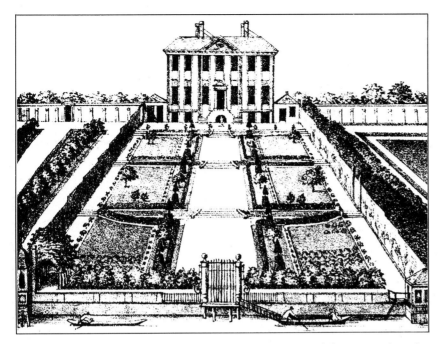

nineteenth-century local historians thought that many of them were kept by Huguenots who arrived after the Revocation of the Edict of Nantes in 1685. There was one 'French Chapel' in Lovers' Walk (now Park Walk), and another in Cook's Ground (now Glebe Place), and a famous Huguenot leader, Jean Cavalier, was buried at the old church in 1740.

Immediately to the south of Little Chelsea was Chelsea Park, estimated as covering forty acres in 1717. It had been part of Sir Thomas More's estate but after its acquisition by the Marquis of Wharton it was known as Lord Wharton's Park. In the early 1700s a company was established to produce raw silk here, and Thomas Crofton Croker claimed in 1860 that 'upwards of two thousand mulberry-trees were soon planted ... this number of trees, was, however, but a small part of what the company intended to plant if they were successful'. Chelsea was thought suitable because of its light soil and 'good air'.

In his *Essay upon the Silk-Worm* (1719), Henry Barham made calculations as to the value of the silk that could be produced at Chelsea which, he decided, showed that 'the profit of this undertaking (if tolerably managed), will be the most considerable which was ever yet known in Great Britain'. But his hopes were never realised. The enterprise failed – perhaps affected by the removal of import tax on raw silk in 1721 – and by the 1870s the mansion that had been built there had been demolished and the ground laid out for the construction of the gaunt Elm Park Gardens estate.

The 'palaces' of Chelsea's riverside began to disappear in the early 1700s, at the same time as new streets arose. In 1717 Sir Hans Sloane leased land in Henry VIII's 'great garden' for building, which was the beginning of Cheyne Walk. One of the best-known houses in the row, No 16 (where Rossetti later lived – see Chapter 33), was long thought to have links with Charles II's wife, Catherine of Braganza, a notion strengthened by the initials RC on the gate. A later occupant named the house 'Queen's House' on the strength of the tale, but the initials are those of Richard Chapman, for whom the house was built in 1717. Other fine buildings in present-day Cheyne Walk are the Georgian Belle Vue Lodge and House, on the corner of Beaufort Street (though the name of Cheyne Walk did not extend west of the church until the embankment was built in the 1870s).

Other streets began to appear in the early 1700s: Cheyne Row, begun in 1708 by Lord Cheyne, Lawrence Street, leading to the old Lawrence family home, Milman's Row and Swan Walk. New mansions were also built:

Cheyne Walk in 1776

Ranelagh House went up to the east of the Royal Hospital in about 1690, and at about the same time a house was built on the western side which was bought by Sir Robert Walpole in about 1721 and altered for him by Vanbrugh. Walpole created beautiful gardens with an octagonal summerhouse and a greenhouse where he entertained Queen Caroline, and his wife built a grotto, well known in its day.

After his death in 1745 the house had various occupants until it was converted to an infirmary for the Chelsea Pensioners by Sir John Soane. The lower part of the garden was leased to Colonel Gordon for the building of Gordon House, which was also later incorporated into the infirmary; but all these buildings were destroyed during the Second World War and later replaced by the National Army Museum.

Between Walpole House and what is now Tite Street, Gough House was built in 1707, taking its name from the Goughs who lived there in the 1720s. In 1866 it was converted to the Victoria Hospital for Children but was demolished in the 1960s after the hospital moved to south London, and was replaced by the present block of flats.

One of the few fine houses surviving in modern Chelsea is Argyll House, which was built in 1723 a little distance away from the heart of the village, fronting the King's private road, over which local landowners and workers had rights of way. It was designed for John Perrin by a Venetian architect, Giacomo Leoni, who described it as a 'little country house' with rooms 'suitable to a private Family . . . The ornaments of the Windows are all of Stone, as is also the great Cornice; the rest is gray Brick, which in my opinion sorting extremely well with white Stone, makes a beautiful Harmony of Colours'. In spite of the loss of those colours as a result of standing on what has become a busy road (the junction of King's Road and Oakley Street), and the threat of demolition early this century, Argyll House remains much as it was built. Its name derives from its owner in 1769–70, the Fourth Duke of Argyll.

Chelsea was the home of several prominent members of political and literary circles in the late seventeenth, early eighteenth centuries; Jonathan

The Naval Academy at 10–11 Paradise Row, demolished and now absorbed by Royal Hospital Road

Swift and Francis Atterbury, Bishop of Rochester, lived in Church Lane, Sir Richard Steele had a house in Cheyne Walk and, later, in the 1750s, Tobias Smollett lived in part of Monmouth House in Lawrence Street. As well as its illustrious scientists, writers and statesmen, Chelsea has several well-known female residents. Mary Astell (1668–1731), the daughter of a Newcastle merchant, was an unusually learned lady who lived in Paradise Row where she wrote books advocating education for women and criticising their servitude to men in marriage. Not surprisingly, her recommendations for a women's community for celibacy and study fell almost entirely on deaf ears, though Bishop Atterbury paid her a back-handed compliment when he wrote that 'Had she as much good breeding as good sense, she would be perfect.'

The other lady of Paradise Row, the Duchess of Mazarin, as she styled herself, was a niece of Cardinal Mazarin and had been brought up in Paris. She became a mistress of Charles II, arriving in England in 1675 and establishing a salon of sorts which was attended almost constantly by the French writer and wit, Charles Saint-Evremond. After the King's death in 1685 the Duchess was reduced to such straits that it was said that the cost of her still lavish entertainments was met by money left under napkins by her guests.

A third female occupant of Paradise Row enjoyed an even more precarious social situation. She was Betty Becke, the mistress of Lord Sandwich, Samuel Pepys's employer. Pepys was thoroughly disapproving of the affair, hearing that Miss Becke was 'a woman of a very bad fame and very impudent'. Fearing that his lordship was being 'debauched by a slut at his lodgings at Chelsy' where he had supposedly gone temporarily for his health, he risked writing him a warning letter in November 1663. People, he wrote, 'insist upon the bad report of the house wherein your Lordship (now observed in perfect health again) continues to sojourne. And by name have charged one of the daughters for a common Courtizan, alleging both places and persons where and with whom she hath been too well known'. Sandwich may have given up Betty Becke for a time, but his fascination with 'this woman at Chelsy' seems to have continued, for their names are linked in Pepys's diary six years later.

Chelsea Old Church from the south-east in 1750

27
Chelsea's churches

Chelsea has a number of churches now, but when Bowack was writing in 1705 there was only one, the church of St Luke on the riverside. Bowack found that it 'appears to have been very Ancient, by the old Wall now standing on the North side, built of Flint and rough Stone, confusedly heap'd together'.

If such a building sounds unfamiliar, it is because the name of St Luke's now belongs to the new church which was built for the parish in the 1820s; and because the old one, now known simply as Chelsea Old Church though its proper name is All Saints, was almost totally destroyed in the Second World War. But its old More Chapel and many of its monuments survived, and the restoration project of the 1950s was so successful that it is still possible to imagine the Old Church a building of the late 1660s/1670s.

It seems that Chelsea first gained a church in the reign of Edward II, the remaining walls of which Bowack described, and that its two chapels, which became the Lawrence and More Chapels, were added soon afterwards. In 1528 Sir Thomas More rebuilt his, and the capitals of its arch – important as work of the early Renaissance – were for a long time ascribed to Holbein, though there seems no foundation for the belief. By 1667 other changes were afoot: the church is described by Bowack as having been 'much decay'd' and 'too small to contain the congregation, (grown very large by the vast Increase of Buildings, about that time in the Town)'. A large part of it was therefore demolished, though the chapels were preserved, 'the old Parts beautified', and 'the whole Roof, Lead, Timber, etc. thereunto belonging' financed by Lady Jane Cheyne.

In spite of various later attempts, the Old Church was never significantly altered. Its old monuments and memorials were treasured, and record a number of names prominent in Chelsea's history: Sir Robert Stanley, several members of the Lawrence family, Lord Dacre of the South, who once owned Beaufort House, Lady Jane Cheyne, Sir Arthur Gorges and of course Sir Thomas More. His memorial bears an epitaph of his own composition which he sent to his friend Erasmus for approval; and the strange gap in one of the sentences (which are in Latin) marks the place where Erasmus deleted the reference to More's unsparing treatment of heretics, for there were rumours that More subjected them to torture, which Erasmus evidently wanted scotched.

In April 1941, two land mines descended on the Old Church and reduced most of it to rubble, although happily – some might say miraculously – the More Chapel escaped damage. Such a disaster might well have marked its passing, but fortunately it was later rebuilt by the architect W H Godfrey, so that the building on the embankment today is a replica of that which once stood crowded on all sides by the houses and wharves of the old village.

Besides its old memorials, it still possesses the Ashburnham Bell, given in 1679 by William Ashburnham in thanks for the occasion when he fell into the river either from a boat or from the road – depending on which story one reads – and was able to find his way to the shore by hearing the church clock strike nine. In the south aisle are the chained books presented by Sir Hans Sloane – the Vinegar Bible (1717), said to be so-called because of a misprint of the Parable of the Vineyard, Foxe's *Book of Martyrs* (1684), a 1723 prayer book and 1683 *Homilies*. The altar, altar rails and part of the pulpit date from the seventeenth century, and outside in the garden is a memorial to Sir Hans Sloane.

In 1736 Sir Hans gave the parish a new burial ground on the King's Road (which survives today as Dovehouse Green, complete with one or two monuments) and additional ground was acquired in 1810. This was to become the site of the new St Luke's Church, which Faulkner greeted with many pages of flowing prose, but which has been found less than satisfactory by later writers.

Chelsea by 1819 had expanded far beyond its old bounds near the river, and so in that year it was decided that a new church should be built – the influence of the rector, Gerald Valerian Wellesley, brother of the Duke of Wellington, no doubt being of assistance in furthering the project. The rather cold, stilted design in Bath stone by James Savage created an early Gothic revival church, with a high tower, a tall, narrow, galleried nave, rows of flying buttresses and an entrance arcade spanning its width.

A ceremony for the laying of the foundation stone in 1820 was somewhat marred by the Duke of Wellington's failure to turn up, but the procession and service went ahead nonetheless, and Faulkner (who seems to have been thoroughly enamoured of the entire project, perhaps because he himself had suggested the building of a new church back in 1810) reported that the 'fineness of the day, and the brilliancy of so many elegantly dressed ladies,

The church in about 1828

James Savage's Holy Trinity Church in Sloane Street

formed altogether one of the most gratifying spectacles than can possibly be conceived'.

Savage's other church in Chelsea was Holy Trinity, Sloane Street, begun in 1828, but this building was short-lived, being demolished sixty years later. In its place arose what Sir John Betjeman later called 'the cathedral of the Arts and Crafts', a new church designed by J D Sedding and paid for by the Earl of Cadogan. Holy Trinity was consecrated in 1890 and though the roof was destroyed by bombs during the Second World War, it is substantially as Sedding designed it: the frieze and the spandrels of the arcades, which he left plain for later decoration, were never filled, though other areas of the church were handsomely decorated and the east window was created by William Morris and Sir Edward Burne-Jones.

The bombs of the Second World War dealt more harshly with the Church of Scotland's St Columba's in Pont Street. But in 1955 a new church was consecrated, an almost totally unadorned, dignified building of Portland stone with a simple statue of the saint and his crane above the main entrance. Its white walls contrast strikingly but not unattractively with the dark red hues of 'Pont Street Dutch' and makes an interesting addition to Chelsea's varied collection of churches.

Opposite page: St Luke's shortly after completion

The 'cathedral of the Arts and Crafts': the new Holy Trinity, Sloane Street, consecrated in 1890

28
Sir Hans Sloane and the Physic Garden

In 1673 the Society of Apothecaries found a suitable site for the building of a barge house, to accommodate their processional barge. It was an area of about four acres on the banks of Chelsea Reach, by Paradise Row, which they leased from the Lord of the Manor, Charles Cheyne, for five pounds per annum. In the following year they built a wall round the land and decided to create a garden, arranging to move plants belonging to the late William Gape, a past master of the society, from Westminster to this new garden; and soon after, they appointed a gardener. The seeds of Chelsea's Physic Garden had been sown.

It was not the first ever physic garden, but it is one of England's oldest – only at Oxford is there one that is older. Physic gardens were a creation of Renaissance Italy, and were intended for the study of botany, and its practical scientific application. London had one or two before Chelsea's was founded, at Holborn (John Gerard's) and Lambeth (John Tradescant's), but neither survived, while Chelsea's grew into one of the finest in the world.

After a shaky start, the garden began to flourish. Fruit trees were planted and the gardener, John Watts – who was also a member of the society – exchanged plants with Leiden University's Professor of Botany, on one occasion bringing back the four cedars of Lebanon which were so prominent in the garden until the last one was felled in 1904. A greenhouse was built which interested John Evelyn when he visited Watts at the garden in 1685: 'What was very ingenious was the subterraneous heat, conveyed by a stove under the conservatory, all vaulted with brick, so as he has the doores and windowes open in the hardest frosts, secluding only the snow.' Later, more greenhouses, a library and a gardener's house were built, but they have since disappeared.

Initially the future of the garden was by no means secure, for it was a large expense for the society. But in 1712 the manor of Chelsea was bought by Hans Sloane, an eminent physician and collector, and in 1722 he gave the garden to the Apothecaries on a perpetual lease, on condition that they continued to run it as a botanical garden, and that they supply the Royal Society with fifty specimens a year until the number had reached 2000.

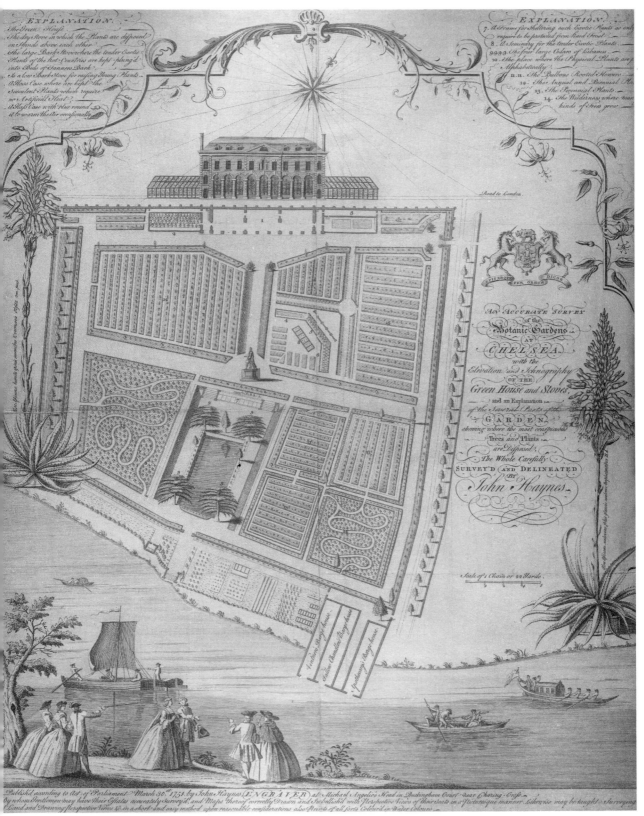

The cedar trees in the gardens of the Apothecaries' company, painted by James Fuge

Sloane was a remarkable man. The youngest son of an Irish receiver of taxes, he came to London to study with a chemist and at the Apothecaries' Garden itself, before pursuing a career which led to a baronetcy in 1716 and to his appointment as Physician to King George II and President of the Royal Society (succeeding Sir Isaac Newton) in 1727. During the course of his studies and travels he amassed a large collection that included scientific and botanical specimens, antiquities, jewels, minerals, books and coins (the left-overs of which ended up in Don Saltero's coffee-house, see Chapter 30).

When he moved to the Manor House at Chelsea in 1742 his collection went with him and was a celebrated private museum, which the Prince and Princess of Wales visited in 1748. Here Sir Hans died in 1753, at the age of ninety-two, an achievement in itself for someone who had shown signs of consumption in childhood. In his will he expressed the wish that the collection 'may be if possible kept and preserved together whole and entire in my manor house in the Parish of Chelsea'; and left instructions for his trustees to offer it, together with the house and the advowson of the church, to the King or to Parliament for £20,000, this sum representing, he believed, less than 'a fourth of their real or intrinsic value'. Parliament accepted the offer, but moved the collection, together with those accumulated by other collectors, to the Duke of Montagu's house in Bloomsbury, thus founding the British Museum, but depriving Chelsea of what might have been its own museum in King Henry VIII's old palace. The house was later demolished (see Chapter 25).

Besides providing the foundation of the British Museum's collections, Sir Hans also secured the fortunes of the Physic Garden, in recognition of which the Society of Apothecaries commissioned a marble statue of him from Rysbrach in 1733. Until 1983 this statue stood proudly on its plinth as the centrepiece of the garden, but in that year its condition was found too decayed to withstand further exposure to the elements. The British Museum made a replica of epoxy resin which now stands on the plinth, while the original is safely inside the museum.

In the same year that its future was settled, in 1722, the garden gained a great botanist as its curator (or Gardener as he was called), Philip Miller, who remained there for nearly fifty years and gave it a worldwide reputation. His famous *Dictionary of Gardening* was written there, in the seventh edition of which he adopted Linnaeus's botanical classification. Linnaeus himself visited Chelsea; and from the garden, thousands of seeds were sent out across the world, including the cotton seeds that began the historic cotton industry in Georgia.

As well as the Gardener, the society appointed a Demonstrator of Plants, who would conduct 'herborising' excursions into the countryside, accompanied by students bearing their collecting boxes. The last herborising took place in 1834, led by the demonstrator of the time, Thomas Wheeler, who by then had been at the Physic Garden since 1778 and was eighty-one years old.

Many eminent names in the world of botany are connected with the garden: among them William Curtis, author of *Flora Londinensis*, who was demonstrator in the 1770s; the great collector Sir Joseph Banks, who donated many packets of seeds in the late eighteenth century and brought basaltic lava from Iceland which was used in the rock garden; and Mrs Elizabeth Blackwell, who produced her beautiful book, *Curious Herbal* in 1737 and 1739 in an attempt to rescue her husband from the debtor's prison. She drew hundreds of plants and engraved them on copper plates while living in Swan Walk, overlooking the garden. Her book was successful, and her husband released from prison; but he stayed only until 1742 when he went to Sweden to expound his agricultural theories, was implicated in some intrigue, and beheaded for treason in 1747.

In the second half of the nineteenth century the Society of Apothecaries found itself again in financial straits, and cut back on expenditure at the garden. The buildings were allowed to deteriorate, the pollution of London's air was taking its toll, and the building of the Chelsea Embankment had adversely affected the soil by lowering the water table (as well as depriving the garden of its picturesque water gate).

At last in the 1890s the society applied to the Charity Commissioners for a scheme by which they could be released from their responsibilities, and the trustees of the London Parochial Charities took over, spending about £6000 on new buildings which are still in use today. They in their turn relinquished their trust in 1983 to new trustees who launched an appeal for the rather more intimidating sum of £1.25 million for an endowment fund, over half of which had been raised by 1987, and opened the garden regularly to the public for the first time.

William Curtis, demonstrator at the garden in the 1770s and author of Flora Londinensis

The Physic Garden today, with the Edwardian flats of Royal Hospital Road in the background

The river front of the Royal Hospital in 1756

29

The Royal Hospital

'1682. 25th May: I was desired by Sir Stephen Fox, and Sir Christopher Wren, His Majesties Surveior, and Architect, to accompanie them to Lambeth, with the plot, and designe of the College to be built at Chelsey for emerited Souldiers, to have the Archbishops approbation: It was a quadrangle of 200 foote square, after the dimensions of the larger quadrangle of Christ Church in Oxon for the accommodation of 440 Persons with Governor and Officers.'

The writer was John Evelyn; and the 'college' at Chelsea that he helped to plan was the Royal Hospital, founded by King Charles II for army veterans. The need to support maimed and superannuated soldiers had become pressing since the formation of a standing army in 1661, and the example set in France by the Hotel Royale des Invalides probably influenced the King. Building began in 1682 and the first residents were installed by 1689. The explanation for the use of the word 'college' to describe the hospital lies in the purpose of an older building on the site. This was a theological college, later nicknamed 'controversy college', founded by James I & VI at the instigation of Matthew Sutcliffe, Dean of Exeter, who was anxious to see the clergy trained in a way that would equip them adequately for debate and the defence of their religion. In his will, Sutcliffe recorded in no uncertain terms that the college had been founded partly to combat 'the pedantry, sophistry, and novelties of the Jesuits, and other the Pope's factors and followers' and 'the treachery of pelagianising Arminians and others, that draw towards popery and Babylonian slavery . . .'.

In spite of Sutcliffe's determination, however, and the expenditure of a good deal of his own money on the project, the college never drew much support, apart from the King, and did not live up to the hopes vested in it. Only a small part of the planned building was constructed, and during the years of the Commonwealth this was used as a prison. It was in this same capacity that it first came within the orbit of Evelyn's responsibilities, when he was given charge of Dutch prisoners of war in 1664. Some of them fell victim to the plague and are thought to have been buried in the college forecourt.

A few years later the old college was given to the Royal Society, of which Evelyn was a member, but their association with it was short-lived, and probably unregretted, since the roof had collapsed and disputes with local tenants and landowners were proving tiresome. In 1681 Sir Christopher Wren, the society's new president, sold the property to Sir Stephen Fox for the building of the hospital.

The question of who conceived the idea of such a hospital has been debated at length, and the romantic legend persists that Nell Gwyn had a hand in its establishment, despite the more prosaic evidence to the contrary. Sir Stephen Fox, if not the originator, was certainly a prime mover in the plan, who, wrote Evelyn, 'had not only the whole managing of this but was, as I perceived, himself to be a grand benefactor, as well it became him who had gotten so vast an estate by the soldiers' (Fox had been Paymaster-General of the army until 1679 and had grown wealthy in the post, see also Chapter 4).

Initially, only the central quadrangle, known as Figure Court, was built to the designs of Wren, funded by a few private donations and by a levy on army pay (this and similar levies continued to support the hospital until 1847 when Parliament assumed responsibility for its maintenance). During James II's reign Wren made additions, building Light Horse Court to the east, and College Court to the west, as well as one or two other buildings in William and Mary's reign. Most of the remaining buildings that flank the east and west roads were designed by Robert Adam and, later, Sir John Soane; Sir Robert Walpole's house in the north-west corner of the grounds was converted to an infirmary, but was destroyed by bombs in 1941.

The hospital grounds gave rise to another story, that Royal Avenue was planned originally as the beginning of a carriage-way linking the hospital with Kensington Palace. It seems clear, however, that the avenue was laid out shortly before William and Mary bought Nottingham House, as the palace was then known (see Chapter 3), and was intended to provide access to the hospital from the King's private road (King's Road). It was lined with horse chestnut trees and hawthorn hedges, and led down to the gates and lodges of the Great Court – now known as Burton's Court – which formed the hospital's main entrance. Later, the gates to the King's Road were closed and ladder stiles put up, giving the avenue the name White Stiles.

In 1687 a porter by the name of James Button was appointed to look after the entrance. The worthy Button took his duties seriously, wearing a costly green uniform and signing his name with a large and unmistakable B. It is from him that the Court is thought to derive its modern name.

The grounds of the hospital were landscaped by Wren, with a fine elevated terrace running the length of the south front and supported by a buttressed wall. Below, running down to the river bank, were two forty-foot canals, between which was a raised path; and the areas to each side beyond the canals

A Chelsea pensioner of 1855

Hannah Snell, 'the female soldier'

Pensioners in the great hall, as depicted in
The Graphic, 1888

were planted with avenues. Planting and maintenance was the responsibility of the indefatigable London and Wise of Brompton Park Nurseries (see Chapter 2). The grounds of Ranelagh House next door were bought for the hospital in 1826 and laid out in 1860; but by then, the lovely seventeenth-century gardens had been swept away and replaced by lawns.

The hospital's administration was planned on military lines, with a Board of Commissioners chaired by the Paymaster-General of the army and a Governor appointed by the Crown. The 'In-Pensioners' (as opposed to those on army pensions who lived outside the hospital, the 'out-pensioners') were formed into nine companies and had to perform guard duties which included an armed patrol of the road to St James's. There are now six companies, formed out of 450 in-pensioners, and the hospital still has a Governor and Lieutenant-Governor, adjutant, medical officers, a chaplain and a quartermaster, as well as six Captains of Invalids (who are retired officers). An annual parade takes place on Founder's Day, 29 May, the birthday of Charles II and popularly known as Oak Apple Day, when the statue of the King in Figure Court (by Grinling Gibbons) is decorated with oak leaves in memory of his famous refuge in the oak tree at Boscobel after the Battle of Worcester.

The main rooms of the hospital are in the north range of Figure Court, which fronts Royal Hospital Road: the octagon porch, the chapel and the great hall where the pensioners dine. The wainscotted cubicles that provide the living quarters are in the 'long wards' running down the east and west sides of the Court, and more wards were made in the north-east wing of Light Horse Court after it was twice destroyed by bombs, in 1918 and 1945.

The Great Hall was the scene of the lying-in-state of the Duke of Wellington in 1852, when the crowds waiting to pay their respects (and satisfy their curiosity) were so great that several people were killed in the crush. J B Ellenor, a local resident, remembered the queues extending up most of Ebury Street, entailing a five or six hour wait. The pensioners themselves, nearly 10,000 of them, were buried in the graveyard laid out in the north-east corner of the grounds by Wren, and included two women, Christina Davis (died 1739) and Hannah Snell (died 1792), who served with the army in disguise at different times in the eighteenth century. No woman has ever become an in-pensioner of the Royal Hospital, but Christina Davis was awarded a pension of five pence a day in 1717, having served for years as a dragoon. Hannah Snell received a pension for serving in the 2nd Marquess Frazers Marines and Guize's Regiment, but died in a lunatic asylum. After 1854 when the Royal Hospital's graveyard was closed, burials took place at Brompton Cemetery, and are now held at Brookwood Cemetery.

Pensioners in one of the 'berths'

The Chelsea Pensioners have something of a reputation for living to a great age. One of them, William Hiseland, died in 1732 aged 112. Dr Monsey, the hospital's physician from 1742 until his death in 1788, lived to the age of ninety-four, and stories of his matter-of-fact approach to life have survived him: one of them tells how he extracted his own teeth when necessary by tying catgut to a bullet at one end and to the tooth at the other, and firing his pistol. Dr Burney, the college organist and father of the novelist Fanny Burney, died in Chelsea in 1814 at the age of eighty-eight. Perhaps the tranquility of the hospital and its grounds had something to do with such longevity, and helps to make the Pensioners such well-loved figures in the Chelsea scene today.

The pensioners' sleeping quarters

Don Saltero's coffee-house at 18 Cheyne Walk

30
Eighteenth-century establishments

In London, the introduction of coffee in the mid seventeenth century had made coffee-houses places of fashionable resort, and it is an indication of Chelsea's popularity that the village should have had one of its own. Don Saltero's, as it was known, was, however, at least as famous for its 'museum' as it was for its coffee, a combination that gave it a secure place in Chelsea's history – it was mentioned as early as 1705 by Bowack.

'Don Saltero' was an Irish barber called James Salter who had served in the household of Sir Hans Sloane. He opened his coffee-house in about 1695, probably in Lawrence Street, and moved to Danvers Street before settling in 18 Cheyne Walk, the house which is always associated with his name; he arrived there in about 1717 and the establishment survived, in varying guises, for another 150 years. Salter's connections with Sloane proved invaluable in establishing the name of the coffee-house. Not only did his old employer give him numerous objects for his 'museum', but he brought him useful introductions to others who could provide more. One of these was Sir John Munden 'who had been much upon the coasts of Spain' and was the person responsible for inventing Salter's rather exotic and enduring nickname, according to *The Gentleman's Magazine* of 1799. Munden was but one of Salter's illustrious customers, for he entertained a number of noblemen and literary figures. Richard Cromwell was often in the coffee-house too and was recalled by one Thomas Pennant, whose father had seen him there, as 'a little and very neat old man, with a most placid countenance, the effect of his innocent and unambitious life'. Another visitor was the young Benjamin Franklin, but he recorded his own 'feats of activity' while swimming back down the Thames to Blackfriars rather than his impressions of Don Saltero's.

The coffee-house museum contained a bizarre collection. Richard Steele wrote in *The Tatler* on 28 June 1709 that in 'the coffee-house where the Literati sit in council' his eye 'was diverted by Ten thousand Gimcracks round the room and on the Sieling' and asked, 'why must a Barber be for ever a Politician, a Musician, an Anatomist, a Poet, and a Physician'. Among the exhibits were 'nuns' stockings', 'petrified mushrooms', 'the spider from Tarantum in Italy the bite whereof occasions madness and death and is curable only by music', and 'manna from Canaan, it drops from the clouds twice in a year in May and June, one day in each month'. Steele took particular delight in exposing a straw hat which Salter had labelled 'Pontius Pilate's Wife's chamber maid's sister's hat'. According to Steele, it had been made 'within three miles of Bedford'. *The Gentleman's Magazine* in 1799 also expressed reservations but decided gravely that 'Such collections, however, aided by those of Tradescant, Ashmole, and

The Chelsea Bun House, by Hogarth

Thoresby, cherished the infancy of Science, and should not be depreciated as the playthings of a boy after he is arrived at manhood.' The magazine's words came at a time when Don Saltero's house and collection were sold, in 1799. Salter himself having died in 1728, the business continued under his daughter and her husband, but in about 1760 it passed into different hands, and in 1790 appears to have been run by a woman from New England. In the nineteenth century it had a 'subscription room', according to the local historian George Bryan, 'where gentlemen met and conversed', but in 1867 it was rebuilt as a private house.

The assembling of collections was not uncommon in eighteenth-century England, and was well represented in Chelsea. While Sir Hans Sloane's was by far the most scientifically based, there was also one belonging to 'Dog' Jennings in Lindsey Row which contained prints, minerals, gems and shells; and that of Mr Haworth at Queen's Elm, which Faulkner said contained no fewer than 40,000 insects and 20,000 dried plants. Even the famous Chelsea Bun House had a modest, if eclectic, collection, though its buns alone were guaranteed to draw a crowd.

The Bun House stood in what is now Pimlico Road, just outside the parish boundary, with a street frontage some fifty feet long. During the eighteenth century it was famous throughout London for its delicious buns, the ultimate seal of fashion being stamped on the premises when both George II and George III called at its windows. The cries of the street vendors – 'r-r-r-r-rare Chelsea buns!' and 'smoking hot, piping hot, Chelsea buns!' – attracted crowds of people: Swift grumbled in his *Journal to Stella*, 'As I walked into the City, I was stopped with clusters of boys and wenches buzzing about the cake shops like fairs. There had the fools let out their shops two yards forward into the streets, all spread with great cakes frothed with sugar and stuck with streamers of tinsel.' But Swift was sold a stale bun, so perhaps he was not among their admirers.

On Good Friday it was the custom to hold a fair in the Five Fields – the area between Ebury Street and Eaton Square – and thousands would gather to enjoy swings, nine-pins, drinking booths 'and all the other vicious "entertainments" which annually disgraced the metropolis in former times', wrote the moralising George Bryan in 1869. Bryan estimated from his own memory of the event that, provided the weather was good, some 200,000 people would gather in the neighbourhood. In 1839 it was said that the Bun House sold 240,000 buns, which would explain why some years earlier Mrs Hands, a member of the family which owned the business for many years, had issued a notice (in

Richard Hand's trade card

March 1793) declaring that 'in consequence of the great concourse of people which assembled before her house at a very early hour, on the morning of Good Friday last, by which her neighbours (with whom she has always lived in friendship and repute) have been much alarmed and annoyed . . . she is determined, though much to her loss, not to sell Cross Buns on that day to any person whatever, but Chelsea buns as usual'.

The Handses became well known, particularly since one of their number, who had been in the Staffordshire militia, was dubbed 'Captain Bun' and took to wearing a long dressing-gown and a fez, being caricatured in 1773 by Matthew Darly as 'Captain Bun Quixote attacking the Oven'. After they sold the Bun House in 1839 a rival shop was opened two doors away, but the best days of the Chelsea bun were over and it is doubtful whether any can be found now to rival those described in a once popular song:

> O flour of the ovens! a zephyr in paste!
> Fragrant as honey, and sweeter in taste!

When they weren't queueing for buns, people in Chelsea could gather at the tea-gardens in the village. There was one called Stromboli's, opposite the

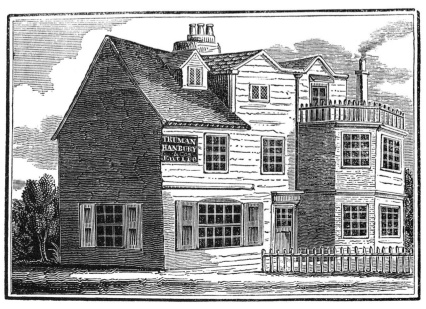

Bun House; another at the Clockhouse in Milman's Row which Faulkner in 1829 said had been 'long famous for the sale of gingerbread and flowers'; and yet another at the World's End Tavern, which stood in large gardens at the junction of Hob's Lane (leading to Chelsea Farm, later known as Cremorne) and the King's Road, and had a slightly questionable though fashionable reputation in the reign of Charles II – it is mentioned in Congreve's *Love for Love*. The rather mysterious name, 'World's End', probably derived from its remote situation at a time when travellers crossing lonely stretches of countryside were easy prey for thieves, as was certainly the case on the roads to Chelsea.

Chelsea's enduring product from this period in its history is its porcelain, though comparatively little is known of the background to the production of these lovely pieces. The pottery was situated somewhere in Lawrence Street, probably in Monmouth House at first, and later, on the north-western side of the street where fragments of pottery have been discovered.

The earliest surviving pieces of Chelsea ware date from about 1745 and are uncoloured. In about 1750 Nicholas Sprimont became director of the factory and designs became more elaborate, with gilding, flowers, shells and mouldings, as well as the famous vegetable and fruit-shaped dishes. In 1770 the owner of the Derby factory, William Duesbury, came to Chelsea, when 'Chelsea Derby' was produced, but fourteen years later he closed the pottery, moved everything to Derby and demolished his Lawrence Street buildings.

There is a popular legend that Dr Johnson used to visit the factory regularly, accompanied by his housekeeper bearing provisions, to experiment with his own 'improvements' on the manufacture of china – which, however, were never successful. Whether this was *the* Dr Johnson has never really been proved. It is known for certain, on the other hand, that Wedgwood had workshops in Chelsea, roughly where Bramerton Street and Glebe Place are now, where the famous Russian service was painted with English scenes, including some of Chelsea.

While Chelsea ware appears to have been highly desirable and valuable from an early date, the work of another well-known Chelsea name was probably mostly, if not entirely, spurious. Doctor Dominiceti established himself at 6 Cheyne Walk in 1765, where he claimed to be able to cure an extremely wide range of afflictions with his 'medicinal baths'. It was said that he spent many thousands of pounds on fitting the property out with baths, 'fumigatory stoves' and 'sweating bed-chambers', and his patients included the blind magistrate Sir John Fielding (half-brother of the novelist Henry Fielding) who lived at Brompton, and the Duke of York; but Faulkner was more sceptical. 'The doctor used to boast', he wrote, 'that no dead man, woman, or child, was ever sent out of his doors; the fact was, that those patients who died under his care were sent out of his garden-gate, at the back of his house.'

One of Chelsea's taverns, the Cross Keys in Lawrence Street

A Chelsea porcelain figure of a fisherman and his companion, dating from circa 1765

31
Ranelagh
Gardens

Ranelagh Gardens in 1752

'To be lett, for the purpose of erecting Houses and Buildings, according to plans to be laid down by the Proprietors, the Land or Ground whereon lately stood Ranelagh House and Rotunda, and the Offices and Buildings thereunto belonging; together also with the Grounds formerly comprising Ranelagh Gardens'. This advertisement, in 1808, was for the great Ranelagh, which only five years previously had welcomed Queen Charlotte to one of its most sumptuous entertainments. A month after her visit it had closed and two years later was razed to the ground.

Only the strip of garden on the eastern flank of the Royal Hospital remains today as a reminder of London's most celebrated eighteenth-century pleasure ground. Ranelagh in its day was visited by kings and queens, writers and artists, politicians and dandies alike. Some thought it splendid, others condemned it as wicked; one or two were bored by it. But few who knew of it and could afford it, stayed away.

Ranelagh House was built in about 1690 by Richard, Earl of Ranelagh, Paymaster-General of the forces and one of the Commissioners of the Royal Hospital. It stood to the east of the Hospital, and was described by Bowack in 1705 as 'not large, but very convenient', with gardens 'which are esteemed the best in England, the size considered'.

A 1776 admission ticket for Ranelagh, drawn by Cipriani and engraved by Bartolozzi

The property was later sold, and in 1741 leased by William Crispe and James Myonet. These two partners planned a great pleasure ground that would rival Vauxhall Gardens, and to this end they commissioned William Jones to design the rotunda which was to become the haunt of fashionable society, and one of the largest buildings in London at the time.

Jones's rotunda was 185 ft in diameter, larger than the Pantheon in Rome. An arcade ran round the outside, and there were four great pedimented entrances leading to the central space and to the boxes above. The ground-level boxes could be approached from inside or directly from outside, through the arcade.

In the centre of the building, lit by sixty windows above the boxes, a huge octagonal pillar rose to support the roof, and was open at its base to accommodate an orchestra, though it was later converted into a large open fireplace. To one side stood an organ (later removed to Tetbury parish church where it was dismantled), and on special occasions the interior was filled with chandeliers and circles of lavishly decorated tables.

Crispe and Myonet opened Ranelagh to the public in 1742, but their ambitions had taken too severe a toll on their purse, and in 1744 the property was divided into thirty-six shares, many of which were bought by Sir Thomas

'A Night Scene at Ranelagh': Mr Mountfort Brown pulling the ear of Dr Hill who has libelled him in The Inspector

Interior view of the rotunda in 1751

Robinson. It was he who steered Ranelagh through its most successful years, and who, in the process, prospered sufficiently to build himself a large house, Prospect Place, nearby. His demeanor, however, does not appear to have matched his prosperity: he was described by one of Ranelagh's fashionable visitors, Mrs Carter, as 'the knight of the woful countenance'.

From the beginning, Ranelagh seems to have been an immense success. A writer in *The Gentleman's Magazine* in 1742 called it 'an enchanted palace', and even Dr Johnson thought it provided 'a gay sensation . . . such as I never experienced anywhere else'. Horace Walpole wrote that it had quite eclipsed Vauxhall and that 'nobody goes anywhere else'.

And yet, on days when no special celebration was held, Ranelagh had little enough to offer: for a shilling or two one could stroll in the gardens, promenade round the rotunda, take a cup of tea or coffee and a bread roll. Even on a popular evening (the most exclusive nights cost two guineas) some visitors remained unimpressed. *The Gentleman's Magazine's* correspondent confessed that, though charmed at first, 'satiety followed; in five minutes I was familiar with the whole and every part; in the five next, indifference took place; in five more, my eyes grew dazzled, my head became giddy, and all night I dreamed of Vanity Fair'. Mrs Carter, also writing in 1742, was not struck 'with

any agreeable impression . . . these scenes to me lose much of their beauty and propriety in a noisy crowd'.

Propriety was certainly sometimes called into question. A German gentleman was shocked when, walking about in 'a garden rather large but sickly in its aspect, unseemly, ill lit and sparsely inhabited', he came across a young lady who 'offered me her arm without introduction and asked me why I was going about all alone. It struck me at that moment that this could not possibly be the magnificent and much recommended Ranelagh!'

The revelries that took place there, often masked, provided plenty of opportunities for those, like the lovely Miss Chudleigh, who were otherwise restricted by polite society. The scene was described scathingly by one contemporary in the tenth number of *The Rambler* as 'an entertainment where the vigilance of jealousy has so often been eluded, and the virgin is set free from the necessity of languishing in silence; where all the out-works of chastity are at once demolished; where the heart is laid open without a blush; where bashfulness may survive virtue, and no wish is crushed under the frown of modesty'.

The enduring picture of Ranelagh, however, is one of glittering gatherings, of music and banquets and finery and fireworks. Handel's new music was

Miss Chudleigh in fancy 'dress' at a masquerade on 26 April 1749

performed here, the child prodigy Mozart played here; there was a regatta in 1775 when the Thames was thick with barges and ablaze with flags, and evenings when the whole of fashionable society seemed to be gathered in the gardens, round its canal and on its Chinese bridge. For fêtes and masked balls the rotunda was magnificently decked out with festoons and flowers, candles and crystal. The road from Westminster was specially lit and patrolled to make it safe for the chairs and carriages that came from town, as well as the pedestrians who thronged the way. Firework nights were advertised with long lists of extravagant displays, and there was always a musical entertainment: 'At Ranelagh House, on Friday May 12, will be a Jubilee Ridotto, or Bal Pare. The Company are desired to come in fancied Dresses or dressed as at the Ridotto, or other Assemblies. No Persons will be suffered to wear Masks.

Besides the usual Entertainments there will be Country Dances and Cotilions, and a new Musical Entertainment in the Manner of the Italian comic Serenatas will be performed about Nine o'Clock.

There will be Music and Illuminations on the Canal and on the Temple, and in other Parts of the Garden.

The best French and other Wines, with Variety of Sweetmeats, are provided for the Sideboard, and Beaufets in the Amphitheatre, which will be opened at Eleven, and Shut up at Two.

The Company are desired to come early. The Doors will be opened at Six, and the Music in the Gardens begin at Seven.

There will be Horse Patrole and an additional Number of Lights on the Road. The Footway from Buckingham Gate is lately mended and enlarged, so as to make it very safe and easy for Chairs.'

After sixty years as one of London's most celebrated social institutions, Ranelagh eventually began to decline in popularity, and closed forever in 1803. In the second edition of *The Environs of London* (1811), Daniel Lysons attributed its failure to the late hour at which it became fashionable to enter the rotunda, midnight, which he said was too late for the 'middle ranks' who formed the majority of the assembly. By 1810, when the site of Ranelagh was visited by Sir Richard Phillips, author of *Morning's Walk from London to Kew* (1817) and who had known it when it was still open and flourishing, there was nothing left but nettles, thistles and 'holes filled with muddy water' marking the foundations.

'A prospect of Chalsea Watter works'

By the early eighteenth century, the supply of water to London's western outskirts had become a problem. From the earliest times London's water had come from streams and wells, and from springs on high ground when the streams became polluted: Henry VIII is said to have built a conduit from a spring at Kensington (in what became Kensington Palace's kitchen gardens) to Chelsea when he bought the manor.

Water was taken to individual houses by bearers, though the influential were sometimes able to arrange for lead pipes to bring it from the conduit head directly into their homes: Sir Arthur Gorges had such a pipe laid to his house from the cistern at Beaufort House. But the provision of spring water by force of gravity proved insufficient to meet the needs of an expanding population in the sixteenth century and, in 1581, the first attempt at mechanical provision was made successfully by means of waterwheels beneath the arches of London Bridge.

In 1722, a prospectus was issued for the establishment of waterworks at Chelsea. It proposed 'to raise Water from the Thames (with Engines working by the Flux and Reflux of the Tide) without prejudicing the Navigation, or any other Part, or Particular belonging to the River, into a Reservatory rais'd on the highest Ground near Oliver's Mount, thence to serve the new Buildings, and all other Parts in the city and suburbs of Westminster, and Parts adjacent'.

Such quantity of water would be reserved 'as will be sufficient not only to supply the ordinary occasions of the Inhabitants, but will also answer all other Calls in case of Fire, the Pestilence, or any Exigency whatsoever'; and 'for the Relief of the labouring Poor, whose livelihood mainly depends on the common uses of Water, either in Washing, Scowering, etc, such Provision shall be made as will supply their necessary Occasions, and ease them of a Burthen which they cannot bear without the greatest Difficulties'.

The Chelsea Water Works Company was duly incorporated, and under royal warrants of 1725 created three reservoirs, one in Hyde Park near Oliver's Mount (after which Mount Street is named), and the other two in St James's Park and Green Park. Water was brought from the Thames into a series of small canals below Ranelagh, and an engine-house was built of materials from the old church of St Martin-in-the-Fields which had been demolished in 1721. The site is now crossed by Chelsea Bridge Road.

32
Chelsea
waterworks

The waterworks in 1752

Here, water was raised by wheels and horse machinery into the reservoirs. Faulkner wrote that the company was so successful that by 1726 'they were in a condition to serve upwards of ten thousand houses with Thames water at a cheaper rate than the New River Company, as they were at comparatively small expense in raising the water; and in their advertisements they asserted, that if there was no other water to serve the cities of London and Westminster, they would be enabled to supply the whole as soon as their pipes could be laid down for that purpose'.

In 1742 the company built its first steam engine at its Chelsea works – which were in fact just outside the Chelsea boundary, beyond the Westbourne, and stretching north to where Victoria station now stands – and this engine, together with another put up in 1747, were, according to Faulkner, 'objects of great curiosity at that time in London'. At about this time also, it seems, they first used iron pipes. Wooden pipes, made of lengths of bored trunks tapered at one end so that they fitted together, were commonly used in London and continued in use in Chelsea until the 1840s, even though they could not withstand much pressure and often leaked.

Leakage, however, was the least of the water companies' problems. In 1827 a pamphlet was published entitled *The Dolphin or Grand Junction Nuisance* which caused a furore that reached the House of Commons. After several years in competition, the water companies had reached a settlement in 1817 and divided London between them, Chelsea retaining only Brompton, Knightsbridge, Chelsea, Pimlico, parts of Westminster and of St Martin-in-the-Fields. Following this arrangement of monopolies, charges were raised.

At about the same time the Grand Junction Water Works Company had found the water in the Grand Junction Canal quite unfit for circulation, and so had built a new pumping station on the Thames, beside the mouth of the Westbourne at Chelsea. The writer of the pamphlet, John Wright, already enraged by the rise in charges, brought the public's attention to the fact that the intake, or 'dolphin', for the Grand Junction's works was almost directly opposite the mouth of the Ranelagh sewer, as the Westbourne River was by this time known. The Thames, he proclaimed, was 'charged with the contents of more than 130 public common sewers, the drainings from dung hills and

laystalls, the refuse of hospitals, slaughter-houses, colour, lead, gas and soap works, drug mills and manufactories, and with all sorts of decomposed animal and vegetable substances'.

In a notice of a public meeting in the same year held to discuss the matter, Wright denounced the water companies. 'That the evils at all times arising out of Monopoly; namely increased Price and deteriorated Quality, should have resulted from such a Confederacy [the ageement of 1817], was to be expected', he wrote. 'But that, in the space of nine years, the Grand Junction Company should have so far departed from every principle of fair dealing, as to sell, at a high price, a necessary of life, so loaded with all sorts of impurities, as to be offensive to the sight, disgusting to the imagination, and destructive to health, appears altogether incredible'.

Official reaction to Wright's complaints was slow to take effect – although a Royal Commission was appointed, its report made few firm recommendations – and it was not until England's population had suffered several rampaging outbreaks of cholera that the Metropolis Water Act of 1852 stipulated that drinking water should come from as pure a source as possible, that it should be filtered and that distribution tanks within five miles of St Paul's should be covered.

But the Chelsea Water Works Company was quicker to take action. In 1827, the engineer James Simpson constructed a prototype filter there, consisting of two settling tanks and a sand and gravel filter. Two years later a larger, permanent version was built, giving Chelsea a pioneering role in water purification until more were adopted elsewhere in the 1840s and 1850s.

The 1852 Act also stipulated that drinking water should not be taken from the tidal stretch of the Thames below Teddington, so the waterworks at Chelsea were closed and moved to Seething Wells (Surbiton), with reservoirs at Putney, and later to Molesey. The offending Grand Junction Water Works Company removed itself to Kew in the 1830s, and later to Hampton; and all the water companies were united in 1904 under the Metropolitan Water Board. The land where Chelsea's extensive waterworks and buildings once lay was quickly covered with the tracks and sheds of Victoria Station.

33
Victorian artists

Turner's house from the river

Chelsea's fame as the home of artists really begins with Turner, though earlier names such as Cipriani and Bartolozzi are linked with the village (Cipriani was buried in the parish). Turner's life in Chelsea is obscure: his attempt to escape the attentions of society was so successful that little is known of the period even today.

He was discovered at Chelsea by his housekeeper, who is said to have followed him there from his home in Queen Anne Street, Cavendish Square. At Chelsea he had taken a cottage by the river (now No 119 Cheyne Walk) at the western end of the village, and assumed his landlady's name, Booth. Here he built a balcony on the roof to enable him to observe the sky and the water; and he was often rowed on the river by Charles Greaves, a local boatbuilder. Leopold Martin, the son of the artist John Martin who also later moved to Chelsea, thought Turner's adopted home 'miserable', in a 'squalid place'. When John Martin came to the waterfront it was to the more respectable Lindsey Row (as the subdivided Lindsey House was known), to the house once occupied by the Brunels, who had added iron balconies to their part of the façade.

Chelsea itself may not figure in the paintings of Turner and Martin but the artists evidently found inspiration in the views of the broad river and big skies. On stormy nights when Greaves had to stay up to watch his boats, Martin would instruct the boatman to wake him if there were clouds and a moon, so that he could capture them on paper.

The inspiration of another famous artist in Chelsea, however, owed little to his surroundings. Dante Gabriel Rossetti came here in 1862, to No 16 Cheyne Walk which was also known as Queen's House or Tudor House (for no good reason since it is a building of the early eighteenth century, see also Chapter 26). His wife had died earlier that year at their Blackfriars home and the move to Chelsea brought the widower a distinctly different style of life, with the company of a number of friends who lived with him at different periods, the best-known of whom was the poet Algernon Swinburne. The writer George Meredith stayed only a short while, repelled, it is said, by Rossetti's habit of eating a plateful of bacon and eggs for breakfast.

Rossetti was one of the original members of the Pre-Raphaelite Brotherhood, the idea of which originated with the artists John Everett Millais and William Holman Hunt, owing to their dislike of painters who claimed to model their work on Raphael's methods. The brooding, mystical quality of Pre-Raphaelite painting is intense in Rossetti's work, and the longer he lived in Cheyne Walk, the more the house seems to have taken on a similar atmosphere. In the early days there were lively dinner parties in exotically decorated rooms, and a menagerie in his garden that included armadillos, wombats and a Brahmin bull. But Rossetti deteriorated, physically and mentally, until he would see no-one but his family and closest friends. He took large doses of chloral, suffered from insomnia and held seances to communicate with his wife. In 1882 he died, shortly before his fifty-fourth birthday, not at Chelsea but in a house lent to him near Margate.

William Holman Hunt had been the first Pre-Raphaelite to come to Chelsea when he moved to Prospect Place – where the Cheyne Hospital for Children is now – in 1849 (he later moved to Campden Hill and then Melbury Road in Kensington). Another Pre-Raphaelite who came to Chelsea was the potter William de Morgan, whose richly coloured tiles once decorated many houses in Kensington and Chelsea. He moved with his mother and sister from Primrose Hill to a house in Cheyne Row, only two doors from Carlyle (see next Chapter), in 1872, and established a workshop in the corner house, where the Catholic Church of the Holy Redeemer now stands.

Later, after his marriage, he lived in The Vale, which was at that time still a secluded rural backwater. But in 1910 it was flattened for redevelopment, its transformation being described in de Morgan's novel, *The Old Man's Youth*. De Morgan and two other residents held a 'house-cooling' party one summer evening in 1909, descriptions of which recall the magical twinkling evenings at Ranelagh a century-and-a-half earlier. The de Morgans moved to Old Church Street, where the potter died in early 1917.

Chelsea's most flamboyant artist, James McNeill Whistler, seems very far in spirit from the Pre-Raphaelites, though he came to the area as early as 1859 and was a friend of Rossetti. An American who had failed as a West Point cadet and become an art student in Paris, Whistler arrived to stay with his half-sister in Sloane Street and make his fortune as an artist. In the following years he had many addresses in Chelsea, at Paradise Row, Cheyne Walk, Lindsey Row and Tite Street, and became known, sometimes feared, and often disliked, as a sharp and pitiless wit. He was well established in the role by the time Oscar Wilde made his entrance, and the two, though friends for a while, engaged in a constant battle of bon mots. They also showed similarities in their rash involvement in libel trials which led both to bankruptcy (see also following Chapter).

Whistler sued Ruskin for libel over his comments on the painting *Black and Gold – The Falling Rocket*. The subject of the picture was the sky over Cremorne but the critic wrote that he had 'never expected to hear a coxcomb ask two hundred guineas for flinging a pot of paint in the public's face'. Whistler was victorious, but he was awarded damages of one farthing, and the bailiffs moved into his new house in Tite Street which he had occupied for less than a

J M W Turner as depicted by The Illustrated London News

The gateway to Rossetti's house, where the initials RC were erroneously believed to stand for Queen Catherine of Braganza, Charles II's wife

year (see also Chapter 40). One morning in 1879, guests arrived for Sunday breakfast there, to find the bailiffs numbering the furniture ready for auction – and serving the meal. Whistler is said to have observed: 'They are wonderful fellows. You will see how excellently they wait on table, and tomorrow, you know, if you want, you can see them sell the chairs you sit on. Amazing!'

Whistler's drollery and biting wit could be highly amusing; but his treatment of the local artist Walter Greaves shows him in a less attractive light. Greaves, the son of the boatbuilder, Charles, who had rowed Turner on the river, was brought up in a house on the corner of Lindsey Row and Milman Street, and had painted with his brother since his early days. He idolised Whistler. Later he recalled: 'I lost my head over Whistler when I first met him and saw his paintings.' The latter was content to give the Greaves brothers the benefit of his advice and was no doubt flattered by their admiration and imitation of him.

Walter Greaves became his assistant and painted many pictures of Chelsea that are now admired for their 'primitive' qualities, besides his famous *Hammersmith Bridge on Boat Race Day*, which he is thought to have painted before meeting Whistler, and which is now in the Tate Gallery. But Whistler dropped Greaves in the late 1870s, and the disciple fell on hard times. He seems to have shown no resentment, despite being unable to sell his pictures

James McNeill Whistler, as seen by Spy

Whister's 'White House' in Tite Street, built for him in 1878

and being denigrated by Whistler's biographers, the Pennells, who destroyed an attempt to revive interest in his work in 1911 by publicly accusing him of plagiarism.

Greaves was a familiar figure in Chelsea, down-at-heel in his tattered black hat and frock-coat as he wandered from shop to shop trying to sell his canvases. He appears to have suffered serious poverty, though there was some support for him from a group of local artists, including Sickert, Wilson Steer and Clausen. In 1922 he was found a place at the Charterhouse in Smithfield, where he died in 1930.

On one occasion the artists held a dinner in his honour at the Chelsea Arts Club. This now famous institution was formed in 1891 at a building since replaced by the Chenil Galleries, and moved to its present home in Old Church Street in 1902 (Charles Chenil opened his gallery in 1905 to help young artists; it closed in 1927). At that time, Chelsea was still the home of many artists, including those of the New English Art Club: Philip Wilson Steer lived at 109 Cheyne Walk until his death in 1942 and Sickert was briefly in The Vale. There was John Singer Sargent, who lived in the same building as Henry James, Carlyle Mansions, Augustus John in Mallord Street and Sir Alfred Munnings whose home from 1920 until 1959 was at No 96 Chelsea Park Gardens.

In 1915 the architect and designer Charles Rennie Mackintosh and his wife Margaret, also a designer, arrived in Glebe Place. He had failed to establish his own architectural practice in Glasgow and the plans he made for local buildings while living in Chelsea were largely unexecuted, though the house he designed for an artist friend, Harold Squire, was built in Glebe Place. The local artistic community also hoped to build a block of studios in Upper Cheyne Row, but the planning authorities took exception to the avant-garde designs by Mackintosh and turned them down. In 1923 the Mackintoshes moved to France, returning only in 1927, the year before Charles died of cancer. The studios once occupied by Chelsea's artists, where they still exist, are of course highly fashionable today, but so much so that only the wealthiest of artists could now afford them.

The home in Cheyne Walk of Daniel Maclise (1806–70), another of Chelsea's artists

Cartoon by Max Beerbohm of Rossetti in his back garden: from left to right at the back, Whistler, Swinburne and Watts-Dunton on the wall, Meredith, Burne-Jones with flower, William Morris declaiming; in foreground, Rossetti, Fanny Cornforth and John Ruskin

Carlyle's house in Cheyne Row with an inset of his birthplace at Ecclefechan

Carlyle's Birth-place, Ecclefechan.

34
Victorian writers

Boehm's statue of Thomas Carlyle on Chelsea Embankment

Chelsea's nineteenth-century writers never formed an identifiable group in the village; indeed quite the reverse, for the story of Chelsea's links with the Victorian literary world is dominated by one man, Thomas Carlyle. And yet it is probably for his personal life rather than for his place in literary history that his house is visited today, for his ideas and the books that express them are scarcely popular in the late twentieth century.

Carlyle came to London in 1834 after he and his wife Jane had endured several years of lonely existence at Craigenputtock in Dumfriesshire. Having house-hunted in Camden Town, Kensington and Primrose Hill, he turned to Chelsea on the recommendation of Leigh Hunt, who lived at Upper Cheyne Row. Carlyle described the area as 'unfashionable; it was once the resort of the court and great, however, hence numerous old houses in it at once cheap and excellent'. One of these was No 5 Great Cheyne Row (now No 24 Cheyne Row), which he described to his wife in a letter.

'We are called "Cheyne Row" proper (pronounced Chainie Row), and are a "genteel neighbourhood", two old ladies on the one side, unknown character on the other, but with "pianos" as Hunt said. The street is flag-paved, sunk-storied, iron-railed, all old-fashioned and tightly done up; looks out on a rank of sturdy old pollarded (that is *beheaded*) Lime trees, standing there like giants in *tawtie* wigs ... Backwards, a garden ... with trees, etc, in bad culture; beyond this, green hayfields and tree-avenues (once a Bishop's pleasure-grounds) ...

'The House itself is eminent, antique; wainscotted to the very ceiling, and has been all new painted and repaired; broadish stair, with massive balustrade (in the old style) corniced as thick as one's thigh; floors firm as a rock ... On the whole a most massive, roomy, sufficient old house; with places, for example, to hang say three dozen hats or cloaks on; and as many crevices, and queer old presses, and shelved closets (all tight and new-painted in their way) as would gratify the most covetous Goody. Rent £35! I confess I am strongly tempted ....'

Carlyle's evident interest and delight in the actual structure of the house conjures up a vivid picture of the place in which he and Jane were to spend the rest of their lives, the domestic details of which have fascinated biographers ever since. Between the austere and unrelenting insistence of his books, and the anguished memories of his dead wife in the *Reminiscences*, there was perhaps a more relaxed and genial Carlyle such as shows through in these letters.

'Chelsea', he wrote, 'is a singular, heterogeneous kind of spot, very dirty and confused in some places, quite beautiful in others, abounding with antiquities and the traces of great men ... Our Row ... runs out upon a beautiful "Parade" (perhaps they call it) running along the shore of the River: shops, etc., a broad highway, with huge shady trees; boats lying moored, and a smell of shipping and tar; Battersea bridge (of wood) a few yards off; the broad River with white-trousered, white-shirted Cockneys dashing by like arrows in their long canoes of Boats; beyond, the green beautiful Knolls of Surrey with their villages: on the whole a most artificial, green-painted, yet lively, fresh, almost opera-looking business such as you can fancy.'

Jane Carlyle replied, concerned about the 'dampish and unwholesome' situation near the river, and the bugs that might populate the house; but having seen the property she approved, and the decision to take it was quickly made. Carlyle recalled the move from their Gray's Inn lodgings in his *Reminiscences*:

'We proceeded all through Belgrave Square hither, with our servant, our looser luggage, ourselves and a little canary bird ("Chico" which she had brought with her from Craigenputtock); our hackney coach rumbling on with us all. Chico, in Belgrave Square, burst into singing, which we took as a good omen ... I don't remember us arriving at this door; but I do the cheerful Gypsy life we had here among the litter and carpenters, for three incipient days. Leigh Hunt was in the next street, sending kind unpractical messages.'

Here in Cheyne Row the Carlyles lived their life of mutual devotion and acute nervous strain that has become famous; here the great scourge of modern degeneracy would sit beneath an awning in the garden, smoking his pipe; here he built an attic storey in an unsuccessful attempt to provide himself with a soundproofed study; and here he wrote his famous works, *The French Revolution* and *Frederick the Great*, besides others.

Many eminent contemporary figures visited him at Chelsea, including Thackeray, who lived in Kensington (see Chapter 9), and Dickens, who had been married in St Luke's Church, Sydney Street. Leigh Hunt, living round the corner in Upper Cheyne Row in his chaotic household, was a cheerful, if unlikely friend who 'is always delighted when I go and rouse him for a walk'. (His less endearing qualities were vividly portrayed in the character of Skimpole in Dickens' *Bleak House*.)

Other nineteenth-century writers in Chelsea had less substantial connections with the village: George Eliot and Mrs Gaskell both lived but briefly in Cheyne Walk, one at the end of her life, the other in her infancy, and Hilaire Belloc also lived there 1900–6. Mark Twain spent a short time in Tedworth Square, and Bram Stoker at Durham Place overlooking Burton's Court; the poet Walter Swinburne was part of the Pre-Raphaelite set which congregated at Rossetti's house (see Chapter 33). Early in the twentieth century, Henry James came to Carlyle Mansions on the embankment from de Vere Mansions in Kensington, where he had had an 'immense bird's eye view

James Henry Leigh Hunt

Mrs Gaskell

From left to right: George Eliot, Henry and Charles Kingsley, and Walter Swinburne

Ape's cartoon of Oscar Wilde in Vanity Fair, 1884

of housetops and streets'. He wrote that the prospect from the reception rooms at Carlyle Mansions, which faced south over the river, was good for his work, being 'so still and yet so animated', and used to enjoy bath-chair promenades, before dying in Chelsea in 1916.

Arnold Bennett came to London as a young man in 1889, and lodged with the Marriott family in Victoria Grove, Chelsea (now Netherton Grove). 'I began to revolve, dazzled, in a circle of painters and musicians who, without the least affectation, spelt Art with the majuscule', he wrote later. As a famous and prosperous author he made his home in No 75 Cadogan Square in 1923, from where he wrote wry letters to his nephew concerning contractors, paint smells and bookshelves. He left Chelsea in 1930.

The Kingsley brothers, Charles, George and Henry, came to Chelsea Rectory when their father received the living of the recently-built St Luke's in 1836. Charles briefly became his father's curate, and his brother Henry enlivened the history of the village in his novel *The Hillyars and the Burtons*, which fictionalises the Lawrence family of Chelsea. An old inhabitant, T B Ellenor remembered that 'The rector and the boys were great favourites with the parishioners as they were courteous and very free with everybody.'

But these nineteenth-century figures seem far away from Chelsea's other notable writer, Oscar Wilde, who did all his well-known work at No 16 Tite Street before his arrest in 1895 put an end to his career. By the time he moved to his house in 1884, Carlyle had been dead three years, and belonged to a vanishing age. Wilde's urbane and witty sophistication had more in common with metropolitan London than with the old village of Chelsea, which was not then the fashionable place it later became. He had known Tite Street from the days when his friend Frank Miles had built a house there (see Chapter 40). Wilde and his new wife, Constance, moved into a red-brick house undistinguished on the exterior but decorated inside by Wilde together with the architect and interior designer E W Godwin and the artist Whistler, with whom Wilde later quarrelled (see also Chapter 34). The study was given a red and yellow colour scheme, the drawing-room ceiling was painted by Whistler, and there was a heavily draped smoking room.

Wilde wrote his famous fairy-tales, *The Picture of Dorian Grey* and his four comedies, including *The Importance of being Earnest*, during his time in Chelsea. He was arrested in the Cadogan Hotel in Sloane Street – an event commemorated in a poem by Sir John Betjeman – and while awaiting trial in 1895 was declared bankrupt, whereupon the contents of his house were sold at auction on the premises. After his release from gaol in 1897 he left England, to die three years later in Paris.

In the twentieth century, Chelsea has been the home of two eminent poets, T S Eliot and Sir John Betjeman, the latter having been taught by the former in Highgate. Eliot lived for many years in Carlyle Mansions, where another American-born writer, Henry James, had lived, but in 1937 he moved with his second wife to Kensington. He was a churchwarden of St Stephen's in Gloucester Road for twenty-five years. Sir John Betjeman lived as a child in Old Church Street and later returned to Chelsea to spend part of his last years at No 29 Radnor Walk.

James Pilton's manufactory at the Manor House in the King's Road

The Pheasantry in King's Road became Chelsea's 'cause celèbre' in the redevelopment battles of the 1970s. Starting life, as far as can be gathered, as a very ordinary building on the King's Road, its architectural pretensions were glamourised in the French fashion in the 1880s in a way which guaranteed a battle when demolition was threatened in 1969. That controversy lasted twelve years; but the Pheasantry's façade has survived to tell the tale.

It was not until the building's future was at risk that its history was considered, and many tales were told about it that have a familiar and suspect ring: it was said, inevitably, that Nell Gwyn had lived there; that it had been Charles II's hunting lodge; that it had been the home of Lord Amherst, who brought pheasants to England from China in the eighteenth century; that it was a Palladian building, or a Victorian building ... the freeholders, the Cadogan estate, thought it simply 'tatty'. Most of what is now known about the building is the result of research done by Nesta Macdonald in the 1970s, during the campaign by local residents to save it from the bulldozer's embrace.

The Pheasantry's first appearance in history seems to be in 1769, when it was marked, though not named, on a map owned by the Cadogan estate. It is shown next to Box Farm, a Chelsea landmark which stood in the King's Road from the seventeenth century until 1899, and at the time these two were almost the only buildings bordering the track: King's Road did not begin to become a commercial thoroughfare until after it was made a public road in 1830. As early as 1809, however, the area possessed a menagerie at a building known as the Manor House, opposite Box Farm, where 'James Pilton's Manufactory' advertised itself and its 'ornamental works for country residences' in *The Gentleman's Magazine*: the advertisement carries an illustration of a large garden with aviaries and peacocks.

At the Pheasantry, a man named Samuel Baker became the tenant in 1864. The family firm was already trading in ornamental poultry, and in 1865 its usual advertisement in *The Field* pointed out its new address: 'Messrs Baker beg to invite their patrons, customers, and gentlemen interested in the breed of PHEASANTS to an INSPECTION at their new Establishment, 152 King's Road, Chelsea, of Specimens of the different varieties of the BREEDING-STOCK'.

The Pheasantry operated as such only until 1878, but its brief period as supplier of pheasants to the gentry had given it an enduring name. Its present appearance was provided by other occupants, the Joubert family, whose name and trades can still be seen inscribed on the walls of the restored building. The Jouberts who came to King's Road are thought to have been descended from a family of French cabinet-makers of royalist sympathies who moved to England in 1831, perhaps as a result of the 1830 revolution. In Chelsea they became versatile decorators in a fast expanding area, describing themselves as 'upholsterers, painters, gilders, ecclesiastical and domestic decorators, cabinet makers, artistic furniture and parquet flooring manufacturers by patent

35
The Pheasantry

machinery'. Some of their furniture was shown at the South Kensington exhibition of 1862.

With a flourish they transformed what was probably a rather plain old building into a miniature stately French manor house, with a flamboyant arch topped by four great galloping horses and their chariot (quadriga), and flanked with caryatids and eagles. The last member of the family to work at the Pheasantry, Felix Joubert, built himself a condensed version of a French château in Jubilee Place (later demolished) and contributed miniature furniture and decorations to Queen Mary's doll's house in the 1920s.

The Jouberts let parts of the Pheasantry to other craftsmen – in the Chelsea library is a letter which mentions wood-carving studios there in about 1900 – and in 1916 they received their most famous tenant, Princess Serafine Astafieva, a Russian ballet dancer who had joined Diaghilev's company in Paris in 1909 and come with it to London in 1911. Five years later she began giving classes in Chelsea. Diaghilev visited her at her studio, indeed, found two of his dancers in her school, Alice Marks – later Dame Alicia Markova – and Anton Dolin. Another pupil who went on to achieve great fame, Margot Fonteyn, had been there only a year when the Princess died in 1934.

By the time of the Princess's death, the Pheasantry was divided between a number of tenants, one of which, the Pheasantry Club, was a leading fashionable venue in Chelsea in that period. Subscriptions in 1933 were ten shillings and sixpence for artists, fifteen shillings for ladies and a guinea for gentlemen – an interesting exercise in social discrimination – and artists were much in evidence. The club continued as a less fashionable discotheque until the 1960s, but in 1969 developers revealed that they had other plans in mind for the building.

A proposal was unveiled for a 266-bedroom hotel; and a lengthy battle began. Already protracted negotiations were stalled by the financial collapse of 1974 and the site changed hands as different developers envisaged different schemes. The buildings around the Pheasantry were demolished; but in 1978 the original permission for development expired, and the owners went back to the drawing-board. Eventually, after standing in solitary dilapidation amid a derelict site for several years, the Pheasantry's façade and entrance arch were retained and restored, so that now, at least from the outside, the building appears quite as splendid as its former French owners once intended.

Below right: The Pheasantry today

Princess Serafine Astafieva, the famous ballet dancer and teacher who lived at the Pheasantry for many years

Henry Holland's house, Sloane Place, which was later known as The Pavilion

In 1830 the amount of open space and land under cultivation in Chelsea was still considerable, but the social composition of the village was changing. In 1821 there had been 275 families engaged in agriculture; ten years later there were only eighty-seven. New streets of terraced houses, though rising piecemeal, were spreading over Chelsea's fields, the Common had disappeared, and with the development of Belgravia immediately to the east, the village was linked to London by a loose spread of buildings.

Nevertheless, its character remained that of a village. Faulkner recalled that only in 1796 he had been 'present at a stag-hunt in Chelsea', and Ellenor, writing as an old man in 1901, remembered seeing 'snipe, teal and wild duck shot on the ground at the west end of Chelsea'. The King's Road became public only in 1830, Markham Square and Carlyle Square were as yet unbuilt, Paulton's Square only just beginning, and in The Vale were just a few small cottages and villas. Chelsea's two earliest squares, which Faulkner called 'new' in 1829, were Trafalgar Square (now rebuilt as Chelsea Square) and Camera Square, later demolished and rebuilt as Chelsea Park Gardens.

Some streets outside the old village centre were already well established, however. Smith Street was lined with houses, and part of St Leonard's Terrace, known then as Green's Row, was built in 1765. A market had been established in about 1790 where the lower half of Sloane Gardens now stands, but judging by Ellenor's memories of the place, it degenerated into something of a slum. The influence of nearby Turk's Row and Jew's Row could not have helped: Faulkner called this area 'without exception, the most disgraceful parts of this Parish' and Ellenor remembered it as a 'labyrinth of courts and passages of small one and two-roomed houses' inhabited by 'the very lowest and most depraved and criminal class . . . all along the curb the low, loose women would sit and insult and rob the passers-by'.

The area surrounding Marlborough Road (now Draycott Avenue) and Keppel Street (now Sloane Avenue) was also densely populated, but immediately north of the Fulham Road the nurseries began again.

36
Chelsea
by 1830

Overleaf: F P Thompson's map of Chelsea, 1836

153

To the Right Honourable

THE EARL CADOGAN,

this Map &c of

CHELSEA,

FROM A NEW AND ACTUAL SURVEY,

Shewing the

Ecclesiastical Divisions of

St. LUKE AND UPPER CHELSEA,

and the

DISTRICT OF HANS TOWN,

and containing that portion of the Parishes of

KENSINGTON AND St. MARGARET'S WESTMINSTER,

lying between the

BOUNDARY of CHELSEA AND THE FULHAM ROAD,

Is by Permission,

Respectfully dedicated,

By his most obedient humble Servant,

F. P. Thompson,

Land Surveyor, &c.

LONDON, PUBLISHED BY F.P. THOMPSON, SURVEYOR &c.

10 BURY STREET NEAR THE NEW CHURCH CHELSEA.

JULY 4th 1836.

This DETACHED PORTION of CHELSEA PARISH

CHELSEA REACH

Scale of Chains

Scale of Feet

ENGRAVED AND PRINTED BY J.& C. WALKER

154

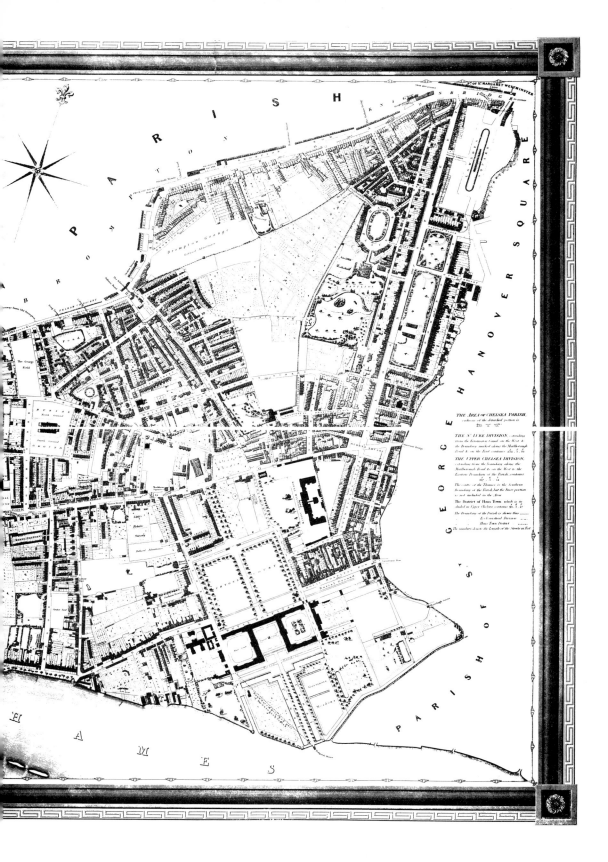

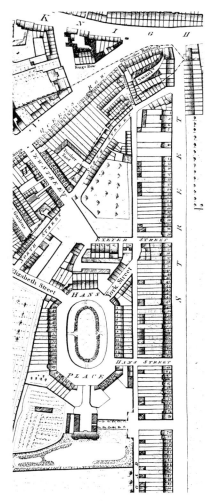

Detail from Horwood's map of London, 1794

The building now known as the Duke of York's headquarters was built in 1801 for a different, though still military, purpose. It was named the Royal Military Asylum for the Children of the Soldiers of the Regular Army, and at first housed and educated orphans of both sexes, an admirable aim thought Faulkner, considering 'the helpless and forlorn condition of many among these orphan objects of commiseration'. The children were divided into companies, with an old soldier attached to each as sergeant; but the boys were moved to Dover in 1909 and by 1913 it was the headquarters of the 2nd London Division of the Territorial Force, and, today, it is still used by the Territorial Army.

When the Asylum was first built it looked across open ground to Whitelands House, which stood on the King's Road (near where the block of flats of the same name stands today at the top of Cheltenham Terrace), and to the houses of Hemus Terrace, which were begun in 1807 and now form part of the western side of Royal Avenue.

The largest unified building project to be undertaken in Chelsea at this time was the creation of Hans Town by the builder and architect Henry Holland. Work began in 1777, long before Belgravia arose from the marshes to the east; but it was near the main road through Knightsbridge and it proved a highly successful speculation. The land on which Hans Town was built belonged to the Second Lord Cadogan, as a result of his marriage to one of Sir Hans Sloane's daughters, but the idea appears to have come not from him but from Holland. Henry Holland had been raised in Fulham and perhaps it was his familiarity with the area between his home and London that enabled him to judge correctly the speed with which demand for houses would reach this part of Chelsea. Agreement was reached initially in 1771, but, according to Faulkner, operations were delayed by the outbreak of war with the American colonies. Most of the houses went up quickly thereafter.

Hans Town stretched from Knightsbridge to a point south of Sloane Square, along the newly created Sloane Street, and the houses on the west side of this new street at first enjoyed an open view across fields to Buckingham House in the distance, until Cadogan Place was built in 1790. Sloane Square was occupied by 1780 and was at first residential, but soon attracted shopkeepers. One establishment on the south side, The Chelsea, Brompton & Belgrave Dispensary, opened in 1812 and was described by Faulkner as having as its object 'the relief of the industrious labourer, the artizan, and the servant'. Behind Sloane Street the land was used to create Hans Place in the shape of a square with its corners shaved off. The northern part of the gardens in front of Cadogan Place are said to have been created by Humphrey Repton, while the southern half was opened as a botanical garden in 1807.

The houses of Hans Town were modest, three-storeyed brick buildings with pleasing doorcases and fanlights. In 1787 an Act of Parliament was passed regulating the maintenance of the streets, and Faulkner wrote that such advantages 'have caused the property to let at great rents, and to be mostly inhabited by the rich and affluent'. If a similar Act could only be obtained for the older part of the parish, he thought, 'it would be a great improvement, and induce persons of independence to reside in it'. Jane Austen used to visit her brother, Henry, when he lived in Sloane Street.

While he was busy creating this 'new town', Henry Holland allocated himself several acres south of Hans Place and built Sloane Place, a fine house whose grounds were landscaped by his father-in-law, 'Capability' Brown. Its entrance was on the north, and inside were intercommunicating, south-facing reception rooms, rich chimney-pieces and mouldings, and mahogany doors. The grounds contained a lake and an ice-house in the form of a folly representing a ruined priory, and Faulkner declared that they helped make Sloane Place 'the most charming villa near London'. It was later known as The Pavilion after Holland's work for the Prince of Wales in Brighton (the Marine Pavilion, later transformed to the Royal Pavilion by Nash), for which it was, erroneously, thought to have been a model; and was demolished in the 1870s to make way for new developments. By the time the smart new houses of the Victorians had been built in fashionable red brick on the estate, there was not a great deal left of Holland's neatly planned design (see Chapter 40), though some of his houses have survived.

37
Cremorne
Gardens

Who now remembers gay Cremorne,
And all her jaunty jills,
And those wild whirling figures born
Of Jullien's grand quadrilles?
With hats on head and morning coats
There footed to his prancing notes
Our partner girls and we;
And the gas-jets winked and the lustres clinked,
And the platform throbbed, as with arms enlinked
We moved to the minstrelsy.

This was how Thomas Hardy recalled Cremorne Gardens in *Reminiscences of a Dancing Man*. Hardy is not normally associated with Chelsea, but Cremorne was more than a merely local phenomenon: it was one of Chelsea's celebrated nineteenth-century 'institutions'. Like its eighteenth-century forerunner, Ranelagh, it drew revellers from far afield, and, in a more democratic age, its advertisements pointed to its accessibility by 'omnibusses from every part of London, Islington, Bethnal Green, Mile End Road'.

The estate on which the pleasure grounds were established lay on the western edge of Chelsea, between the river and the King's Road, south-west of World's End. Here, in about 1740, the Ninth Earl of Huntingdon built himself a villa overlooking the river known as Chelsea Farm, where his pious wife, the famous Countess Huntingdon of the Methodist movement, liked to invite one

A music cover from the 1860s depicting Cremorne's dance-floor

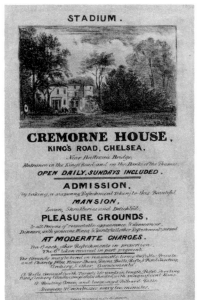

A hand-bill advertising Baron de Berenger's pleasure grounds

of the leading evangelists of the day, George Whitfield, to preach to her aristocratic friends.

The house acquired the name of Cremorne in 1778 when it became the home of Thomas Dawson, later Viscount Cremorne, who remodelled it to designs by James Wyatt. From him it descended to the Penn family of Buckinghamshire and Pennsylvania, and in 1830 was bought by Baron Charles de Berenger. At the time, it was described by Faulkner as a 'charming villa', with grounds enclosed by an iron rail and chain, 'laid out with taste and simplicity; it is screened with a variety of handsome trees and commands extensive views on the Thames, whilst it constitutes the most ornamental object on its banks'.

On the western side of the property stood Ashburnham House, built in 1747 by Dr Benjamin Hoadley and acquiring its name later from another owner, the Earl of Ashburnham. Lady Mary Coke lived here after leaving Aubrey House in Kensington (see Chapter 5) and the grounds, with magnolias, orange trees, a cedar of Lebanon and other rare species, were later absorbed by Cremorne Gardens.

Baron de Berenger was the first owner of Cremorne to see the possibilities of opening it to the public. He established a 'stadium' where, for a subscription of two or three guineas, members could learn various manly accomplishments such as shooting, fencing, swimming and rowing. But the scope of the establishment soon widened to include fireworks and balloon ascents, as well as demonstrations such as that given by a 'rope-dancer', who claimed to be able to hang by the neck from his rope, and nearly killed himself in the process. By the time Cremorne came up for sale, it was becoming a popular place.

A set of sale particulars of 1840 describes it as a 'splendid place of entertainment', which could replace Vauxhall Gardens in the public affection if managed by 'a spirited individual, with a moderate capital and well furnished head'. By 1843 Cremorne was in the hands of another 'baron' of dubious origin, Renton Nicholson, who was infamous for the scandalous mock trials staged by his Judge and Jury Society, which he removed from Bow Street to Cremorne.

Nicholson also held two 'One Thousand Guinea Three Days' Fêtes' there, during which were promised 'minstrelsy, music, dancing', as well as novelties such as 'Mr Alexander Burke's celebrated poney, "Bobby"', who 'will trot seven miles and a half in 30 minutes, with a monkey on his back'; and the singing of 'Tippitywitchet', 'Hot Codlins' and other songs by the clown Tom Matthews. During 1845 the management of Cremorne was briefly the responsibility of Matthews and the caterer there, Littlejohn, but they were soon succeeded by Thomas Bartlett Simpson, in whose care the gardens became a roaring success.

To the beautiful grounds were added a variety of embellishments which, combined with the large numbers of visitors, must sometimes have given the impression of a fairground rather than a garden. The Ordnance Survey map of 1867 shows a marionette theatre, circus, 'fernery', diorama, shooting gallery, hermit's cave, gipsy's grotto, firework gallery, bowling saloon, two large halls,

Vincent de Groof, 'the flying man'

a 'stereorama', pagoda, maze, several fountains and other unidentified buildings.

In the large Ashburnham hall, which stood on the boundary of the two old estates, horticultural exhibitions were held, while in the hermit's cave 'a man of celebrated prophetic knowledge' foretold the future. There was also a 'monster oyster-shell grotto' in which the air was perfumed 'most appropriately with Rummell's Sea-weed Bouquet, diffused by means of a vaporiser' and where customers were served shellfish by 'young ladies dressed as mermaids'.

The most splendid edifice in the gardens was probably the bandstand (shown on the map as the pagoda) and dance-floor, the latter encircling the pagoda and 'capable, it is said, of affording full space for the mazy movements of 4000 dancers at the same time', according to *The Illustrated London News*. The paper added that 'Lavender bowers, Chinese walks, trees illuminated with jets of gas, and flower-beds glittering with coloured lamps, are among the other attractions of the grounds'.

The events staged at Cremorne to hold the attention of its public were varied and ingenious. In 1858 a crowd gathered to watch 'The Italian Salamander' walk through a frame of burning brushwood to demonstrate his fireproof clothing; in 1861 the 'Female Blondin' set off to cross the river on a tightrope, though she had to abandon the attempt when the rope slackened; the gymnast Leotard performed various feats; the 'Man-frog' ate, smoked and slept in a tank full of water; there were appearances by 'Signor Devani, the celebrated Ourang-Outang contortionist' and by the 'hirsute Kostroma people from central Russia' who were claimed to have the heads of dogs; there was a mock tournament, an aquatic battle and an aristocratic fête which was washed out by a downpour; a staging of the battle of Sevastapol during which the stage collapsed; numerous concerts and several balloon ascents, one of which ended in tragedy in 1874 at St Luke's Church in Robert Street, as Sydney Street was known then.

A 'flying man' named Vincent de Groof had agreed to demonstrate his bat-like machine by attaching it to a balloon from which he would be cut free at an appropriate height. When this was done, however, it simply spiralled down to earth and left de Groof dead on the pavement. Eleven years earlier the tightrope walker, Carlo Valerio, had also come to grief at Cremorne when he 'alighted on his head on the gravel of the promenade', as *The Penny Illustrated Paper* delicately put it.

The deaths of performers probably added fuel to the fire kindled by opponents of Cremorne, though it was not their only cause for complaint. The gardens had a reputation for their attraction of 'fast' types, both male and female, and for its liberal dispensation of alcohol. Admission was free, but 'every visitor is expected to take Refreshment to the amount of sixpence', and some took a good deal more. 'Decorous hard drinking is the order of the day', said one contemporary of Sundays at Cremorne.

Canon Cromwell of St Marks College complained vociferously – and was pilloried for his pains in *The Day's Doings* (October 1871), which envisaged a day when the rules of Cremorne would stipulate that 'No gentleman can be admitted unless accompanied by a nurse holding a license from the bench of Middlesex magistrates.'

Cremorne's opponents won the day when its owner, John Baum, was forced to bring a libel action against the author of a defamatory pamphlet which called the gardens a 'nursery of every kind of vice', the author being a local Baptist minister. Baum won the case, but with damages of only a farthing, and his costs crippled him. A sale took place in 1878 of everything from the dance-floor to the standing timber, Ashburnham and Cremorne Houses were demolished and in 1880, L'Estrange described the site as 'a desolation of broken ground'.

Soon afterwards, building began on both estates and on the strip of ground between Ashburnham House and the river known as The Lots. The power station in Lots Road was opened in 1904 and now only a small patch of 'open space' at the riverside preserves the memory of the gardens, together with the old iron gates that once guarded the King's Road entrance.

*View of the Thames and old
Battersea Bridge in 1793*

It is difficult now to imagine the Thames filled with colourful pleasure barges, and being the source of rich harvests of fish, let alone being a pleasant place to swim, now that its role in the life of London is so diminished. It was once all of these, however, and Chelsea Reach was a good place to see such activities, for it was a fine broad expanse of water bordered by fields and gardens, and the village of Chelsea itself.

The river held a variety of fish. Faulkner wrote in 1829 that it produced 'salmon, trout, pike, carp, roach, dace, perch, chub, barbel, smelt, gudgeon, and of flounders there are numbers in this river; it abounds also with fine eels and lampreys. At Chelsea, the angler's boat should be fixed almost opposite the church, so as to angle in six or seven feet of water. Here, as well as under Battersea Bridge, are caught good roach and dace in their season.' The scales of roach and dace, he said, were 'sold to the Jews for the purpose of making false pearls', while salmon 'bear a most extravagant price in the London markets, having been sold at twelve shillings a pound'.

Fishing at Chelsea as a full-time occupation, however, seems to have died out by the time he was writing, partly at least because of the use of unlawful nets. In 1869 George Bryan remembered that 'two or three fishermen earned a scanty living by selling the fish they caught', but that otherwise it was not profitable. Another old resident, John Munday, remembering the river in the 1840s, recalled seeing the water 'so low that we walked across without our shoes and stockings on'.

The river's importance as a transport route in London was also declining with the provision of better roads and more bridges; but in earlier times it must have presented a busy and sometimes a picturesque appearance, as Steele evidently felt when he wrote in August 1712 in *The Spectator*:

'When we first put off from Shore, we soon fell in with a Fleet of Gardeners bound for the several Market-Ports of London; and it was the liveliest Scene imaginable to see the Chearfulness with which these industrious People ply'd their way to a certain Sale of their Goods. The Banks on each Side are as well

38
The
River

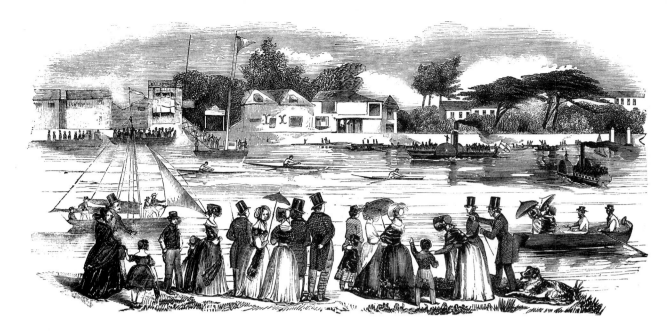

The finishing line of Doggett's race, with the cedars of Chelsea's Physic Garden on the right

A waterman wearing Doggett's coat and badge

peopled, and beautified with as agreeable Plantations as any spot on the Earth; but the Thames it self, loaded with the Product of each Shore, added very much to the Landskip.'

It was the role of the Thames as a thoroughfare that prompted the creation of its famous tradition; the race for Doggett's Coat and Badge between London Bridge and Chelsea. Thomas Doggett (circa 1650–1721), a highly successful Irish actor and manager, was as familiar with the river as might be expected in an age still dependent on river transport; indeed the watermen found valuable customers in the theatre-going public and the theatres in turn were indebted to the watermen for delivering audiences to their doors.

In addition, the watermen held plenty of informal races among themselves for wagers – Pepys came across one planned to finish at Chelsea in 1661 – so there were good reasons why Doggett should establish a race for watermen fresh from their apprenticeships, between what was then the city's only bridge across the Thames, and Chelsea Reach. And Doggett had another reason: he was an ardent Hanoverian and the race was his way of celebrating the accession of George I, for which, say the records of the Watermen's Company, he went to his grave 'endeared to Whigs and Watermen'.

So it was that he instigated the famous race in 1715, giving an orange-coloured coat and a silver badge depicting the Hanoverian horse. His will provided for 'the laying out ffurnishing and procuring yearly on the ffirst day of August for ever the following particulars that is to say, ffive pounds for a Badge of silver weighing about twelve ounces and representing Liberty to be given to be rowed for by Six young Watermen according to my Custom, Eighteen Shillings for Cloath for a Livery whereon the said Badge is to be put, one pound one shilling for making up the said Livery and Buttons and Appurtenances to it and Thirty shillings to the Clerk of Watermens Hall'.

The race took place on the first day of August, at the time when the tide was strongest against the rowers, which meant that it sometimes took two hours, rowing a heavy passenger wherry, to cover the five miles between the Old Swan at London Bridge, and the White Swan at Chelsea, which stood on the water's edge below Swan Walk. When the White Swan was converted to a brewery in about 1780, the finishing line was moved to another tavern of the same name on the western side of the Physic Garden, where Norman Shaw's Swan House (see Chapter 40) stands now.

The local historian Bryan was given a rhyme said to have been written by a waterman which one can imagine having been sung in Chelsea's taverns after the race:

F.Bartolozzi sculp. 1775

Let your oars, like lightning flog it,
Up the Thames as swiftly jog it,
An' you'd win the prize of Doggett,
The glory of the river!
Bendin', bowin', strainin', rowin',
Perhaps the wind in fury blowin',
Or the tide agin you flowin',
The coat and badge forever!

Admission ticket for the Ranelagh regatta ball in 1775, drawn by Cipriani and engraved by Bartolozzi

The riverside taverns of the village were vital community institutions – the local historian Reginald Blunt worked out that there was at one time one every eighty yards between Battersea Bridge and the Royal Hospital – and were part of a crowded, bustling waterfront scene. There were several wharves in the village, for coal, timber and lime, in addition to the stairs at various points where boats and ferries could be boarded.

It was a place full of interest for a boy, as Thomas Bell Ellenor demonstrated when he wrote in 1901, 'Rambling Recollections of Chelsea and the Surrounding District as a Village in the Early Part of the Past Century' – by an old inhabitant, telling of his memories of childhood there. Good Fridays at the Swan Brewhouse were particularly memorable, for then the drains from the brewery, which naturally ran into the river, were all plugged with bags of sand when the tide was low, so that the hot liquid running from the coppers would force rats into the yard 'by the score'. Everyone let loose his dog, and pandemonium ensued.

163

Ne Sutor ultra
Crepidam

*Thomas Doggett dancing the
Cheshire Round*

Ellenor also recalled the characters of the place: 'a half-witted fellow, who got his living by collecting corks and drift wood'; Jamie Cator, 'a remnant of the old press gang . . . morose, dark-featured, heavily marked with the small-pox'; and the family who lived in an old jolly-boat and came twice a week to sell 'bundles of rush grass cut in the marshes on the river's bank, to sell to the local tradesmen to feed their horses'.

Such characters were far removed from the fashionable life of the neighbourhood and from the fabulous regatta that took place on the river at Ranelagh in 1775 when the Thames resembled 'a floating town'. The river was covered with boats, all flying flags, there was scaffolding on the banks for the benefit of spectators and in Ranelagh Gardens a temporary octagonal building was decorated with the colours of the navy's flags, with streamers and lustres, while 2000 people dined and danced in the rotunda.

Later regattas at Chelsea, usually held at Whitsun, were rather more modest, but nevertheless animated occasions. Cheyne Walk and Battersea Bridge were crowded with spectators in carriages or on horseback, and the pleasure boats would be covered with flags. Sometimes there would be musicians aboard. Ellenor remembered sailing matches between 'small tubby-looking, half-decked boats', rowing competitions and riverbank performers including clowns who 'played a kind of river tournament, sitting straddle-legged on beer barrels afloat, tilting at each other with long poles' and an 'old woman drawn in a washing tub by four geese'. The last regatta, held in 1871, was painted by the local artist, Walter Greaves (see Chapter 33).

Bryan stated in 1869 that steamboats had made it impracticable to continue the regattas at Chelsea; one wonders in any case what might have been the fate of anyone falling into the water by that time – the Thames had only a few years previously been responsible for producing the 'Great Stink' of 1858. Nowadays the river, though still decidedly murky, is much cleaner, but barely used save for a few pleasure boats and one or two barges. Doggett's race still takes place in July, however, between London Bridge and Cadogan Pier, and there are plans for a commuter service now that people are rediscovering the pleasures of living by London's river.

*View of the Royal Hospital from
Battersea (circa 1834)*

The first Battersea Bridge, seen from Cheyne Walk in 1825

The building of Chelsea Embankment in the 1870s was probably the most significant and far-reaching change the area has ever seen; not necessarily for the benefits it was built to provide, but because it swept away the heart of the old riverside village, the wharves, the old streets and waterfront taverns. With the embankment in place, Chelsea lost its old identity forever. The residents of the original part of Cheyne Walk found themselves observing the river across a newly planted garden; the Physic Garden and the Royal Hospital lost their river gates and access to the water was restricted to a stroll beside a massive granite wall.

Chelsea was different in 1772, the year in which its first bridge was built across the river on the route of a ferry which had been plying the waters for centuries. The low brick embankment beside the Thames was pierced in many places by steps and interrupted by the walls of houses and wharves that overhung the river on the south side of Duke Street and Lombard Street. Between Cheyne Walk and the water there were only the front gardens of the houses, a road and an avenue of trees.

When Battersea Bridge was built, of wood, in 1772, it was the only bridge over the river between Westminster and Putney. A newspaper report claimed that it would be 'one of the strongest and most compleat works of the kind in the kingdom', and its opening ceremony was held 'amidst the Concourse of many Thousand People' and the ringing of the church bells in both parishes. Its irregular construction, the slight curve it made before it reached the Chelsea shore and the boats that were moored in the 'bay' beside it made it the subject of many paintings and drawings, particularly those of Walter Greaves, the Chelsea boatboy (see Chapter 33) and Whistler, whose *Nocturne in Blue and Silver* has made the ricketty old bridge the subject of one of the best-known pictures in English art. Faulkner commented that people liked to 'resort to the bridge for the benefit of the air, and the pleasure of viewing the scenery from it'.

39
The Embankment and three bridges

Building of the embankment and
Albert Bridge in 1873

But others were less inspired. George Bryan, writing in 1869, called it 'a most unsightly structure'. The number of deaths and barge collisions it caused were 'really painful to contemplate', he said. 'It is a sad contrast, in every respect, to the elegant structures that now span the river.'

One of the 'elegant structures' in Bryan's mind was probably the new Chelsea Bridge, known at first as Ranelagh or Victoria Bridge, which was opened by Queen Victoria in 1858 to give access to Clapham and the newly opened Battersea Park. Constructed of cast iron, with ornamental towers and octagonal lodges, this suspension bridge gained the approbation of *The Illustrated London News* (10 April 1858) which enthused:

'Looked at from the gardens of Chelsea Hospital, or, better still, from a distant boat on the middle of the river, the new bridge appears like a fairy structure, with its beautiful towers, gilded and painted to resemble light-coloured bronze, and crowned with large globular lamps, diffusing sunny light all around.'

The public would have been equally enthusiastic had it not been for the toll exacted from them on crossing the bridge. As it was, there were immediate protests and a demonstration, but it was not until 1879, when Chelsea's three bridges – Albert, Chelsea and Battersea – as well as those at Lambeth and Vauxhall, were acquired by the Metropolitan Board of Works, that they became public highways and free of toll. The occasion was celebrated by the Prince and Princess of Wales who crossed each of the bridges, the Prince declaring the measure an 'incalculable boon to all classes of the inhabitants'.

By the time Chelsea Bridge was opened, and a new road made to it from Sloane Square, the embankment of the north side of the Thames from Westminster had reached the Royal Hospital, where the road ended in a carriage sweep outside the south gates (still to be seen today). The embankment of Chelsea Reach itself, as far as Battersea Bridge, was begun in 1871 by the Metropolitan Board of Works under its chief engineer, Joseph Bazalgette (later Sir Joseph), as an extension to his scheme for the drainage of the metropolis.

At Chelsea, land was reclaimed so that a new sewer could be laid to relieve western London, rather than allow the sewers to empty into the river at Cremorne. At the same time a road was built above it, and a new suspension bridge thrown across to Battersea at the bottom of Oakley Street (said to be the first London street to be planted with trees – in 1851).

Albert Bridge, as the bridge was named, was opened in 1873 to provide better access to London from Battersea for the growing amount of traffic with which the old wooden Battersea Bridge could not easily cope. Proposals for a bridge at this point, where the Cadogan Pier had stood for many years, were voiced several years earlier, but held up while the course of the embankment was decided. The bridge later needed costly remedial work, when the first weight limits were imposed, but fortunately it has survived to decorate the Thames with its icing-sugar wrought ironwork, its little toll kiosks and gaily lit suspension chains. Notices still remind troops crossing over to break step.

Chelsea Embankment was completed in 1874 and opened by the Duke and Duchess of Edinburgh. The river had been reduced to a uniform width of about 700 ft, instead of its old 700–850 ft; gardens had been planted on the reclaimed area in front of Cheyne Walk and a junction was made with the south-western end of the Queen's Road (now Royal Hospital Road). The official pamphlet issued on the occasion by the Metropolitan Board of Works pointed out that, although the chief purpose of the embankment in London had been to find a site for the low-level sewer, it had also removed the stinking mud-banks which had formerly been 'forced upon the attention of more than one of the senses' on warm sunny days, and replaced them with 'pleasant drives and ornamental gardens'.

The original Chelsea Bridge, opened in 1858

Albert Bridge (circa 1880)

When the extension of Chelsea Embankment from Battersea Bridge to Lots Road was proposed in the 1890s, similar ornamental gardens were envisaged in front of the part of Cheyne Walk that faced the river there. *The Westminster Gazette* of 20 July 1896 spoke of the 'unsanitary condition of this portion of the shore; the little bay is at low tide a malodorous stretch of mud' but the residents of Cheyne Walk protested, submitting to the House of Commons a petition which claimed that such a scheme would 'for ever destroy one of the most characteristic and picturesque portions of the foreshore'.

The extension was never built, though it was proposed again in 1951. Instead, the road was widened slightly, and later, in 1954, a new concrete wall replaced the old. The bay and the moored barges remained; but modern residents must sometimes wonder today if the decision in favour of the picturesque was wise. Traffic on the embankment in 1932 was already bad enough for the Chelsea Society to be seriously concerned about both noise and speed; one wonders whether they would not have been more enthusiastic about a screen of gardens between the road and the houses had they been able to foresee the thundering onslaught of today's embankment traffic.

The major changes to Chelsea's riverside had been completed by 1874; but the bridges themselves were not immune from change. In 1883 old Battersea Bridge was declared unsafe for traffic. It had been bought by the Albert Bridge Company in 1873 under an arrangement made when its profitability was threatened by the building of the latter. When both bridges later came under the control of the Metropolitan Board of Works, it was dismantled and replaced by the present iron bridge, and opened, complete with two tracks of tramlines, in 1890. The decorative Chelsea suspension bridge was demolished in 1935, despite loud protests, and replaced by the present steel and granite structure. All three of Chelsea's bridges, however, contribute greatly to the scenery of the river with their gay colours and bright lights.

Tite Street in 1886, a sketch by Pennell

Chelsea's reputation as the home of artists was well established by the second half of the nineteenth century. Its original attraction for them had been that it was old-fashioned and therefore inexpensive; but inevitably, once it had acquired such repute, its status began to change. It became fashionable, and consequently attractive to a much more affluent type of resident. So when the architectural revolution of the 1870s occurred, many of the new houses that seemed so appropriate in such a setting, were affordable only for the wealthy.

The change that took place in domestic architecture in the 1870s had a major effect on London. It brought the building of great Italianate stuccoed terraces to a halt, and introduced red brick into the streets (see also Chapter 18). The change was gradual and led to only a partial alteration in central London's appearance, since most of the area was already built up, but it was particularly evident in Chelsea.

The houses of the architect Philip Webb were forerunners of this movement. Two of them were built in Kensington – Val Prinsep's studio house in Holland Park (see Chapter 17) and the house on Palace Green for the future Earl of Carlisle (see Chapter 8) – and a third was built in Glebe Place, Chelsea. This was the home of George Pryce Boyce, designed in 1868 and already showing the influence of seventeenth and eighteenth century vernacular traditions which were later to give the brick architecture of the period its name, 'Queen Anne'.

Webb's houses were sometimes received with great mistrust; but the speed with which the new domestic style was accepted can be seen in the redevelopment of much of Hans Town in the 1870s, an area first built up less than a hundred years earlier (see Chapter 36). The Cadogan estate's pioneering response to architects' complaints about standard London streetscapes cleared away much of Henry Holland's earlier buildings and created a rare enclave, with houses designed by influential architects such as Richard Norman Shaw,

40
Chelsea's 'domestic revival'

*Houses on Chelsea Embankment
by E W Godwin, 1878*

George Devey, Ernest George and others. The area was favourably judged and immediately populated by the upper class, though the riot of detail in such confined spaces as Cadogan Square might be thought less than totally successful.

'Queen Anne' has been described by its historian, Mark Girouard, as 'a kind of architectural cocktail, with a little genuine Queen Anne in it, a little Dutch, a little Flemish, a squeeze of Robert Adam, a generous dash of Wren, and a touch of François Ier'. All these influences were abundantly evident in the transformed Hans Town as attempts were made to give each house a distinct character in contrast to the anonymity of earlier terraces. Osbert Lancaster nicknamed the result 'Pont Street Dutch'.

The attractive compositions of steeply pitched roofs, oriel windows, carved brickwork and shaped gables that are characteristic of Queen Anne are sometimes missed in the confined quarters of London's streets; but the building of Chelsea Embankment in 1874 gave architects a superb opportunity: a riverside, tree-lined setting adjacent to the old houses of Cheyne Walk. Sadly the charms of these houses and the opportunity to contemplate them have been diminished by the traffic that now pounds along the road. But Shaw's Swan House, standing on the site of the second Swan Inn, remains a fine example of his work with its elegant façade and oriel windows, despite its present function as a neon-lit office.

Behind the embankment, the Metropolitan Board of Works had extended Tite Street southwards and made it available for building, and it was here that

Chelsea's 'artistic' character was concentrated in the 1870s and 1880s'. It was more outrageous (and less affluent) than the establishment world of Melbury Road in Kensington – chiefly as a result of the presence of Whistler – and rather grand for Chelsea, most of whose artists worked in more modest studios dotted around the village.

The architect most associated with Tite Street was E W Godwin, a practitioner of 'Queen Anne' who, however, moved swiftly on to startlingly avant-garde designs (particularly with furniture and wallpapers) – or would have done if the Board of Works had let him. As it was, the board was affronted. Godwin's spare, pale brick and green slate design for Whistler's house, which became known as The White House, began to take shape in early 1878 on land leased from the board, but without its clearance, and when the

A J Adams's design for houses in Cadogan Square, published in 1880

board's members saw his drawings they refused to let building continue until modifications were made. The same thing happened when Godwin designed another house across the street for Frank Miles, a wealthy young artist who planned to live there with his friend, Oscar Wilde (see also Chapter 34).

This design would have done away altogether with the favoured Queen Anne skyline of shaped gables, substituting a solid rectangular studio window. The board thought this idea worse than The White House, and so both buildings, like Webb's at Palace Green a few years earlier, were given more conventional stone dressings, sculpted panels, and, in the case of Miles's property, a shaped gable and door pediment. Whistler's house was demolished in the 1960s, but Miles's survives relatively little changed, though with a few inappropriate window frames.

At the other end of the original stretch of Cheyne Walk are two other houses that are remnants of the elevated architectural theories of the late nineteenth century. They were designed by the Arts and Crafts architect C R Ashbee, in 1894, and stand just to the west of Oakley Street, numbered 38 and 39 Cheyne Walk. Ashbee had started a crafts school and workshop in the East End in the 1880s, and went on to found the Guild of Handicraft, which he took to the Cotswolds in 1902 (to Chipping Campden, where Baptist Hicks had built his country house in the seventeenth century and from which he took his title – see Chapter 1). Before he left London, Ashbee designed several houses in Chelsea, including No 37 Cheyne Walk for his mother, on the site of the Old Magpie & Stump tavern. This, a tall brick house with three stories of stone-dressed oriels, was demolished in the 1970s, together with the highly popular Blue Cockatoo restaurant and the Pier Hotel, to make way for the present mundane block of flats above a car showroom. Next-door he built the two that survive, with tall narrow windows, steeply pitched roofs and a great white gable – two pleasingly appropriate descendants of gentle, well-mannered old Cheyne Walk.

Nos 38 and 39 Cheyne Walk designed by C R Ashbee

Opposite page: Swan House on the embankment, designed by Richard Norman Shaw

The glaciarium in King's Road

Ellenor, in 1901, made some revealing comments on his childhood in Chelsea in the early nineteenth century. He described various antics on the river (see Chapter 38) which sound captivating for a small boy; but distinguished between such occasions and 'entertainment'. The latter, he stated, 'was very poor'. But he was writing at a time when expectations had changed greatly among the working class: having begun life with little but his surroundings and local people to rely on for amusement, he had lived to see Cremorne open and close, and the creation of vast palaces of entertainment such as Earl's Court and the White City.

Chelsea's inhabitants lived in a crowded, working village; apart from the events of the river, entertainment came, if at all, in small doses from outside the parish. For example, one occasion Ellenor recalled was the visit of a 'professor of mesmerism and clairvoyance' to a skittle ground behind a public house. 'He was a thin, shabby old man, dressed in black with very dirty linen. With him were his wife, and two girls – his daughters, he informed us – one about twelve and the other about fourteen, with ringlets, shabbily dressed and closely covered up in old cloaks.'

The man would perform some conjuring and card tricks before putting one of the girls into a 'trance', balancing her across the backs of two chairs, and standing her sister on top of her. 'At the end, as an extra, a pale, sickly youth was introduced, and sang "Wapping Old Stairs", and "Sally in our Alley", the young lady playing the accompaniment, much to the satisfaction of the company.'

By the 1870s entertainment had become more sophisticated. Ice-rinks appear to have been popular in the parish, and the press devoted considerable space to a description of the methods by which Mr John Gamgee produced 'artificial cold at a low cost' at his 'Glaciarium' or 'real ice skating rink' behind the Old Clock House in the King's Road. The ice was two inches thick, covering an area twenty-four feet by sixteen, and was opened in 1876 in a canvas-

41
Entertainment

covered building. It was depicted complete with ladies in bustles and gentlemen with folded arms, gliding around in a genteel fashion.

There is another skating-rink mentioned in a contemporary account of Chelsea in *Old and New London* (1879) as being in Royal Avenue; but the grandest was at Prince's Club, between Cadogan Square and Walton Street, where Lennox Gardens now stands. The club covered a large area, boasting a cricket pitch and tennis courts, adjacent to Henry Holland's Pavilion and opened in 1870. A skating-rink was added to its facilities, on which the authors of that same account of Chelsea, Walter Thornbury and Edward Walford, had decided views:

'Prince's was always rather select and exclusive, but of late its exclusiveness has been increased, the price of admission being raised, and all sorts of stringent regulations being introduced by the committee, in order to keep it "select". So "select" indeed has it become, that a cricketing husband, though an old subscriber, may not take his wife into its precincts, nor can a skating wife introduce her husband, or even her daughter. Nay, further, an edict has gone forth from the despots of "Prince's" – "that no lady is to be admitted at all unless she has been presented at Court". Of course, therefore, the members are "very select"; no "nobodies" are there; "Lady Clara Vere de Vere" has the skating rink all to herself, or shares it only with other "daughters of a hundred earls". How delightful! Yes, delightful for Lady Clara and her friend, but not so for the outside public.'

George and James Prince established their cricket ground on land that had been nurseries, and within two years had the satisfaction of seeing it described in Wisden as 'one of the truest playing grounds in England'. In the same year, Middlesex County Cricket Club moved here from Fulham, but left again in 1876 to establish itself in its present situation at Lords. Prince's Club's reputation for good cricket was short-lived: by 1879 Thornbury and Walford claimed that it had 'long been a cricket ground of second-rate importance', though this apparent exaggeration – the place had been open in all only nine years – may be explained by the writers' disapproval of the club's exclusivity.

Any attempt to improve matters was cut short by the expiry of its lease in 1885, though the laying out of Lennox Gardens appears to have been begun even earlier: a map of 1879 shows the southern half of it already in place, and by 1887 it was complete, together with Clabon Mews behind Cadogan Square, and the Prince's Club had closed. It reopened later under the same name, however, in Knightsbridge, and revived its skating-rink in a building in Trevor Place for a time.

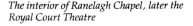

The interior of Ranelagh Chapel, later the Royal Court Theatre

The interior of the Royal Court in Sloane Square

The Royal Court Theatre was opened in 1870 in the old Ranelagh Chapel – built in 1818 on the west side of Lower George Street, now Sloane Gardens – 'for the performance of comedies, farces, and the lighter order of dramas', and was known initially as 'The New Chelsea Theatre', but almost immediately closed. After an elaborate face-lift it reopened as the Royal Court and enjoyed great success. But its life was cut short in 1887, when it was demolished to clear the way for Sloane Gardens.

The new Royal Court was built next door to Sloane Square station and opened in 1888. Initially a poor successor to the old theatre, it blossomed suddenly and memorably under the management of Barker and Vedrenne with six matinees of Shaw's *Candida* in 1904 and went on, during the next three years, to present 988 performances of thirty-two plays, 701 of which were of eleven plays by Shaw.

The critic Desmond MacCarthy wrote in 1907 that, in contrast to 'the stock London play', with 'its hackneyed situations, its vapid sentiments ... its reach-me-down solutions and superficial problems', the Vedrenne–Barker formula was a revelation. Its attractions over what had gone before may seem obvious now, but in 1904 it was a novelty to find a management aiming, as MacCarthy put it, at 'truth as opposed to effect ... the whole play had to be tugged at and tested in rehearsal until the coherence of its idea and the soundness of its sentiment were perfectly established'.

The trail-blazing character of the Royal Court was thus established by Vedrenne and Barker. And though the theatre became a cinema in the 1930s, was bombed during the war and put on musicals in the early 1950s, this character reasserted itself in 1956 when the English Stage Company bought the lease and began to support the new generation of playwrights. One of the earliest productions in their opening year was the now historic first performance of John Osborne's *Look Back in Anger*, with Kenneth Haigh as Jimmy Porter, Alan Bates as Cliff and Mary Ure as Alison.

The theatre was turned into a private club in 1965 so that the contentious Osborne play, *A Patriot for Me* could be shown, and there were many battles with the Lord Chamberlain over censorship. Nowadays the need for such measures against censorship has evaporated but the Royal Court has retained its reputation as a focus for challenge and change in the theatre. Paradoxically, however, one of its latest controversies has involved *not* staging the play *Perdition* by Jim Allen, because of its contentious theme of Hungarian Zionists' collaboration with the Nazis.

Skating at Prince's in 1914, after the rink had reopened in Trevor Place

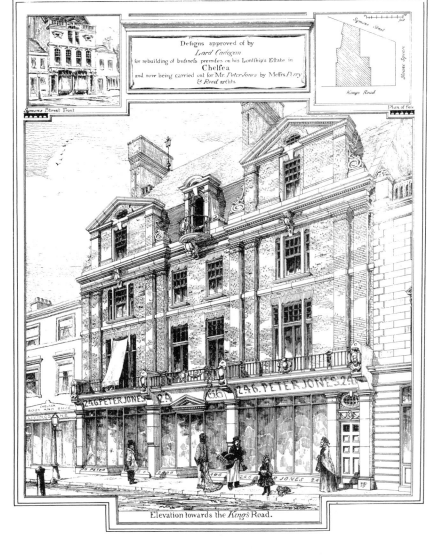

42
Peter Jones sets the shopping scene

Peter Jones

On 1 September 1905, *The West Middlesex Advertiser* made a solemn announcement: 'It is our painful duty to record the death of Mr Peter Jones, the founder of the great drapery establishment at Sloane-square, which occurred at six o'clock on Wednesday morning at the home of his daughter and son-in-law in Rydal-road, Streatham. The deceased gentleman, who was sixty-two years of age, passed away peacefully in his sleep – a quiet ending to one of the most strenuous and remarkable careers which the metropolis presents.'

The 'great drapery establishment' had grown from a modest store occupying two buildings to one which spread into another twenty-six before being rebuilt in the 1880s. By the time of its founder's death it could be described as 'silk mercers, costumiers, and complete house furnishers'; and in 1936 it was transformed into the sleek, curving form and all-embracing 'department store' that we know today. Throughout this metamorphosis it never lost sight of its local role as an extended corner shop, a role which present residents of the area would confirm it continues to play.

Peter Jones was the son of a hat maker in Monmouthshire and came to London from Newcastle Emlyn in the 1860s. After working for drapers in Newington and Leicester Square, he established his own business in Marlborough Road, now Draycott Avenue, and was soon enthusiastically knocking the premises about to provide more space. Unfortunately his efforts did not take into account the principles of construction and the weakened party wall between his two buildings collapsed, temporarily burying Mrs Jones in the rubble and killing an apprentice boy.

The event evidently did not constitute much of a setback, for five years later he had moved to King's Road. At that time, as *The West Middlesex Advertiser* recorded in his obituary, 'the complexion of the neighbourhood was very different to what it is to-day ... Lower Sloane-street and other streets in the neighbourhood, now adorned with high-class houses and flats, were then streets of working class dwellings, occupied by respectable artizans'.

Jones was shrewd in the running of his business, catering efficiently for the needs of these clients and adjusting his stock to suit a different type of customer as the area became popular with the middle classes (his own home was in Redcliffe Square). By the early 1900s he was selling everything from linoleum to tea-gowns, employing more than 300 people and turning over £157,000 a year.

His new building enabled him to display the goods in grand fashion. Constructed during the 1880s, ponderous in red brick and red Mansfield stone under a green slate roof, it prompted an equally turgid appreciation in *Illustrated London* (1893): 'The famous emporium conducted by Mr Peter Jones in Sloane Square possesses a paramount claim to prominent mention in any review of the great mercantile houses of western and south-western London ... the establishment now forms one huge block, of harmonious design and handsome appearance. . . .'

Inside, the new store was luxuriously fitted out in a style which would probably gain fashionable approval today, now that such places hardly exist. A review in *The Builder* of 19 January 1889 described it: 'The costume department, which is two storeys high, surrounded by galleries, has been very elaborately fitted with walnut and ebony cases, decorated with carvings of natural foliage. The premises were among the first of their character to be lighted by electricity, when Messrs Crompton supplied the installation, worked off two 16 hp gas-engines; but the whole of the shops are now lighted by incandescent lamps, supplied from a local centre.'

Photographs taken at the turn of the century show the cluttered departments, decorated with potted palms, which were lined with wooden shelves and polished counters. Ranged along the counters were chairs for the customers while assistants took from the shelves cretonnes, dimities, serges, frillings, collars and cuffs. Heavy jardinières and parasols decorated the tops of cabinets and jugs, basins, plates and teacups filled the china department.

Nos 4 and 6 King's Road, taken over by Peter Jones in 1877 when he moved from Marlborough Road

Sloane Square in the early 1900s: at that time, Peter Jones (with awnings) was still separated from the Square by the Star and Garter public house

The King's Road frontage in 1893

The 'oriental fancy' department at the turn of the century

Above the departments were quarters for the staff, where many of them lived. These, said Peter Jones's obituary, were 'replete with every appointment conducive to social enjoyment' and included a library, a piano and two billiard tables.

Such was the Peter Jones store when John Lewis bought it in 1906. Tradition has it that Lewis walked from his own shop in Oxford Street to Sloane Square with twenty £1000 notes in his pocket for the purpose. His association with the place was not, at first, a happy one – turnover dropped £20,000 almost immediately and by 1909 was below £95,000 – and in 1914 he handed over control to his son Spedan, who was keen to introduce ideas on partnership conceived while he was recovering from a riding accident a few years earlier.

In 1915 the store made a net loss and was grateful for the profit generated by the public house which stood between it and Sloane Square, and which it now owned. Spedan Lewis told his shareholders: 'I regret we are thriving exceedingly by being publicans.' But his policies at Peter Jones weathered the Depression and when his father died in 1928, the partnership scheme – profit-sharing for all the staff – was extended to the John Lewis store.

The greatest change of all came to Peter Jones when Lewis decided on the construction of a totally new building. The store had kept abreast of changing fashions as far as content was concerned – for example it had opened a painted furniture department, where the great interior decorator, John Fowler, worked in the early 1930s – but its Victorian buildings were hopelessly outdated by the standards of the modern movement. Over a period of four years, 1932–6, the old building came down and there arose – out of extraordinary confusion since the store was kept open all this time – a new one, more like an ocean liner than a department store, swathed in the glass and steel of its avant-garde curtain wall.

Such a transformation might be expected to have aroused nostalgia for the cluttered comfort of the old Peter Jones, but, on the contrary, there was great enthusiasm. In a review of the capital's new shops, which included Simpsons in Piccadilly and D H Evans, *Vogue* announced: 'The curved line of Peter Jones' new glass façade against the mottled sky proves that there is romance – the realisation of something that somebody visualised in a moment of inspiration.'

The architectural press, though less lyrical, was equally pleased. 'This new store', proclaimed *The Architect and Building News* in June 1936, '. . . is a notable object lesson in the advantages of a rational approach to civic design. Of all the London squares, Sloane Square is perhaps the most stupidly and unskilfully overdressed, and, by contrast with the drab façades of 'Renaissance' brick and terra-cotta which surround it, the new building proclaims itself a paragon of lucidity and taste.'

The building was designed by the architects Slater and Moberley, with the associated architect William Crabtree and the consulting architect C H Reilly, so that the supporting structure was invisible behind walls seemingly made of nothing but glass and slender bronze mullions. The display windows of the ground floor ran without interruption round two sides of the store beneath a broad canopy and, inside, open floors and large light wells gave a feeling of space far removed from the dingy departments which the Victorians had known and approved.

In a poll taken in 1939 by *The Architects' Journal* to discover which was the most popular modern building among a number of representative laymen, Peter Jones triumphed, coming top of the list. The journal, slightly puzzled at such success – though pleasantly surprised that the new architecture was proving popular at all – decided that the store 'seems to have some quality that inspires confidence'.

Customers certainly found it full of new ideas. There was a secretarial agency, a dry-cleaning department, and a 'livestock' section selling creatures as diverse as squirrels, fish and pink flamingoes. After the Second World War, kennels were established in the basement so that customers could deposit their pets before shopping, and in the 1950s the 'pram park' kept an eye on as many as a hundred babies a day. Until 1945 an 'artists' market' flourished, until Spedan Lewis found it selling contemporary art including drawings by Mervyn Peake and Jacob Epstein, which he branded as 'thoroughly bad stock . . . smelly mud'.

Fortunately, the reconstruction programme spared the building on the north-west corner of the block that Peter Jones monopolised. This, No 25 Cadogan Gardens, was designed by A H Mackmurdo in 1893 for the Australian artist Mortimer Mempes and has six fine double-height windows, three of them oriels, in the Anglo-Dutch style. It was bought by the store in 1939 and although the façade is still in existence, the interior has been remodelled for use as management offices. Next to it in Symons Street, at the back entrance to the store, are the last remaining walls of Mr Jones's emporium of 1889.

'A paragon of lucidity and taste': the 1936 building

Visitors to the RHS show in
the Temple gardens, 1901

43
The
Flower
Show

To visitors unaware of Chelsea's past, there may seem no better reason for the location of the great Flower Show than tradition – it has after all been held in the grounds of the Royal Hospital since 1913. But Chelsea is also a highly appropriate site for a horticultural celebration, for its gardens have had a prominent place in its history for 400 years. Dr John King wrote in the early 1700s that Sir Thomas More built a house in Chelsea 'with gardens, orchards, and all conveniences about it', and Danvers House nearby possessed a renowned seventeenth-century Italian garden. Later, in 1829, Thomas Faulkner stated that there were several 'nursery gardens' in the vicinity of the King's Road 'much frequented by the Nobility and Gentry in the spring of the year'.

These nurseries, wrote Faulkner, 'besides furnishing the choicest variety of early raised flowers, have, each succeeding season, something new to present to the Botanical world'. There was Mr Colvill at Blacklands, with a large conservatory and hothouses fronting the King's Road; a botanical garden between Cadogan Place and Sloane Street first laid out in 1807; Mr Knight's large nursery near Stanley House; and a minor 'physic garden' at the Clock House near World's End on part of Sir Thomas More's old garden, where there were vines, fig trees and pomegranates, and where the owners sold distilled waters of 'medicinal value'; not to mention the Apothecaries' Garden itself.

At the time that Faulkner was writing, the Royal Horticultural Society had already started to take shape. In 1801 John Wedgwood, son of Josiah, wrote to George III's gardener at Kensington, William Forsyth, proposing 'the formation of a Horticultural Society', and asking Forsyth, if he saw Sir Joseph Banks, 'to ask him his opinion of the plan'. Banks was President of the Royal Society and Royal Adviser to the gardens at Kew; he approved the idea, and a 'Society for the Improvement of Horticulture' was founded in 1804 by the three men and four others, meeting at Hatchard's Bookshop in Piccadilly.

The society's interest at first centred on the reading of papers on the cultivation of fruit and vegetables, but in 1822 it leased thirty-three acres at Chiswick in order to establish a garden, which was later opened to the public. General interest proved so great that the society (which became the Royal Horticultural Society in the 1860s) went on to create gardens at Kensington (see Chapter 12) and at the Inner Temple, where an annual show was held between 1888 and 1911. But by 1911 relations with the Inner Temple were deteriorating and a proposal from the RHS for an international horticultural exhibition focussed attention on the need for a larger site. The company formed to organise this exhibition settled on the grounds of the Royal Hospital in Chelsea.

Now that Chelsea finds itself in the heart of London it comes as a surprise to hear that there were worries about its distance from the centre, compared with the convenience of the Temple. However, the station at Sloane Square was a point in Chelsea's favour; there were two good entrances to the Royal Hospital grounds, one in Queen's Road (now Royal Hospital Road) and one on the embankment; and there was more space than the Temple had provided. This was just as well, since applications for exhibition space increased during preparations and the show eventually covered twenty-eight acres. The main marquee was the largest ever erected at the time, covering over three acres, and there were other tents for exhibits from overseas. Electricity was installed throughout the grounds and Leopold de Rothschild sent his plants from Gunnersbury in twenty vans.

Visitors thronged down the Queen's Road and in trams across Battersea Bridge, and King George V and Queen Mary paid a visit, as did the ill-fated Archduke Franz Ferdinand of Austria and his wife. Their assassinations, at Sarajevo two years later, were to precipitate the havoc of the First World War which put an end to the great private establishments of England whose owners and head gardeners had been so amply represented that first year at Chelsea.

A total of 178,389 visitors came to the show between 22 and 30 May 1912, and the RHS determined that its May show should be held there in future. This was a splendid site for the exhibition of floral displays, topiary, exotic orchids in a specially heated marquee and the particularly popular rockeries along the embankment railings. It was highly appropriate that these should enjoy such prominence, since it is Forsyth who is said to have been the first to create a rock garden, in 1774, when he was in charge of the Physic Garden.

Associated trades were also keen supporters: there was a variety of displays of advanced methods for heating greenhouses, and a firm from Streatham exhibited leather 'horse boots' which prevented hoof prints marking lawns during mowing or rolling.

The outbreak of war in August 1914 did not close the annual show, except in 1917. Contemporary reports stressed that it was certainly not held in a festive atmosphere, but that it could make a valuable contribution to the difficult times, not only by supporting a stricken industry, but by fostering the urgently necessary increase in the cultivation of fruit and vegetables – echoing the early interests of the RHS. Early in the war the society had distributed leaflets for this purpose, and during the years that followed it sent seeds to the army in France and collected money for more to be sent later to restock the battered fields and gardens of the Low Countries. A Shetland pony was used to publicise this fund at the show in 1916.

The atmosphere during the First World War is evident in a report of the show in *The Gentlewoman* of 15 May 1915:

'Chelsea Flower Show is not a gala; there is no merrymaking or essence of the carnival, all of which in these times would be most offensive to the English mind, plunged as it is in so much sadness. It is purely a year's record of horticultural enterprise ... Even our soldiers, wounded or otherwise, where they have been obliged to stay long in some place, have written home for

King George VI and Queen Elizabeth visiting the Chelsea Flower Show when it reopened after the war

plants and seeds . . . We all turn to our gardens for a little peace and comfort in these troublous times; and I venture to predict that, after this War, there will be a no more popular pursuit than gardening, for many a year to come.'

The years following the war saw a democratising influence at the show, though it has never lost its place in the social calendar; but in 1939 it was closed for eight years. When it opened again in May 1947 there were gardens for pre-fabs, and ideas for those in bombed areas on how to 'make the rubble blossom'. The show recovered with the rest of the country, and during 1951, the year of the Festival of Britain, there was another record-breaking marquee to cope with the extra visitors.

Chelsea's flower show today remains highly popular: 215,000 people visited it in 1986. Debates about removing it to a larger site in London have been held over many years and become more urgent as the society's lease on the present site runs out in 1990; but there remains a strong body of opinion which holds that, were it not in Chelsea, it would no longer be the same show; and so it remains. Other aspects of this annual event are unchanging too. The fashion for fussy rock gardens may have waned but early photographs reveal a familiar scene: huge crowds, umbrellas, muddy grass – and sometimes a little sunshine.

In 1901 Chelsea had a population of 95,000. Today the number is more than 40,000. The difference is less dramatic than it appears however, since the borough of Chelsea, until its reorganisation in 1899 under the London Government Act, included a 'detached' area immediately to the north of the borough of Kensington, which had somehow become part of the manor back in the middle ages.

Cheyne Walk

Until the 1870s this 'outland' remained largely undeveloped apart from the hamlet of Kensal, but in that decade the Artisans', Labourers' and General Dwellings Company built a grid of streets known as Queen's Park, neatly laid out as terraces of vaguely Gothic cottages. Unlike its near neighbour, Kensal New Town, (see Chapter 21) it was highly respectable. Booth wrote that the occupants were 'of the regularly employed class: railway men or police, artisans, small clerks, and others. The competition for these popular little houses is great.' In 1901 the estate became part of the borough of Paddington.

Old Chelsea was changing too. Crosby Hall, a late-medieval banqueting hall that had stood in Bishopsgate, was rescued from demolition and moved to the corner of Danvers Street and Cheyne Walk, to become a hostel for female graduates. Dr Phene's fantastical house on the corner of Oakley Street and Upper Cheyne Row was demolished in about 1920; and the late seventeenth-

Crosby Hall, moved to the embankment in 1909–10

century houses of Paradise Row came down, to be replaced by blocks of flats. Between 1910 and 1930 the area known as Chelsea Park was flattened and redeveloped. This included The Vale, where there had previously been only about four houses, and Camera Square, an area of small terraced houses that had a reputation as a den of vice. The houses that went up in their place are an attractive, Queen Anne influenced garden suburb of a type, with ornamental niches and plaques, decorative paving, gables, the occasional Venetian window, some studios and communal gardens.

Such developments obviously raised the tone of places that had been the home of Chelsea's indigenous population, though other old, overcrowded corners remained. Booth wrote of the area just to the west of the expensive new houses of Hans Town that it was 'a group of mean streets reminding one of parts of Mile End or Bethnal Green'. But some new provision was also made for the poor in the building of those familiar, austere blocks that the Victorians and Edwardians thought would deal with the problems of urban poverty: the Samuel Lewis Trust Dwellings and the Sutton Dwellings went up in the area between Cale Street and Fulham Road in the early years of this century. Much later, in the 1970s, old World's End was swept away by the council and replaced by their own answer to the perennial problem of housing – the huge russet brick towers that dominate the western end of the borough.

The popular image of Chelsea is perhaps of a rather pretty London 'village' full of brightly painted artisans' cottages, artists' studios and houseboats; but in fact much of Chelsea has been redeveloped, which is no doubt why those cottages that remain are so very desirable – and so very unlike they were when occupied by their original tenants (Paradise Walk, for example, was originally known as Bull Walk and was one of the few places in Chelsea marked on Booth's map of 1902 as being of the very lowest class.)

Pupils of Hill House School, Hans Place

In the 1930s fourteen acres around Draycott Avenue and Sloane Avenue were razed and rebuilt; the row of houses known as Lombard Terrace next to the Old Church finally disappeared; the last vestiges of Shrewsbury House were lost; Whitelands House at the northern end of Cheltenham Terrace, which for a spell was used as the headquarters of the British Union of Fascists, was pulled down and replaced by a block of flats; and Trafalgar Square was rebuilt as Chelsea Square, losing Catharine Lodge, a house dating from about 1800, and gaining in its place two white classical houses by Oliver Hill. The Chelsea Society was founded by the local historian, Reginald Blunt, in 1927, just in time to see all this happen, and has been an important agitator for sensitive development and conservation in the borough.

There have been escapes from redevelopment too. An extraordinary proposal by the Cadogan estate for two tower blocks, each thirty-three-storeys high, in the Tedworth Square area was mercifully rebuffed in 1968 by the Minister of Housing and Local Government following a public inquiry. Plans for an inner ring road which would run along the embankment until a bridge was built across the river near Lots Road were eventually shelved, though the rather sensible idea of turning the Extension Railway track into a by-pass that would alleviate the Shepherds Bush/Earl's Court one-way system was also dropped in the process. That would seem unlikely to happen now that Chelsea Harbour, an up-market group of apartment blocks round what used to be the old railway dock, is being built, just beyond the Chelsea boundary.

Chelsea has a great sense of its own intriguing history and its identity as an old village. Its artistic traditions have helped preserve this, though that in itself is an invitation to the wealthy to colonise it and dilute the old variety of the place. The emphasis changed in the 1960s when, because of its bohemian reputation, it became the focus for a trendy young generation, and King's Road, which had never before been the centre of the village, turned into a cross between a street market and a fashion parade.

But the real challenge to Chelsea's individuality came when it was amalgamated with the Royal Borough of Kensington in 1964. There was a good deal of anger and unhappiness at the thought of being only a part of a larger administrative district, even though the only other part would be its next-door neighbour, with which it is closely linked at certain points in its history. Chelsea's affairs are no longer run from the attractive old town hall in King's Road (though that building has been made into a fine library), and so in that respect it has lost some of its identity; but Chelsea as a place with character of its own seems alive and well. Its residents come and go, and many of them are considerably better off than those of the old days; but it takes only a very short while for them to be enchanted by the spell of the place and as anxious as the rest to prolong the magic.

Bibliography

An Historical and Topographical Description of Chelsea – Thomas Faulkner 1829
Chelsea in the Olden and Present Times – George Bryan 1869
Old and New London – Walter Thornbury and Edward Walford 1879
The Antiquities of Middlesex – John Bowack 1705
Survey of London, Volumes II (1909), IV (1913), VII (1921), XI (1927), XXXVII (1973), XXXVIII, XLI and XLII (1986)
The Village of Palaces – A G L'Estrange 1880
By Chelsea Reach – Reginald Blunt 1921
The Wonderful Village – R Blunt 1918
The Lure of Old Chelsea – R Blunt 1922
Illustrated Historical Handbook to Chelsea – R Blunt 1900
In Cheyne Walk and Thereabout – R Blunt 1914
Red Anchor Pieces – Reginald Blunt 1928
Paradise Row – Reginald Blunt 1906
Old Chelsea – Benjamin Ellis Martin 1889
Rambling Recollections of Chelsea – by an Old Inhabitant (Thomas Bell Ellenor) 1901
Memorials of Old Chelsea – Alfred Beaver 1892
Kensington and Chelsea – William Gaunt 1975
Georgian London – Sir John Summerson (revised ed) 1978
Arts and Crafts Architecture – Peter Davey 1980
Lives of Eminent Men – John Aubrey (lived 1626–97) pub 1931
The Environs of London – Daniel Lysons, 1795
A Tour through the whole Island of Great Britain – Daniel Defoe 1724–7
Diary – Samuel Pepys (lived 1633–1703) first pub in entirety 1893–6
Diary – John Evelyn (lived 1620–1706) pub 1955
St Thomas More – Christopher Hollis 1961
Thomas More – R W Chambers 1935 reprinted 1957
Sir Thomas More – Angela Cox/Pitkin Pictorials 1977
In the Shadow of a Saint: Lady Alice More – Ruth Norrington 1983
The Romance of the Apothecaries' Garden at Chelsea – F Dawtrey Drewitt 1922
Memoirs of the Botanic Garden at Chelsea – Henry Field, revised by R H Semple 1878
The Chelsea Physic Garden – Trustees of the Chelsea Physic Garden
Chelsea Old Church – Randall Davies 1904
A Guide to London's Churches – Mervyn Batch 1978
Parish Churches of London – Basil F L Clarke 1966
Old London Gardens – Gladys Taylor 1977
The Royal Hospital Chelsea – Captain C G T Dean 1950
An Historical and Descriptive Account of the Royal Hospital – Thomas Faulkner 1805
Guide Book – The Royal Hospital
Chelsea Porcelain Factory: Papers – Chelsea Local History Library
The Water Supply of London – Metropolitan Water Board 1961
Man and Water – Norman Smith 1976
The London Water Supply – Richard Sisley 1899
Arnold Bennett's Letters to his Nephew – ed Richard Bennett 1936
Walter Greaves and the Goupil Gallery – Michael Parkin Fine Art Ltd, 1984
Dante Gabriel Rossetti – Brian and Judy Dobbs 1977
Henry James at Home – H Montgomery Hyde 1969
The World of James McNeill Whistler – Horace Gregory 1959
Chelsea Reach – Tom Pocock 1970
William de Morgan and his Wife – A M W Stirling 1922
Oscar Wilde – Vyvian Holland 1960
I too am Here, Selections from the Letters of Jane Carlyle – ed Alan and Mary McQueen Simpson 1977
Carlyle's House – The National Trust 1975
Carlyle's Chelsea Home – Reginald Blunt 1895
The Cheyne Book of Chelsea China and Pottery – ed Reginald Blunt 1924, republished 1973
The Pheasantry – Nesta MacDonald 1977
Henry Holland: His Life and Architecture – Dorothy Stroud 1966
Town Planning in London – Donald J Olsen 1964 and 1982

Cremorne and the Later London Gardens – Warwick Wroth 1907
Thomas Doggett Deceased – Theodore Cook and Guy Nickalls 1908
Crossing London's River – John Pudney 1972
Thames Crossings – Geoffrey Phillips 1981
London under London – Richard Trench and Ellis Hillman 1985
C R Ashbee: Architect, Designer and Romantic Socialist – Alan Crawford 1985
The Growth of Victorian London – Donald J Olsen 1976
Sweetness and Light – Mark Girouard 1977
A Place Called Chelsea – ed John Gullick 1975
Victorian Architecture – Roger Dixon and Stefan Muthesius 1978
The Court Theatre 1904–1907 – Desmond MacCarthy 1907
Recreation – J A R Pimlott 1968
The Swinging Sixties – Brian Masters 1985
At the Royal Court – ed Richard Findlater 1981
The Chelsea Flower Show – Hester Marsden-Smedley 1976
The Chelsea Flower Show – Faith and Geoff Whiten 1982
The Story of the Royal Horticultural Society – H R Fletcher 1969
The Old Court Suburb – Leigh Hunt 1855
History and Antiquities of Kensington – Thomas Faulkner 1820
Gardener to Queen Anne – David Green 1956
Lady Mary Coke, Letters and Journals 1756–74 – pub by Kingsmead 1970
Kensington – Geoffrey Evans 1975
Notting Hill in Bygone Days – Florence M Gladstone 1924, updated by Ashley Barker 1969
Kensington Palace – John Hayes (DoE) 1984
Kensington Palace and Gardens – W J Loftie 1900
Kensington Palace – Derek Hudson 1968
Old Kensington Palace – Austin Dobson 1910
The London Museum at Kensington Palace – Ernest Law 1912
Kensington Palace and Sir Christopher Wren: A Vindication – G H Chettle and P A Faulkner, Journal of the British Archaeological Association Vol XIV 1951
Holland House – Leslie Mitchell 1980
Holland House in Kensington – Derek Hudson 1967
The Home of the Hollands 1605–1820 – Earl of Ilchester 1937
Chronicles of Holland House 1820–1900 – Earl of Ilchester 1937
Holland House – Princess Marie Liechtenstein 1874
A Walk from London to Fulham – Thomas Crofton Croker 1860, revised by Beatrice E Horne 1896
Little Chelsea – W S Scott 1940
Aubrey House Kensington 1698–1920 – Florence M Gladstone 1922
Mendelssohn and his Friends in Kensington – Rosamund Brunel Gotch 1934
Blessington D'Orsay: A Masquerade – Michael Sadleir 1933
Kensington Picturesque and Historical – W J Loftie 1888
The Thackeray Country – Lewis Melville 1905
The London of Thackeray – E Beresford Chancellor 1923
The Great Exhibition of 1851 – C H Gibbs-Smith 1950, 1981
The Great Exhibition: 1851 – Yvonne ffrench 1950
Paxton's Palace – Anthony Bird 1976
The Art and Architecture of London – Ann Saunders 1984
Alfred Waterhouse and the Natural History Museum – Mark Girouard 1981
The Natural History Museum at South Kensington – William T Stearn 1981
'The Brick Palace of 1862' – Betty Bradford, The Architectural Review, July 1962
The Archdeacon and the Architect – Michael Barney (St Mary Abbots Centenary Essay) 1972
The Story of St Mary Abbots Kensington – Judith D Guillum Scott 1942
Travels in South Kensington – Moncure Daniel Conway 1882
The Royal Albert Hall – Ronald W Clark 1958
The West London Joint Railways – J B Atkinson 1984

The History of Railways in Britain – F Ferneyhough 1975
History of London Transport – T C Barker and Michael Robbins (Vols I and II, 1963 and 1974)
Building the Inner Circle Railway – from The Railway Gazette 1946.
100 Years of the District – London Transport 1968
The Shell Book of Firsts – Patrick Robertson, revised 1983
The Making of the Serpentine – W L Rutton, The Home Counties Magazine April and July 1903
J M Barrie and the Lost Boys – Andrew Birkin 1979
England's Michelangelo – Wilfrid Blunt 1975
Lord Leighton – Leonee and Richard Ormond 1975
Letters of the Honourable Mrs Edward Twisleton 1928 Leighton House Essays
The London Oratory Centenary 1884–1984 – ed Michael Napier and Alistair Laing 1984
Old Kew, Chiswick and Kensington – Lloyd Sanders 1910
Earl's Court – Claude Langdon 1953
Theatre Notebook Vol 13 No 4, 1959 (article on Royal Kent Theatre)
London: The Western Reaches – Godfrey James 1950
Royal Borough – Rachel Ferguson 1950
Four National Exhibitions in London – Charles Lowe 1892
Life and Labour of the People in London (Third Series, Religious Influences) – Charles Booth 1902
A History of Shopping – Dorothy Davis 1966
Shopping in Style – Alison Adburgham 1979
A Garden in the Sky – A W Peel 1960
Harrods: the Store and the Legend – Tim Dale 1981
Life in Victorian London – L C B Seaman 1973
Kenna's Kingdom – R Weir Brown 1881

Acknowledgments

We should like to thank the following people who have helped us collect the pictures for this book: Chris Christodoulou – official photographer at the Royal Albert Hall; Adrian Hodges – publicity officer at the Commonwealth Institute; Mrs P K Pratt – Chelsea branch librarian; Paul Senior – manager of Derry & Toms roof garden; Mrs I E Shaw – photographic records officer at the Museum of London; Mrs Deborah Wearing – manager of print and merchandise information at the John Lewis Partnership.

Picture sources and illustrations

The following abbreviations are used:–

BL British Library
BM British Museum
HPL Hulton Picture Library
ILN Illustrated London News
KL Kensington Library
LTS London Topographical Society
MF Mirror Features
NMR National

Monuments Record
NPG National Portrait Gallery
PJ Peter Jackson Collection
SI Syndication International
TPL Topham Picture Library
V & A Victoria & Albert Museum

End Papers. Photographic copy of a manuscript map drawn in 1717 by J P Desmaretz endorsed 'Art and Science Department 10 December 1862'. The location of the original is unknown. Public Records Office.

Frontispiece. Chromolithograph by W Loeillot. From *The National Memorial to . . . the Prince Consort*. 1875. PJ

10 Eng. after a painting by Van Dyck. PJ
12/13 Drawings by John Thorpe. Sir John Soane's Museum.
12/13 Detail from eng. by I Kip after L Knyff. Plate from *Britannia Illustrata c.* 1707. KL
14 ILN 1 Oct. 1853. PJ
15 *top* Painting by unknown artist. Dept. of the Environment.
15 *bottom* Eng. after a drawing by Chatelain. From *Fifty Original Views*, 1750. PJ
16/17 Eng. re-published by Laurie & Whittle. Originally engraved between 1750 & 1753. PJ
18 *bottom* Eng. from Faulkner's *Kensington*, 1820. PJ
18 *top* Eng. Detail from *Topographical Survey of the Parish of Kensington*, 1766. Published by Joshua Rhodes. KL
19 Watercolour by Buckler, 1826. BM. Dept. of Prints & Drawings. Crace. IX, 22.
20 & 21 Engs. by J Houbraken after G Kneller. From Birch's *Heads*, 1744. PJ
20/21 Eng. after Mark Anthony Hauduroy. From *Nouveau Theatre de la Grande Bretagne*, 1724. PJ
22 *top* Photo. NMR
22 *top* Eng. by Sutton Nicholls, *c.* 1690.
23 Mezzotint by Samuel Reynolds after a painting by C R Leslie, 1847. KL
24 Eng. from *Universal Magazine*. PJ
25 *top* Eng. by Benoist. PJ
25 *bottom* Plate from Dore's *London*, 1872. PJ
26 Lithograph after Thomas Maisey. PJ
26/27 Watercolour by J Salway drawn in 1811 for the Kensington Turnpike Trust. Facsimile published by the London Topographical Society from the original in BM. Dept. of Manuscripts. Add. 31325.
27 Watercolour by George Scharf, 1822. BM. Dept. of Prints & Drawings. Box 17a. 1900–7–25 (10)
28 *top left* Photo. KL
28 *top right* Pencil drawing by Robert Banks. PJ
28/29 Continuation of Salway's drawing (Pages 26/27).
29 Photo. *Evening News*.
30/31 *Historic Times*, 11 Jan. 1850. PJ
32 Plate from *Ragged Homes and How to Mend Them*, by Mrs Bayly, 1859. PJ
33 Drawing reproduced in *Notting Hill in Bygone Days* by Florence M Gladstone, 1924.
34/35 Aquatint by Reeve after Henry Alken Jnr. PJ
35 Plate from *Sporting Review*, 1841. PJ
36 Lithograph by T Allom, 1853. KL
37 ILN 22 Feb. 1845. PJ
38 Watercolour by Thomas Hosmer Shepherd. KL
39 *top* Stipple eng. by H I Ryall after A E Chalon, 1844. PJ
39 *bottom* Eng. by & after J Scott. From Faulkner's Kensington, 1810. PJ
40 Eng. by Josiah Neele after L Stewart, *c.* 1832. PJ
41 *top* Graphic, 30 June 1877. PJ
41 *bottom* Lithograph by 'Ape'. From *Vanity Fair*, 21 Feb. 1874. PJ
42 Lithograph by T Madeley, *c.* 1842. KL
43 Photo Victorian Society.
44 Detail from 'Plan of the Parish of St. Mary Kensington' engraved by Thomas Starling, 1822. KL
45 Detail from 'Map of Kensington' issued by Henry Lovibond & Son, Cannon Brewery, 1880. PJ
46 *Mirror*, 28 April 1838. PJ
48 *top Historic Times*, 1849. PJ
48 *bottom Gentleman's Magazine*, 1828. PJ
49 *Historic Times*, 1849. PJ
50/51 Steel eng. by & after T A Prior. PJ
51 ILN 19 July 1851. PJ
52 *top* Litho. by Philip Brannon. Plate from *The Park & the Crystal Palace*, 1851. PJ
52 *bottom* ILN 7 Dec. 1850. PJ
53 Detail from 'Odds & Ends, in, out & about, The Great Exhibition of 1851.' Etching by George Cruikshank. PJ
54 Steel eng. Drawn by T Boyes from the original design, 1862. PJ

55 *top* ILN 27 June 1857. PJ
55 *bottom* Photo from original neg. PJ
56 Steel eng. Plate from Cassell's *Old & New London*. PJ
57 From Cassell's *History of England*. PJ
58 & 59 ILN 2 Jan. 1869. PJ
60 Photo. KL
61 Eng. by Schnebbelie. *Gentleman's Magazine*. Vol C. pt. 1, 1830. PJ
62 ILN 8 Sept. 1871. PJ
64 & 65 Photos by Chris Christodoulou.
67 Pen and wash by Walter Greaves.
68 *bottom* Map drawn & engraved by B R Davies. From Faulkner's Hammersmith, 1839. PJ
69 *top* ILN 14 Oct. 1911.
70 Eng. after J Sargeant. PJ
71 *top* Eng. by S Soringsagots. PJ
71 *bottom* Eng. after H West. From Partington's *National History and Views of London*, *c.* 1835. PJ
72 Photo. HPL
73 *top* Photo. MF
73 *bottom* Graphic, 15 Aug. 1874. PJ
74 From *Building News*, 7 Oct. 1881. PJ
75 *top* From *George Frederick Watts*, by M S Watts, 1912.
75 *bottom* ILN 1 Feb. 1896. PJ
76 NMR
77 Perspective by Axel Haig, 1880. PJ
78 *top* NMR
78 *bottom* Pen drawing by Frederick Griggs. Reproduced in *George Frederick Watts*, by M S Watts, 1912.
79 Woodburytype. PJ
80/81/82 From *Building News*, 25 June 1875, 20 Sept. 1878, 4 June 1875. PJ
83 Plate from H Muthesius, Die Englische Baukunst der Gegenwart, 1900. PJ
84 & 86 From *Building News*, 2 May 1879 & 19 May 1882. PJ
87 Photo *c.* 1890. KL
88 Watercolour, probably by Robert B Schnebbelie. KL
89 ILN 7 June 1851. PJ
90 ILN 10 May 1851. PJ. Original handbill. PJ
91 ILN 16 April 1887. PJ. Photo from original neg. PJ
92 ILN 9 March 1895. PJ
93 Original invitation card. Etching by Tristram Ellis, 1882. PJ
94 Etching by Robert Banks. PJ
95 Photo. Harrods.
96 *top* From *Illustrated London & Its Representation of Commerce*, 1893. PJ
96 *bottom* HPL
97 NMR
98 *bottom* Illustration from *Living London* by George R Sims, 1903.
98 *top* Photo. Courtesy of The Roof Gardens.
99 *top* Photo. TPL
99 *bottom* Photo. *Evening Standard*.
100 TPL
101 *top* SI
101 *bottom* ILN 14 Aug. 1880. PJ
102 *top* Cephas Picture Library.
102 *bottom* TPL
103 HPL
106/107 Eng. by I Kip after L Knyff. Plate from *Britannia Illustrata*, *c.* 1707. KL
107 Eng. by J Houbraken after Holbein. Plate from Birch's *Heads*, 1741. PJ
108 *Saturday Magazine*, 7 June 1834. PJ
109 Drawing by Hans Holbein. Offentliche Kunstsammlung, Basle.
110 *top* Graphic, 8 June 1872. PJ
110 *bottom* Eng. by J Barlow, 'Drawn from the original' by Edward Ward. From Faulkner's *Chelsea* (1st. ed. 1810).
111 From Cassell's *Old & New London*. PJ
112 *top* Detail from Kip's View. See page 106.
112 *bottom* Photo by Jack Scheerboom.
113 *Gentleman's Magazine*, June 1829. PJ
114 Redrawing for the Survey of London Vol. IV from the Thorpe manuscript in the Soane Museum.
115 Eng. after J B Chatelain, 1750. PJ
116 Litho. after S H Grim, 1780. PJ
117 *top* Litho. after Henry Warren. From Faulkner's *Chelsea*, 1829. PJ
117 *bottom* Wood eng. by F W Fairholt. From Croker's *Walk from London to Fulham*, 1860. PJ
118 Watercolour by James Miller dated 1776. V & A
119 Eng. *c.* 1795. PJ
120 Eng. after Chatelain. From *Fifty Original Views*, 1750. PJ
121 Eng. after T H Shepherd. From *London in the Nineteenth Century*, 1829. PJ
122 *top* Eng. from *Gentleman's Magazine*, April 1831. PJ
122 *bottom Builder*, 6 Oct. 1888. PJ
123 Eng. after T H Shepherd. From *Metropolitan Improvements*, 1828. PJ
124 Painting by Stephen Slaughter, 1736. NPG
125 Eng. by John Haynes, 1751. PJ
126 Litho. by H Warren after Jas Fuge, *c.* 1835. PJ
127 *top* Stipple eng. 1800. PJ
127 *bottom* TPL
128/129 Eng. by B Cole. From Maitland's *London*, 1756. PJ
129 Litho. published by Ackermann. PJ
130 *top left* Stipple eng. by G Scott. PJ
130 *Graphic*, 4 Feb. 1888. PJ
131 *top* SI
131 *bottom Graphic*, 11 Feb. 1888. PJ
132 Pen drawing by Joseph Pennell. Illustration in *Century Magazine* Vol. XXXIII, Nov. 1886. PJ

133 *top* Eng. by William Hogarth, *c.* 1730. PJ
133 *bottom* Trade card engraved by William Hogarth, *c.* 1718. PJ
134 *top* Etching by & after R B Schnebbelie, 1835. From Smith's *Historical & Literary Curiosities*, 1840. PJ
134 *bottom Gentleman's Magazine*, 1828. PJ
135 Watercolour. CL
135 *bottom* By courtesy of Christie's.
136/137 Eng. 'Canalet delint./C.Grignion sculp.' 1752. PJ
137 Eng. admission ticket by Bartolozzi after Cipriani, 1776. PJ
138/139 Eng. 'Caneleti delin./N.Parr sculp.' 1751. PJ
138 Eng. 'Clody invt./Telltruth sculpt.' *c.* 1752. PJ
140 Detail from anonymous engraving 'Printed for & Sold by Geo. Foster at the White Horse opposite the Old Bailey on Ludgate Hill . . .' July 31 1749., PJ
141 Anonymous drawing.
142/143 Eng. by & after J Boydell, 1752. PJ
144 Pen drawing by Joseph Pennell. Illustration from *Century Magazine*, Vol. XXXIII, Dec. 1886. PJ
145 *top* ILN 10 May 1851. PJ
145 *bottom* Same as p. 144 above.
146 *top* Litho. by 'Spy'. From *Vanity Fair*, 12 Jan. 1878. PJ
146 *bottom* ILN 7 May 1870. PJ
147 *top* Pen drawing by Malcolm Fraser. PJ
147 *bottom* Cartoon by Max Beerbohm. PJ
148 *top* ILN 19 Feb. 1881. PJ
148 *bottom* Eng. by E Roffe. *Art Journal*. PJ
149 *top* Etching by A Trowquill. PJ
149 *bottom* Bust by D Dunbar. PJ
150 *top* Etching by P Rajon after F W Burton. PJ
150 *top* Three carte-de-visite photographs. PJ
150 *bottom* Litho by 'Ape'. From *Vanity Fair*, 24 May 1884. PJ
151 *Gentleman's Magazine*, April 1809. PJ
152 *right* John Stidolph. PJ
152 *left* CL
153 From Faulkner's *Chelsea*, 1829. PJ
154/155 Map of Chelsea by F P Thompson, 1836. LTS publication No. 111.
156 Detail from Horwood's Plan of London (1794). PJ
157 Anonymous litho. (Dated by hand, 1856). PJ
158 *left* Handbill. Litho. *c.* 1830. PJ
158 *right* Music cover. Litho. by Alfred Concanen. *c.* 1862. PJ
159 Litho. 1831. PJ
160 ILN 18 July 1874. PJ
161 Aquatint by J Farington after J C Stadler, 1793. From Boydell's *History of the Thames*, 1794/6. PJ
162 *top* Pictorial Times, 5 Aug. 1843. PJ
162 *bottom* Litho. Published by Ackermann, 1855. PJ
163 Eng. by Bartolozzi after Cipriani, 1775. PJ
164 *top left* Etching copied from a painting formerly preserved at Lyme Regis. PJ
164 *bottom* Steel eng. 'Tombleson delt./S.Lacey sculp.' From Tombleson's *Thames* (1834). PJ
165 Steel eng. by Chas. Heath after P. DeWint. From Heath's *Views of London* (1825). PJ
166 ILN 14 June 1873. PJ
167 Tinted litho. by E Dolby from a photo by J A Spencer. From Nolan's *Great Britain as It Is*, (1859). PJ
168 Plate from Cassell's *Old & New London*. PJ
169 Pen drawing by Joseph Pennell. Illustration from *Century Magazine*, Vol. XXXIII, Dec. 1886. PJ
170, 171 & 173 From *Building News*, 15 March 1878, 16 July 1880 and 15 June 1877. PJ
172 Photo by H Felton, NMR
174 ILN 13 May 1876. PJ
175 ILN. PJ
176 ILN 4 Feb. 1871. PJ
177 ILN
178 Pen drawing for *The Architect*, 17 May 1879. PJ
178/181 All courtesy of John Lewis Partnership.
182 Painting by Frank Craig. Graphic, 1 June 1901. PJ
184 Photo. CL
185 MF
186 NMR
187 TPL

Index